The Independent Fiduciary

INVESTING FOR PENSION FUNDS AND ENDOWMENT FUNDS

Russell L. Olson

John Wiley & Sons, Inc.

New York • Chichester • Weinheim • Brisbane • Singapore • Toronto

To Jeanette,

my wife

and my best friend

Published by John Wiley & Sons, Inc.

Published simultaneously in Canada.

This publication is designed to provide accurate and authoritative information in regard to the subject matter covered. It is sold with the understanding that the publisher is not engaged in rendering professional services. If professional advice or other expert assistance is required, the services of a competent professional person should be sought.

Library of Congress Cataloging-in-Publication Data:

Olson, Russell L., 1933–
    The independent fiduciary : investing for pension funds and
endowment funds / Russell L. Olson.
        p.   cm. — (Wiley frontiers in finance)
    Includes index.
    ISBN 0-471-35387-6 (cloth : alk. paper)
    1. Pension trusts—Investments. 2. Endowments—Finance.
I. Title. II. Series.
HD7105.4.037   1999
332.67'254—dc21   99–22802

Printed in the United States of America.

10 9 8 7 6 5 4 3 2 1

Preface

I remember well when in 1971, after having enjoyed 15 years in the field of public relations, I was offered a position in corporate treasury work. My reaction was: *Me? Working in investments? I hardly know a stock from a bond!*

The area that seemed to need the most attention at the time was pension investments, a field I had to learn from the ground up. I had taken one course on investments in business school and audited two others. That was it. My baptism was rugged.

After preparing a presentation for our treasurer to give to Kodak's management about our pension trust fund's 1973 investment performance, he turned to me and said, "Rusty, why don't you give the presentation?" So I told management about how our trust fund's investment return for 1973 was *minus 20%*. And a year later I told them our 1974 performance was *minus 26%*. It's a wonder they kept me on the job!

I discovered there were many people to learn from, almost all of whom were selling something. Even academics, I discovered, are selling something—an idea, on which their reputation is based. The fact that a person is selling something has not caused me a problem, as long as I keep their interests in the back of my mind. Therein has been my education.

One of the greatest sources of my education has been half a dozen off-site two-day investment strategy conferences we set up for the committee in charge of the Kodak pension fund—an idea originated by John Casey and Steve Rogers, who moderated these conferences. These conferences have done more than anything else, by far, to educate our committee, our staff, and me, and to help our pension fund set its strategic course for the years ahead. We have been amazingly fortunate to have benefited at these conferences from some of the greatest investment minds of our time, several of whom have never managed any money for us. Our conference participants have included:

Peter Aldrich	Peter Lynch
John Angelo	Ed Mathias
Jack Bogle	Meyer Melnikoff
Gary Brinson	Roy Neuberger
Gary Burkhead	Hilda Ochoa
Bill Crerend	Alan Patricof
Ray Dalio	Steve Robert
Gilbert deBotton	Barr Rosenberg
Francis Finlay	Lew Sanders
David Fisher	Rex Sinquefield
Dale Frey	Jeff Skelton
Jeremy Grantham	Mark Tavel
Fred Grauer	John Templeton
Hank Herrmann	Antoine vanAgtmael
John Hill	Brain Wruble
Phil Horsley	Buzz Zaino
Dean LaBaron	Dick Zecher
Scott Lummer	

A great many others have also played a significant role in my education. At the risk of making some egregious omissions, I would like to list some of them: Rob Arnott, Doug Breeden, Richard Brignoli, Sam Eisenstadt, Charley Ellis, Teddy Forstmann, Dick Michaud, Eric Nelson, Eric Oddleifson, Ed Peters, Julian Robertson, and Grant Schaumburg.

Perhaps I should have started this list with the names of my key senior partners at Kodak through the years—Duff Lewis, then Bob Spooner, Kat Mandel, and Dave McNiff. These dedicated people have shared fully the task at hand and in the process have taught me a great deal. Critical to everything we've done have been our staff support people through the years: Betsy Blackburn, Dick Clouser, Peggy Clutz, Narvilla Coley, Kathleen Emert, Dick McCarthy, Patty Pearce, Mary Jane Pocock, Usha Shah, Jean Tuffo, Jim Vance, and Barb Veomett; our attorneys, Greg Gumina and John Purves; and associates abroad such as Peter Armstrong, Larry Seager, and Mike Stockwell.

Another group of people I must acknowledge are the seven treasurers I have worked for—Don Fewster, Gene Radford, Don Snyder, Mike Hamilton, Dave Vigren, Jesse Greene, and Dave Pollock—all of whom have been wonderfully supportive.

I must also pay tribute to all the various persons who through the years have served on the Kodak Retirement Income Plan Committee. I am grateful for their unswerving focus on doing the right thing and for their willingness to listen to things that, initially at least, sounded strange and perhaps scary to them. Few pension staff people have been blessed with as fine a group of committee members. Their names, besides the treasurers mentioned above, include: Colby Chandler, Ken Cole, Walter Fallon, Paul Holm, Harry Kavetas, Jack McCarthy, Mike Morley, Cecil Quillen, Bob Ross, Bob Sherman, Charles Singleton, Paul Smith, Virgil Stephens, Carl Stevenson, Bill Sutton, Gary Van Graafeiland, and Gerry Zornow.

I must express especially deep gratitude to a number of people whose opinion I value highly, who took the time to read my manuscript critically when it was in draft form and give me their advice and suggestions, or who provided useful data for the book. This book is far better as a result of their input. I refer here to my current partners Bob Spooner, Kathleen Emert, and Jean Tuffo, and my ERISA attorney, Greg Gumina; my previous partner, Duff Lewis; Joe Grills, former head of pension investments at IBM; Bob Mainer, Trish Carr, and Eve Kingsley at The Boston Company; Chris Lyon of BARRA RogersCasey; Ray Dalio of Bridgewater Associates; Dave Rosso, Amy Dalnodar, and Dick Wendt at the actuarial firm of Towers Perrin; Fred Giuffreda of Horsley, Bridge and Associates; Bob Sterrett, a friend and member of our church endowment committee; Kirsten Sandberg of Harvard Business School Publishing, who provided helpful constructive criticism on the writing of the manuscript; and the staff at Publications Development Company.

Author's Note: Throughout this book, in referring to individual investors or investment managers, I shall for convenience sake use the masculine pronoun. In all such cases, the "he" is used in the classical sense as a shorthand to designate "he or she." In the current age, this may open me to criticism, and I'm sorry if it does.

Clearly, investing is every bit as much a woman's world as a man's world. But I personally rebel against the imprecision of modern usage. "Each person does their own thing." And I find terribly cumbersome the repetition in, "Each person does his or her own thing." That leaves me with only the classical approach.

One could ask, why not use the pronoun "it" in referring to investment managers, because the manager of an investment program is usually an institution. I do often use the pronoun "it" in referring to institutions. But I also frequently and purposefully choose the personal pronoun in these pages to remind us that all investment decisions are made by persons—often an individual, sometime a small group—and, in either case, the particular person or persons really matter.

RUSSELL L. OLSON

Rochester, New York
August 1999

Contents

Introduction

These pages deal with institutional *taxfree* investing—whether by pension funds, endowment funds, or foundations.

Investment returns on a pension fund impact directly a company's cost of doing business and thereby its competitiveness in the marketplace. Income from endowment funds is the lifeblood of many universities and charitable organizations. A 1% increase (or decrease) in its long-term rate of return will have a dramatic effect on both kinds of institutions. If the concepts discussed in these pages help these funds prudently to achieve higher rates of return, then I will feel well repaid for the effort in putting it together.

I chose the title, *The Independent Fiduciary,* to emphasize two key considerations:

- If we have responsibilities for a pension fund, endowment fund, or foundation, we are a *fiduciary.* Legally—and morally—we must operate in the *sole interest* of the beneficiaries of that fund.
- Too often, fiduciaries look at what fiduciaries of other funds are doing and strive to do likewise, on the assumption that that must be the way to go. The underlying theme of these pages is that this is *not necessarily* the way to go. A fiduciary should do his own *independent* thinking. He must educate himself as much as he reasonably can about investments and then apply the independent logic and good old common sense with which God endowed him.

These pages are about *institutional taxfree* investing because that is where the author's experience lies. Individuals may find many of the

One of the best definitions of *fiduciary* may be the following: "Many forms of conduct permissible in a workaday world for those acting at arm's length are forbidden to those bound by fiduciary ties. A trustee [fiduciary] is held to something stricter than the words of the market place. Not honesty alone, but the punctilio of an honor the most sensitive, is then the standard of behavior. As to this there has developed a tradition that is unbending and inveterate."—Justice Benjamin N. Cardozo, 1928.

concepts applicable to their 401(k) and IRA investments, but the prime focus is on *institutional taxfree* investing.

Some of the principles discussed in these pages will apply to *taxable investing* as well. But as every personal financial advisor knows so well, there is a lot more to it, and we shall not try to deal in these pages with that "lot more." We shall let those readers who are mainly interested in taxable investing use their own common sense and logic to decide to what extent these pages apply.

I hope the book will be helpful to anyone connected with institutional investing—committee members, pension and endowment staff members (junior as well as senior), and also their legal counsel and others who consult with them.

The book is not intended to be a cookbook for how to invest institutional assets. Rather, it is intended to suggest the tools—and give the encouragement—for readers to have the confidence to use their own good minds in dealing profitably with the challenge of investing institutional assets.

Unfortunately, for readers who are not professionals in the field, the first two chapters on keeping score—on return and risk—may be among the more difficult in the book. They introduce many terms and concepts that may be unfamiliar. I believe, however, these concepts are worth grasping to get the most out of the subsequent chapters.

For professionals in the field, an appropriate approach may be to skim the book and read closely those portions that seem relevant to you. You might, for example, feel that the meaning of "investment returns" is elementary and not worth devoting much time to. I would suggest, however, that you skim such sections, not skip them altogether, as the section might still include a thought or two worth pondering—and might well include a statement or two with which you might downright disagree!

Throughout this book, I have freely stated the opinions and prejudices I have accumulated in more than 25 years of looking after a large corporate pension fund and working with half a dozen endowment funds ranging in assets from $50,000 to $100 million. If I feel strongly about something, I have said so. If I have doubts about something, I have tried to express my reservations.

Over these years, I have discovered more often than I would like to admit that I am not always right. I learned that elements of investment philosophy in which I believed strongly at one time were not as sound as I had thought, or perhaps not sound at all. What makes the job of institutional investing so fascinating is that it's a bottomless barrel of challenge: There is no end to the opportunity for meaningful learning. If I could continue this work for another 100 years, I would still have a lot to learn. If I had written this book 10 years ago, the book would have been quite different, and if I waited another 10 years to write it, the book would probably be quite different yet.

Don't take what's written in this book, or any other book about investing, as the last word. Do your own independent thinking. Everything comes down to facts and logic. Do we have all of the relevant facts? Are the facts accurate? Does the logic hold up? Ask questions, ad nauseum if necessary. Does it make sense to you? If not, challenge it. Work hard to articulate your reasons.

Organization of the Book

In organizing this book, I begin with the basic concepts of *return* and *risk* (Chapters 1 and 2). Understanding those concepts is a prerequisite for everything else.

The next step is *setting investment objectives* for our fund (Chapter 3). This leads naturally to the all-important decision of asset allocation (Chapter 4). Only then can we think about selecting and monitoring investment managers (Chapters 5 and 6).

We discuss real estate and alternative assct classes (Chapters 7 and 8) and negotiating private agreements (Chapter 9). We follow with an introduction to the fund's master trustee (Chapter 10) and some special investment opportunities that a master trustee can help to facilitate (Chapter 11).

The remaining chapters deal with special topics:

- The importance of a good information retrieval system—files (Chapter 12).
- A treatise on liabilities, which are of central importance to pension funds (Chapter 13).
- A commentary on governance—on how decisions are made, and by whom (Chapter 14).
- A discussion about how a global company can go about coordinating the pension programs of overseas subsidiaries (Chapter 15).
- A contrast of the pros and cons of defined benefit and defined contribution pension plans (Chapter 16).
- Special considerations relative to endowment funds and foundations (Chapter 17).
- Finally, a catch-all chapter I have labeled "Aphorisms" (Chapter 18).

I don't expect everyone to agree with all of my points of view. I have taken pains at least to avoid factual errors, but I have found that even factual perfection can be elusive. In any case, when you disagree with something I have said, I would be most appreciative if you would take the time to let me know.[1] Inviting challenges to my thinking is my recipe for continuous learning.

---

[1] My e-mail address is rlolson@rochester.rr.com.

Chapter 1

Keeping Score I: Investment Returns

During a particular 10-year interval, let's say our fund earned a return of 10% per year. What does that mean? And is that good or poor? These are questions Chapter 1 will deal with.

What is the basic purpose of institutional investing, whether for a pension fund, an endowment fund, or a foundation? The basic purpose is to *make money*—more specifically, to make as much money as we can within a level of risk that is appropriate to the financial circumstances of the fund's sponsor. That sounds rather simple . . . at least until we begin to define terms.

Whatever game we are learning, whether it is tennis, bridge, or some other, one of the first things we should learn is how to keep score. How can we know how we are doing if we don't know how to keep score? This is equally true of investing, which I view as a "game" in the classical sense of the term, an extremely serious game.

How do we keep score in investing? The money we earn (or lose) is called *investment return*. Let's talk about keeping score of investment returns . . . and then, in Chapter 2, about risk.

Total Return

What constitutes investment return? Investment return on stocks and bonds includes income (such as dividends and interest) and capital gains, net of all fees and expenses. That's a definition of *total return*.

As basic as that is, we need to keep it in mind. The stock and bond indexes as reported in the newspaper reflect only *price*—even though dividends have provided investors with close to half of their total return on stocks over the past 70 years. We must add dividends (or interest) to an index to obtain the total return on a stock or bond index.[1]

Our focus should always be on *total return*—the sum of income and capital gains (or losses), whether realized or unrealized.[2] Fundamentally, there is little difference between income and capital gains, in that a company or an investor can manipulate the composition of income and capital gains, but one cannot manipulate total return. A company that wants to shield its investors from taxes can pay very low (or no) dividends and reinvest most (or all) of its earnings, either in its business or in the repurchase of its common shares. As investors, we can easily build a portfolio with high income or low income, depending on whether we invest in securities that pay high or low dividends and interest. But achieving a high *total return* remains a difficult challenge.

---

[1] The *timing* of a dividend or interest payment impacts the total *rate* of return. For example, an 8% bond purports to pay interest at 8% per year, and if we receive that 8% at the end of the year, exactly 8% is the rate of income we would get. But bonds generally pay interest twice a year—4% every six months. We can use the interest payment we receive halfway through the year, perhaps to invest in another 8% bond. Per dollar invested, our wealth at the end of six months was $1.04, and at the end of the year it is 4% higher—1.04 times $1.04—for a year-end wealth of $1.0816, or an internal rate of return of 8.16%.

If instead, we invested in a high-yielding stock whose dividend equaled 8% of its price, our internal rate of return, assuming the price of the stock doesn't change, would be 8.24% because stocks pay dividends four times a year—providing more opportunity to reinvest.

[2] We *realize* a capital gain (or loss) when we sell a security for a price that's different from what we paid for it. We have an *unrealized* capital gain (or loss) if the price of a security *we currently own* is different from the price we paid for it.

The final part of the definition of total return is: ". . . net of all fees and expenses." The only return we can count is what we can spend. We must therefore deduct all costs—mainly investment management fees, transaction fees, and custodial expense.

Total return is what investing is all about.

Valuing Our Investments

To find the total return on our investments for any time interval, we must know the *value* of our investments at the start of the interval and at the end of the interval. But what value? Book value (the price we paid for an investment) or market value? Or some other value, such as amortized book value?[3] Or some combination, such as the lower of book or market value?

To understand our investments at any time, we must focus on a single value—*market value*—the price at which we could most realistically sell those investments at that time. That's what our investments were worth.

Book values are helpful to auditors, and accounting rules require that book values be taken into consideration. (Book values are extremely important to taxable investors.) But for purposes of understanding our taxfree investments, book values are not helpful.

I often refer to book values as an historical accident. Book value is the price we happened to have paid for our investment on the day we happened to have bought it. A comparison of an investment's market and book values is not enlightening. If the value of our investment is up 50% since we bought it, is that good? If we bought it only a year ago, that's probably good (unless the market rose even more than 50% in that time). But if we bought it 10 years ago, a 50% increase is not very exciting.

Book values also can be manipulated. If we want to show a higher book value for our portfolio, we can sell a security with a large unrealized appreciation (whose price is much higher than its cost), and the book value of our portfolio will rise by the gain we have just realized. Or if we want to

---

[3] Amortized book value would apply to a bond if we paid more or less than par value (the principal amount we will receive when the bond matures, usually $1,000), and if we *amortize* the amount above or below par value little by little over the life of the bond.

show a lower book value, we can sell a security whose price is much lower than its purchased price, and the book value of our portfolio will decline by the loss we have just realized.

Market values *cannot* be manipulated. The moral of the story: Always focus on market values. When making reports about our fund to its board or its membership, we should stick with market values. Forget about book values.

What's a Good Rate of Return?

What does it mean when the newspaper says that Mutual Fund X had an annual rate of return of 10% for the past three years. That's simple. It means that if we put a dollar into the mutual fund three years ago, it would have grown by 10% per year. We know that's not 3 times 10 equals 30% for the three years because it's a *compound* rate of growth. The dollar theoretically became worth $1.10 after year 1, plus another 10% was $1.21 after year 2, and another 10% was $1.33 after year 3. A return of 33% over three years is the same as 10% per year.

Fine. But, is 10% per year *good*? And if we've invested in a whole series of mutual funds over a period of years, what is our rate of return, and is that good? These are much tougher questions.

First, is that 10% per year good? That depends. Based on the way Mutual Fund X generally invests money, what opportunity did it have to make money? How did the fund's total return compare with that of its benchmark—usually the most appropriate unmanaged index?

Let's say that Mutual Fund X invests mainly in large, well-known U.S. stocks, sticking pretty close to the kinds of stocks included in Standard & Poor's (S&P) 500 index and that we should expect Mutual Fund X to incur about the same level of risk. In that case, the S&P 500 is a good reflection of the opportunity that the mutual fund faced—the S&P 500 is a sound benchmark. If the total return on the S&P 500 was 13% per year, then the 10% return on Mutual Fund X was not so hot. On the other hand, if the S&P's total return was only 7%, then 10% represents very good performance.[4]

---

[4] A technicality for those who want to be precise: There can be a material difference between any given year's return on an index, such as the S&P 500, depending

Now wait a moment. Let's turn that around. What if Mutual Fund X returned *minus* 10% per year, and the S&P was off 13% per year. Are we saying that Mutual Fund X performed very well?

Absolutely. Investing in the stock market is a relative game. We know the market can drop precipitously—and *will* sometime. And at that time, Mutual Fund X is just as likely to drop precipitously. We must be aware of that before we buy into Mutual Fund X. As Harry Truman once said, if you can't stand the heat, get out of the kitchen. If we have selected a valid benchmark for Mutual Fund X, then the most we can ask of Mutual Fund X is to do well *relative to* that benchmark. I view that as a cardinal rule of investing.

So if the S&P returned 7% and Mutual Fund X returned 10%, then Mutual Fund X is pretty good, right? Not necessarily.

Virtually every mutual fund that has underperformed its benchmark over a long time can select intervals of years when it looked like a hero. And almost every fund with outstanding long-term performance has run into intervals of years when it couldn't meet its benchmark. Hence, evaluating the performance of a mutual fund (or an investment manager) on the basis of only one or two intervals, such as the past 3 or 5 years, is fraught with danger.

I prefer to look at a manager's performance over *all* relevant intervals. How can we best do this? Let me illustrate with one of the best performing mutual funds over recent decades, the Sequoia Fund.

A graph typically displayed by mutual funds shows how $100 invested in the fund at the beginning of an interval would have grown over the years. (We arbitrarily selected January 1, 1972, as the date when we theoretically invested $100 in the Sequoia Fund.) This kind of graph (Figure 1.1), although perhaps most often used, is of little value for analysis.

At the very least the graph should include a comparison with its benchmark to show how much value it has added over the years, as shown in Figure 1.2.

---

on *who* calculates the return. The difference usually amounts to only 0.1 to 0.2% in a year but has at times amounted to as much as 0.5%. Differences are due mainly to the assumed timing of the reinvestment of dividends.

The return on an index such as the S&P 500 should be calculated the same way as for an index fund. The index should accrue dividends on their ex-date (the first day that buyers of the stock will *not* receive the dividend), but the index should not assume reinvestment of those dividends until their payment date.

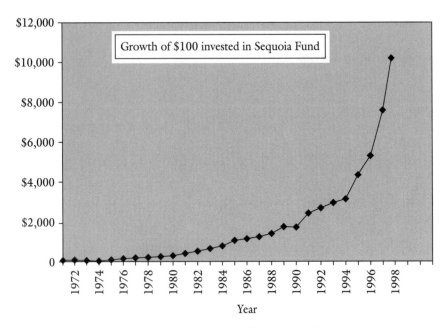

Figure 1.1   A Typical Historical Chart.

Figures 1.1 and 1.2 make it look as if all the good performance occurred in recent years, because a 10% increase in value in a recent year
translates into a much larger dollar increase than a 10% increase in the early
years. To correct this misimpression, the vertical axis should not be *arithmetic,* but *logarithmic,* as in Figure 1.3.

In Figure 1.3 a 10% increase in value will have the same upward tilt,
whether the increase occurred in the first year or the last. Here we can see
which years were best and worst (by the slope of the line) and when performance vs. benchmark was best and worst (by the widening or narrowing
of the distance between the two lines).

Even this is not adequate for analysis. I much prefer a triangle of numbers as in Table 1.1. Triangle A shows that, over the 27 years from the
start of 1972 to the end of 1998, the Sequoia Fund has compounded 19%
per year (the upper left number), even though the fund had negative returns in three of those years, in 1973, 1974, and 1990. The hypotenuse

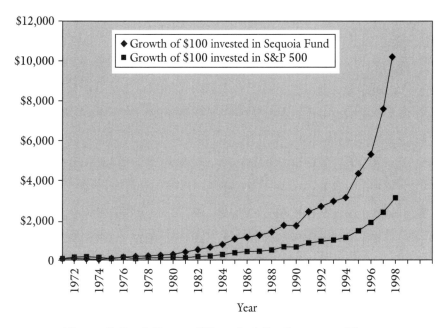

Figure 1.2   A Better Historical Performance Chart.

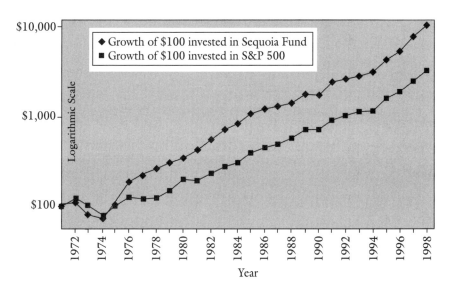

Figure 1.3   A Much Better Historical Performance Chart.

Table 1.1 Triangle A: The Sequoia Fund

From Start of

To End of	72	73	74	75	76	77	78	79	80	81	82	83	84	85	86	87	88	89	90	91	92	93	94	95	96	97	98
98	(19)	19	22	23	22	20	20	20	20	21	21	20	20	20	19	20	21	22	21	25	23	25	28	35	33	39	35
97	18	19	21	23	21	19	19	19	20	20	20	19	19	19	18	18	19	20	19	23	21	23	26	35	32	43	
96	17	18	20	22	20	18	18	18	18	19	18	18	17	17	16	16	17	18	16	20	17	18	21	31	22		
95	17	18	20	22	20	18	18	18	18	17	18	17	17	16	15	15	16	17	16	20	15	17	21	41			
94	16	17	19	21	19	17	17	16	17	17	17	15	14	14	13	13	13	14	11	15	8	7	3				
93	17	17	20	22	20	18	18	17	18	18	18	17	16	15	14	14	15	16	13	19	10	11					
92	17	18	20	23	21	19	18	18	18	19	18	17	16	16	14	14	16	17	14	24	9						
91	17	18	21	24	22	19	19	18	19	20	19	18	17	17	15	15	18	20	16	40							
90	16	17	20	23	21	18	17	17	17	18	17	16	14	13	11	10	11	11	(4)								
89	18	18	22	25	23	19	19	18	19	19	19	17	17	16	11	15	19	28									
88	17	18	21	25	22	19	19	18	19	19	19	17	15	15	11	9	11										
87	17	18	22	26	23	19	19	19	20	21	21	19	17	16	10	7											
86	18	19	23	27	25	22	22	20	22	23	23	22	20	20	13												
85	18	20	23	29	26	22	22	20	22	25	26	25	23	28													
84	18	19	24	29	26	21	21	20	23	25	26	23	19														
83	18	19	24	30	27	21	21	21	23	27	29	27															
82	17	18	24	30	26	20	20	19	22	26	31																
81	15	17	23	30	26	18	17	15	17	22																	
80	15	16	24	32	26	17	16	15	13																		
79	15	17	25	36	30	19	18	12																			
78	15	18	28	42	37	22	24																				
77	14	16	29	49	44	20																					
76	13	15	33	66	72																						
75	2	1	16	61																							
74	-13	-20	-16																								
73	-11	-24																									
72	4																										

Note: The numbers on the left and at the top reference the year.

Table 1.2 Triangle B: The S&P 500 Index

To End of	From Start of																										
	72	73	74	75	76	77	78	79	80	81	82	83	84	85	86	87	88	89	90	91	92	93	94	95	96	97	98
98	14	14	15	17	16	16	17	18	18	17	18	18	18	19	18	18	19	19	18	21	20	22	24	31	28	31	29
97	13	13	14	17	16	15	17	17	17	16	18	18	17	18	17	17	18	18	17	20	18	20	23	31	28	33	
96	13	12	14	16	15	15	16	16	16	15	17	16	16	17	16	15	16	16	14	18	15	17	20	30	23		
95	12	12	13	16	15	14	15	16	16	15	16	16	15	16	15	14	16	15	13	17	13	15	18	38			
94	11	11	12	15	13	13	14	15	15	13	15	14	14	14	13	12	13	12	9	12	6	6	1				
93	12	11	13	15	14	14	15	16	16	14	16	16	15	16	14	13	15	14	11	16	6	10					
92	12	11	13	16	14	14	15	16	16	15	17	16	15	17	15	14	16	16	11	18	8						
91	12	12	13	16	15	14	16	17	17	15	18	17	17	18	16	15	18	18	12	30							
90	11	11	12	15	14	13	15	16	15	14	16	16	15	16	13	12	14	13	-3								
89	12	11	13	17	15	15	17	18	18	16	19	19	18	20	18	17	24	31									
88	11	10	12	16	14	13	15	16	16	14	17	17	15	18	13	11	17										
87	10	10	12	16	14	13	15	16	16	14	17	16	15	18	12	5											
86	11	10	12	16	15	14	16	18	18	15	20	19	18	25	18												
85	10	10	12	16	14	13	16	18	18	15	20	20	19	32													
84	9	8	10	15	12	11	14	15	15	11	16	14	6														
83	9	8	11	16	13	12	15	17	17	12	22	23															
82	8	7	9	15	12	10	14	16	15	7	21																
81	6	5	8	14	11	8	12	14	12	-5																	
80	8	6	10	17	14	12	19	25	33																		
79	5	3	7	15	10	5	12	18																			
78	3	1	4	14	7	-1	7																				
77	3	-0	4	16	7	-7																					
76	5	2	8	30	24																						
75	1	-5	1	37																							
74	-9	-21	-26																								
73	1	-15																									
72	19																										

Note: The numbers on the left and at the top reference the year.

Table 1.3   Triangle C: Value Added—The Sequoia Fund Minus The Benchmark (S&P 500)

To End of	From Start of 72	73	74	75	76	77	78	79	80	81	82	83	84	85	86	87	88	89	90	91	92	93	94	95	96	97	98
98	(5)	6	7	6	6	4	3	2	3	4	2	2	2	1	1	2	2	3	3	4	3	3	4	5	5	8	7
97	5	6	7	6	6	4	3	2	2	4	2	2	1	1	1	1	1	2	3	3	3	3	3	4	4	10	
96	5	6	6	6	6	4	2	2	2	3	2	1	1	-0	0	1	1	1	2	3	1	1	1	1	-1		
95	5	6	7	7	6	4	3	2	2	4	2	1	1	0	0	1	1	2	3	3	2	2	3	4			
94	5	6	7	7	6	4	3	2	2	4	2	1	1	-0	0	1	0	2	3	3	2	1	2				
93	5	6	7	7	6	4	3	2	2	4	2	1	1	-1	-0	0	0	1	2	3	2	1					
92	5	6	8	7	7	4	3	2	2	4	2	1	1	-1	-0	0	0	2	2	4	2						
91	6	7	8	8	7	4	2	1	2	4	1	1	1	-1	-1	0	-0	1	5	(10)							
90	5	7	8	8	7	4	2	1	2	4	1	0	-1	(-3)	-2	-2	-0	1	4								
89	6	7	8	8	7	4	2	1	2	4	1	0	-0	-3	-3	-2	-3	-4									
88	6	8	9	9	8	5	3	2	3	5	2	1	0	-3	-3	-2	(6)										
87	7	8	10	10	9	6	4	3	4	7	3	2	2	-2	-3	2											
86	7	9	11	11	10	7	4	3	4	8	4	2	1	-1	-5												
85	8	10	12	12	11	8	6	4	6	10	6	5	5	-4													
84	9	11	14	13	13	10	7	5	7	14	9	9	12														
83	9	11	14	14	13	9	7	5	6	14	9	5															
82	9	11	15	14	14	10	6	3	6	19	10																
81	9	12	15	16	15	10	5	1	5	26																	
80	7	10	14	14	13	5	-3	-13	-20																		
79	10	14	19	21	21	13	6	-6																			
78	12	17	24	29	30	22	17																				
77	11	17	26	33	37	27																					
76	8	14	25	36	49																						
75	1	6	16	23																							
74	-3	1	11																								
73	-12	-9																									
72	-15																										
Actual	4	-24	-16	61	72	20	24	12	13	22	31	27	19	28	13	7	11	28	-4	40	9	11	3	41	22	43	35

Note: The numbers on the left and at the top reference the year. (Circled values in the original: 5 at End 98/Start 72; –3 at End 90/Start 85; 6 at End 88/Start 88; 10 at End 91/Start 91.)

consists of the fund's performance in each calendar year. For example, from the start of 1990 to the end of that same year, the fund's total return was −4%.

We just said, however, that a manager should be judged relative to a benchmark. If we use the S&P 500 index as Sequoia's benchmark, then we need to know the performance of the S&P 500 (including dividends, of course). See Table 1.2 on page 13. The Sequoia Fund's performance *relative* to the S&P 500 therefore equals the first triangle *minus* the second triangle as in Table 1.3 on page 14. Each number in Value Added Triangle C is simply the corresponding number in Triangle A minus the corresponding number in Triangle B, that is, $A - B = C$. The line at the bottom labeled "Actual" shows the Sequoia's actual performance in each calendar year.

If you compare Triangle C with Triangles A and B, you will find numerous rounding differences. This is because Triangle C is derived from the

---

Again for the Sequoia Fund relative to the S&P 500, we can derive a more precise triangle of Value Added—although less intuitively understandable—by *division* instead of *subtraction:* by dividing 1 + the fund's return in Triangle A by 1 + the benchmark's return in Triangle B ($D = (1 + A)/(1 + B) - 1$), as shown in Table 1.4 on page 16.

This measures the *annual percentage change in wealth* for each year and for every combination of years. It reflects the fact, for example, that beating our benchmark by 5 percentage points when the benchmark is down 25% is as good as beating our benchmark by 10 percentage points when our benchmark is up 50% [That's $(1 - .20)/(1 - .25) = (.8/.75) = 1.067$, or 6.7% ... and $(1 + .60)/(1 + .50) = (1.6/1.5) = 1.067$, or 6.7%—the same percentage advantage over our benchmark in each case].

Another elegance of this approach is that the numbers in Triangle D all relate mathematically to one another. For example, if three successive years (such as 1983, 1984, and 1985) had Value Added of +4%, +12%, and −3%, the compound annual rate of Value Added for the three years is not 5% as shown in Triangle C but 4% $[(1.04 \times 1.12 \times .97)^{1/3} - 1 = .0415)]$. Did you follow that explanation easily? If not, you understand why we use Triangle C for most purposes.

Table 1.4 Triangle D: Value Added—The Sequoia Fund Divided by The Benchmark (S&P 500)

To End of	From Start of																										
	72	73	74	75	76	77	78	79	80	81	82	83	84	85	86	87	88	89	90	91	92	93	94	95	96	97	98
98	4	5	6	5	5	4	2	2	2	3	2	2	1	1	1	2	2	2	3	3	3	3	3	4	4	6	5
97	4	5	6	5	5	3	2	2	2	3	2	1	1	0	1	1	1	2	2	3	2	2	3	3	3	7	
96	4	5	6	5	5	3	2	1	2	3	1	1	1	-0	0	1	1	1	2	2	1	1	1	1	-1		
95	4	5	6	6	5	4	2	1	2	3	2	1	1	0	0	1	1	2	2	3	2	2	2	3			
94	4	5	6	6	5	4	2	1	2	3	2	1	1	-0	0	0	0	1	2	3	1	1	2				
93	5	5	7	6	5	4	2	1	2	3	1	1	1	-0	-0	0	0	1	2	3	1	1					
92	5	6	7	6	5	4	2	1	2	4	1	1	1	-1	-0	-0	-0	1	2	3	2						
91	5	6	7	7	6	4	2	1	2	4	2	1	1	-1	-0	0	-0	1	3	7							
90	5	6	7	7	6	4	2	1	2	3	1	0	-0	-2	-2	-2	-3	-2	-1								
89	5	6	7	7	6	4	2	1	2	4	1	0	-0	-3	-3	-2	-4	-3									
88	6	7	8	8	7	5	3	3	2	5	2	1	0	-3	-2	-2	-5										
87	6	8	9	9	8	6	4	2	3	6	3	2	1	-2	-1	2											
86	7	8	10	9	9	6	4	2	3	6	3	3	2	-4	-4												
85	7	9	11	11	10	7	5	3	5	9	5	(4)	4	-3													
84	8	10	12	12	12	9	6	4	6	12	8	8	12														
83	8	10	12	12	12	8	5	3	5	13	6	4															
82	8	11	13	12	12	9	5	3	5	17	8																
81	8	11	14	13	13	9	5	1	4	28																	
80	6	9	12	11	11	5	-2	-10	-15																		
79	10	13	18	18	19	12	5	-5																			
78	12	17	23	25	28	23	16																				
77	11	17	25	28	34	29																					
76	8	14	23	28	40																						
75	1	6	16	17																							
74	-4	1	15																								
73	-12	-11																									
72	-13																										
Actual	4	-24	-16	61	72	20	24	12	13	22	31	27	19	28	13	7	11	28	-4	40	9	11	3	41	22	43	35

Note: The numbers on the left and at the top reference the year.

unrounded numbers from Triangles A and B. For most purposes, Value Added triangles rounded to the nearest full percentage point are quite adequate.

Triangle C provides a lot of meaningful information. It shows that the Sequoia Fund outperformed the S&P 500 by 10 percentage points in 1991 but underperformed the index by 6 percentage points in 1988, that for the entire 27-year interval 1972–1997 the fund outperformed the index by 5 percentage points per year but it had a bad era in the six years 1985–1990, when it underperformed the index by 3 percentage points per year.

Triangle C is good for our analytical needs, and it is excellent as a graphic to use with our committee in discussing a manager's performance. In fact, to keep the committee members focused on long-term performance, I prefer not to show them a manager's performance *without* using a triangle to put it in perspective. But I would show it in color to emphasize the times the manager outperformed its benchmark and the times it underperformed (Table 1.5 on page 18).

Benchmarks for a Manager

The analysis provided by the triangle in Table 1.5 can be very helpful—but only if we have chosen a valid benchmark for that manager. If we have chosen the wrong benchmark, this analysis is not only useless, but it might even motivate us to part company with a strong manager at the wrong time (or to keep a mediocre manager).

So how do we select an appropriate benchmark? Volumes have been written about that. But in essence, a benchmark should represent the particular universe of stocks (or other securities) from which the particular manager we are evaluating selects his stocks.

We can run sophisticated statistical analyses that are designed to tailor a unique benchmark for a particular manager. Many people believe strongly that this is the best way to derive a valid benchmark. I have always been somewhat skeptical, however, as to whether the monumental effort to develop a thoroughly tailored benchmark is worth it.

If we are evaluating a manager of U.S. stocks, we should first ask whether he invests mainly in large, well-known stocks. If the answer is yes, then the S&P 500, which is weighted very heavily toward large stocks, is probably a good benchmark. It should be a reasonable benchmark for an interval of 10 years or more. For shorter intervals, we need to use a lot of judgment in evaluating a manager's performance.

Table 1.5 Triangle C: Value Added—The Sequoia Fund Minus The Benchmark (S&P 500)

To	*From Start of*																										
End of	*72*	*73*	*74*	*75*	*76*	*77*	*78*	*79*	*80*	*81*	*82*	*83*	*84*	*85*	*86*	*87*	*88*	*89*	*90*	*91*	*92*	*93*	*94*	*95*	*96*	*97*	*98*
98	5	6	7	6	6	4	3	2	3	4	2	2	2	1	1	2	2	3	3	4	3	3	4	5	5	8	7
97	5	6	7	6	6	4	3	2	2	4	2	2	1	1	1	1	1	2	3	3	3	3	3	4	4	10	
96	5	6	6	6	6	4	2	2	2	3	2	1	1	0	0	1	1	1	2	3	1	1	1	1	1		
95	5	6	7	7	6	4	3	2	2	4	2	1	1	0	0	1	1	2	3	3	2	2	3	4			
94	5	6	7	7	6	4	3	2	2	4	2	1	1	0	0	1	0	2	2	3	2	1	2				
93	5	6	7	7	6	4	3	2	2	4	2	1	1	1	0	0	0	1	2	4	1	1					
92	5	6	8	7	7	4	3	2	2	4	2	1	1	1	0	0	0	2	3	5	2						
91	6	7	8	8	7	5	3	2	2	4	2	1	1	1	1	0	0	1	4	10							
90	5	7	8	8	7	4	2	1	2	4	1	0	1	3	2	2	3	2	1								
89	6	7	8	8	7	5	3	1	2	4	1	0	0	3	3	2	5	4									
88	6	8	9	9	8	5	3	2	3	5	2	1	0	3	3	2	6										
87	7	8	10	10	9	6	4	3	4	7	3	2	2	2	1	2											
86	7	9	11	11	10	7	4	3	4	8	4	2	1	5	5												
85	8	10	12	12	12	8	6	4	6	10	6	5	5	4													
84	9	11	14	14	13	10	7	5	7	14	9	9	12														
83	9	11	14	14	13	9	6	3	6	14	7	5															
82	9	11	15	15	14	10	6	3	6	19	10																
81	9	12	15	16	15	10	5	1	5	26																	
80	7	10	14	14	13	5	3	13	20																		
79	10	14	19	21	21	13	6	6																			
78	12	17	24	29	30	22	17																				
77	11	17	26	33	37	27																					
76	8	14	25	36	49																						
75	1	6	16	23																							
74	3	1	11																								
73	12	9																									
72	15																										
Actual	4	−24	−16	61	72	20	24	12	13	22	31	27	19	28	13	7	11	28	−4	40	9	11	3	41	22	43	35

White = outperformed benchmark (we use blue numbers)
Gray = underperformed benchmark (we use red numbers)

Note: The numbers on the left and at the top reference the year.

If the manager invests mainly in growth stocks, stocks expected to achieve rapid increases in their earnings per share, our manager might underperform the S&P 500 by a material degree for a period of years when growth stocks happen to be out of favor. A better benchmark for shorter intervals might be an *index of large growth stocks.* A variety of consultants make such indexes available. The results of their various indexes differ from one another somewhat because there isn't and never will be a precisely uniform definition of growth stocks.

Or the manager may invest mainly in stocks with a low price-to-book-value ratio, typically known as value stocks. Similarly, we can find a range of indexes of large value stocks—again, all providing somewhat different results, because the definitions of value stocks are even less uniform than of growth stocks.

These specialized indexes can be somewhat helpful. But they can't substitute for a thorough understanding of how our manager invests and for good judgment about how the market has treated his particular investment style over the past few years.

You wouldn't use the S&P 500 as the benchmark for a manager of small U.S. stocks because small stocks perform very differently from large stocks. A good measure of returns on small stocks is the Russell 2000 index, which measures the performance of the 2,000 largest stocks *after* first eliminating the 1,000 largest stocks. You can see from Table 1.6 how the Russell 2000 has performed relative to the S&P 500.

We can see from Table 1.6 that for the years 1979 (inception of the Russell 2000 index) through 1983, small stocks outperformed large stocks (as defined by these two indexes) by 9 percentage points per year. Then from 1984 through 1990, large stocks outperformed small stocks by 10 percentage points per year. Contemplate the wrong conclusions we might reach if we were using the wrong benchmark for a particular manager!

Again, consultants make available various indexes of small growth stocks and small value stocks. The same caveats as for large growth stocks apply here.

What if we have a manager who invests in all kinds of stocks—big ones and small ones, and different kinds of stocks at different times? The best benchmark for such a manager may be the Wilshire 5000 index, which tries to measure the returns of all stocks that are publicly traded in the United States, or the Russell 3000 index, which measures the returns of the largest 3,000 U.S. stocks. The results of these two indexes are very close.

Table 1.6 Triangle E: Russell 2000 Index vs. S&P 500 Index

To End of	\<From Start of\> 79	80	81	82	83	84	85	86	87	88	89	90	91	92	93	94	95	96	97	98
98	3	4	5	5	6	7	6	6	6	5	6	5	3	6	9	12	15	17	22	31
97	1	3	3	4	4	5	4	4	4	2	3	2	1	1	4	7	9	9	11	
96	1	2	3	3	4	4	4	4	3	1	3	1	3	0	2	6	8	6		
95	0	2	2	3	4	4	3	4	2		2	0	4	2	1	6	9			
94	0	1	2	3	3	4	3	3	2	0	1	2	7	5	3					
93	0	1	2	3	3	4	3	3	2	1	0	3	12	10	9					
92	0	2	3	4	4	5	4	5	3	1	3	1	13	11						
91	1	3	4	5	6	7	6	7	6	4	7	4	16							
90	2	5	5	7	8	(10)	9	11	10	9	16	16								
89	1	3	4	5	7	9	7	9	8	3	15									
88	1	2	3	4	5	7	6	7	4	8										
87	0	3	4	6	8	11	10	13	14											
86	2	1	2	4	6	10	7	13												
85	4	1	0	2	4	8	1													
84	5	1	0	2	5	14														
83	(9)	6	6	5	7															
82	10	6	5	4																
81	12	7	7																	
80	16	6																		
79	25																			
Actual	43	39	2	25	29	-7	31	6	-9	25	16	-20	46	18	19	-2	28	17	22	-3

White = outperformed benchmark
Gray = underperformed benchmark

Note: The numbers on the left and at the top reference the year.

20

Other indexes are also available—mid-cap indexes and mini-cap indexes, for example. Selecting the right benchmark for a manager is not an easy matter. We might ask the manager with what benchmark he chooses to compare himself. That can be helpful, but not always, because some managers compare their results with the S&P 500 only because that's the index they think most investors are familiar with. One must remember that the S&P 500 measures only some 85% of the value of all U.S. stocks, and it is heavily weighted toward the few very largest stocks.

We just used the words mid-cap and mini-cap. What do we mean by "cap"? Cap stands for market capitalization—the price of a stock times the number of its shares outstanding. Almost all stock indexes are *cap-weighted*. That is, a stock like GE, which may have a cap of $300 billion, is weighted 3,000 times as heavily as a mini-cap stock with a cap of only $100 million. There is an elegance to cap-weighted indexes:

- They reflect the total market value of all stocks included in the index.
- The number of shares of each stock in the index never needs to be rebalanced as stock prices change (unless a company issues more shares or repurchases some of its shares).
- We can create a portfolio that contains the same stocks in the same proportions as the index (an index fund), and if properly assembled the portfolio's performance should very precisely mirror that of the index. We'll talk more about index funds in Chapter 5 in the context of selecting investment managers.
- Cap-weighting is appropriate because all investors together *must* hold the same aggregate value in each stock as its capitalization, and they can hold no more aggregate value in each small stock than its capitalization. Although any individual investor can be different, all investors together cannot.

We haven't even mentioned the most popular stock index of all—the Dow Jones Index of 30 Industrial Stocks. Why not? After all, it's the market barometer most often referred to in the press.

The Dow is not a cap-weighted index. Each stock is weighted by a factor relating to its price, unrelated to how many shares are outstanding. It is difficult to manage an index fund of the Dow Jones Industrials. For this reason, while The Dow serves well as a rough measure of the performance of very large stocks, it is not a very useful analytical tool.

Returns on a Portfolio of Investments

Now let's get back to the question raised earlier: If we've invested in a whole series of mutual funds over the years, what is our rate of return?

Let's say we invested an increasing amount of money over a period of years, some years more, some years less. In some years, we withdrew some money from our investments. Also, we invested in not one but in multiple kinds of mutual funds. We thus invested in a *portfolio* of funds such as that held by an institutional investor.

How do we keep score on a portfolio like that? There are two basic ways : (1) dollar-weighted returns, and (2) time-weighted returns. It's important to understanding the differences between them—what the differences mean, when to use each, and why. We can illustrate the difference most easily with a simple example.

If we put $1,000 into Mutual Fund X and it returns 20% the first year, then we invest another $5,000 in Mutual Fund Y, and they both return 10% the second year, what is our rate of return on our *portfolio* of the two funds for the two years?

First, how much money do we have (what is our wealth) at the end of year 2? Our wealth after year 2 is $6,820:

Date	Cash Flow (Contributions & Withdrawals)	Investment Wealth	Rate of Return	Return
1/01/00	$+1,000	$1,000	—	
12/31/00	—	1,200	$200	20%
1/01/01	+5,000	6,200	—	—
12/31/01	—	6,820	620	10%

If we weight the results in each year equally (as a mutual fund does), then the annual rate of return for the two years is about the average of 10% and 20% or roughly 15%.[5]

---

[5] But be careful of taking simple averages. It's not as simple as it might seem. In this case, the precise annual time-weighted rate of return for the two years is 14.89% $[(1.10 \times 1.20)^{1/2} - 1 = .1489]$. For a technical discussion of time-weighted and dollar-weighted rates of return, see Appendix A at the end of this chapter.

But we did not earn 15% per year on every dollar. We earned 20% on $1,000, then 10% on a little more than $6,000. What is the dollar-weighted annual rate of return on every dollar we had invested? The most accepted way to derive the dollar-weighted rate of return is to calculate its *internal rate of return*—which turns out to be 11.5%.[6]

So what rate of return did we earn on our money—15% or 11.5%? Both figures give us useful information. The important thing is to use them for the right purpose.

The 11.5% is what we actually earned on our money. That may be good or bad compared with our long-term aspirations. But it is very difficult to compare that with our opportunities (i.e., with any benchmark) to determine whether that is good or bad, because no benchmark invested money with the same *timing* as we.

Weighting each year equally gives us a figure—15%—that we can compare with other similar funds or with an appropriate benchmark.

Because time-weighted returns ignore the timing of investments or redemptions, time-weighted returns implicitly relieve the investor of the responsibility for the timing of his investments. That is a critically important assumption. But is it an *appropriate* assumption?

It depends.

Let's say we placed $1,000 with Investment Manager A, and the second year after he achieved a 10% return, we gave him an additional $5,000, and then the stock market dropped 10% and Manager A's investment did also. His *time-weighted* rate of return is about zero (actually –0.5% per year)[7] and his *dollar-weighted* rate of return is –7.4% per year.[8] Shouldn't Manager A have known better than to put the money in the stock market just before it went down? If we rely on his *time-weighted* performance, we're saying no, he shouldn't have known better. But isn't that why we place our money with a professional investment manager?

Manager A had an opportunity to be a hero by keeping the money in cash equivalents for the second year, but we are unrealistic if we expect our manager to be a good market timer. After 25 years of investing, I still don't know of a really good market timer. It is realistic to expect a good

---

[6] Note that $6,820 = 1,000(1.1152)^2 + 5,000(1.1152)$. The methodology for calculations like this is described in the Appendix to this chapter.

[7] $(1.10 \times 0.90)^{1/2} - 1 = .995$, or –0.5%.

[8] $1,000 \times 1.10 = 1,100$; $1,100 + 5,000 = 6,100$; $6,100 \times 0.90 = 5,490$; $1 - .074 = .926$; $5,490 = 1,000 \times (.926)^2 + 5,000 \,(.926)$.

manager of stocks or bonds to perform well over the long-term *relative* to an appropriate benchmark, but not to be clairvoyant enough to know when to go in or out of the stock market.

Therefore, *time-weighted* rates of returns are best for evaluating a manager of stocks or bonds. They are also the *only way* to compare the performance of our overall fund with other funds that have had different timing of cash flows (contributions or withdrawals), or with an overall benchmark for our fund.

But, ultimately, time-weighted rates of return are not what count. *Dollar-weighted* rates of return—also known as internal rates of return—determine our ending wealth. Also, dollar-weighted rates of return are the only meaningful way to measure returns on private investments, where the manager controls the timing of when money goes into and out of the fund.

In Short

All rates of return should be based on market value. Calculating rates of return is simply a matter of applying the right arithmetic.

Determining whether a fund's rate of return is good or not—now that's another matter. We must use appropriate benchmarks, thoughtful analyses, and judgment.

Appendix A

Calculating Rates of Return

Dollar-Weighted Rate of Return
[also referred to as internal rate of return (IRR) or cash-flow rate of return (CFRR)]

Measure

The dollar-weighted rate of return is the compound (usually annual) growth rate of every dollar in a fund, with due weight given to the time it was in the fund. As more dollars are contributed over time, proportionately greater weight is given to more recent time intervals—or vice versa.

Use

For a pension fund, the dollar-weighted rate of return is the best measure to show how the fund is growing relative to the pension plan's actuarial interest assumption. It is also generally the best performance measure for private investments, such as real estate.

Where recent contributions (or withdrawals) have been large, relative to the market value of a fund, the dollar-weighted rate of return may be quite different from the time-weighted rate for the latest year or several years. On the other hand, where contributions (or withdrawals) have been relatively small, the two rates of return will be quite similar.

Mathematics

The dollar-weighted rate of return is calculated by solving for R in the following equation:

$$0 = F_1(1 + R / 100)^{Y_1} + F_2(1 + R / 100)^{Y_2} + \ldots + F_n(1 + R / 100)^{Y_n} + MV$$

where MV is the market value of the fund at the end of the time interval being measured.

F_1 is the first cash flow (usually the market value of the fund at the beginning of the time interval being measured, which would be considered a negative cash flow).

F_2, F_3, F_4, etc., are contributions (negative cash flows) or withdrawals (positive cash flows), and F_n is the last cash flow.

Y is the number of years (or other base period, such as a quarter of a year) that has elapsed from the beginning of the interval to the end of the interval being measured.

Needless to say, this equation is best solved by computer.

Time-Weighted Rate of Return

Measure

The time-weighted rate of return measures the compound annual growth rate of a dollar that was in the fund from the beginning of an interval to the end of that interval. In effect, the fund's performance in each unit of time is given equal weight.

All rates of return pertaining to mutual funds, for example, are time-weighted rates of return.

Use

The time-weighted rate of return is used to compare the performance of one fund with that of another despite different flows of contributions into (or withdrawals out of) each fund. It is also used to compare the performance of a pension fund with that of stock indexes, bond indexes, mutual funds, or other pension funds or endowment funds.

Time-weighted rates of return are generally regarded as the best performance measure of a manager of stocks or bonds. The manager has no control over the amount or timing of contributions (or withdrawals), and the time-weighted rate of return removes these considerations from his performance evaluation.

A time-weighted rate of return is not a measure of the return on all dollars invested and therefore is not designed to measure past performance of pension funds on the same basis as the actuarial interest assumption, for example.

Mathematics

Absolute precision would require that the total market value of a fund (including accrued interest, dividends, receivables, and payables) be calculated every time a contribution (or withdrawal) is made—just as is done with mutual funds, which are priced daily. Obtaining the total market value of a pension or endowment fund so frequently is not practical.

Many pension plans obtain the market value of each of their trust funds (including the above accruals) only at the end of each month or each quarter. They calculate the dollar-weighted return for that month or quarter, then *link* these returns. Two examples of dollar-weighted quarterly calculations:

	Example A	*Example B*
31 March market value	$(6,543,286)	$(6,543,286)
Contributions:		
15 April	(250,000)	(250,000)
15 May	(250,000)	(250,000)
15 June	(250,000)	(250,000)
30 June market value	7,443,981	7,021,359
Dollar-weighted rate of return:		
On an annual basis	+9.028%	−4.848%
On a quarterly basis	+2.178%	−3.928%

The conversion from an annual basis to a quarterly basis is made as follows:

Example A	*Example B*
$(1 + 9.028/100)^{91/365} = 1.02178$	$(1 - 14.848/100)^{91/365} = .96072$
$100(1.02178 - 1) = 2.178\%$	$100(.96072 - 1) = -3.928\%$

The exponents in Examples A and B reflect the number of days in the quarter (91) divided by the number of days in the year (365). The exponent for the first quarter would normally be 90/365 and for the third and fourth quarters, 92/365.

Time-weighted performance records are kept by means of an index, which is often set arbitrarily at 1.0000 at inception (or 10.000 or 100.00). We then adjust that index at the end of each month or quarter by the rate of return for that month or quarter, thereby *linking* the monthly or quarterly returns. For example, if the above rates of return were for the first quarter of a fund's existence, its index at the end of that first quarter would be:

Example A: 1.0000(1 + 2.178%) = 1.0218

Example B: 1.0000(1 − 3.928%) = .9607

Of course, if the fund had been in existence for some years and its index at the start of the quarter had been 1.8931, then we would *link* the quarterly return to that index, and the new index at the end of the quarter (using Example A) would be:

$$1.8931(1 + 2.178/100) = 1.9343$$

An index record, after a few years, might look like this:

31 Dec. '00—1.0000	31 Mar. '02—1.3223
	30 June '02—1.2491
31 Mar. '01—1.1212	30 Sept. '02—1.1826
30 June '01—1.1734	31 Dec. '02—1.2275
30 Sept. '01—1.2671	
31 Dec. '01—1.2579	31 Mar. '03—1.2938

The time-weighted rate of return for any time interval can then be found by dividing the latest index by the first index and taking the answer to the power of one over the number of years in the interval. For example:

The latest 12 months:

$$(1.2938/1.3223)^{1/1} = .9784, \text{ or } -2.16\%$$

Performance since inception:

$$(1.2938/1.0000)^{1/2.25} = 1.1213, \text{ or } 12.13\%$$

Performance from 30 June '01 to 31 December '02:

$$(1.2275/1.1734)^{1/1.5} = 1.0305, \text{ or } 3.05\%$$

Comparisons with Stock Indexes

If we are comparing the performance of our fund with that of a stock index, we must be sure that the stock index is a *total return* index, including dividends. Most indexes published in the newspaper are simply price indexes, without inclusion of dividends—an inappropriate benchmark for a fund.

Chapter 2

Keeping Score II: Risk

Over a 10-year interval, Fund A earned 12% per year while Fund B earned only 10% per year. Both funds had negative returns in some years, but in their negative years Fund A was down 5% more than Fund B. Which was the better fund?

The answer may depend on our willingness to take on risk. Risk is the flip side of investment return. The higher the expected return, the higher the expected risk. That's a truism—and pretty true. It doesn't necessarily work the other way, however. The higher the risk *does not* necessarily mean the higher the return. Casinos, for example, can be high risk, but for the gambler they all have a negative expected return.

What is risk?

When someone talks about the risk of a particular investment, we should first ask what he means—because one can define risk many ways.

Most fundamentally, risk is the probability of losing money—or that the value of our investment will go down. Most investments other than U.S. Treasury bills and insured bank accounts have some reasonable probability of losing money. Other risks include:

- *Loss of buying power.* We could go many years without losing money and have suffered from very real risk. A passbook savings account, for example, would not have lost money, but its buying power at the end of a long interval could be lower than when it started if its rate of return failed to keep up with inflation.

- *Theft.* The risk of dealing with someone, perhaps several times removed from the person we are dealing with directly, who turns out to be a thief. Some mighty sophisticated investors have at times put large amounts of money into a company only to find out that the inventory the auditor signed off on simply wasn't there, and the company was heading for bankruptcy. There are countless ways for dishonest people to separate us from our money. We can never afford to compromise relative to the character and trustworthiness of the people with whom we do business. Trust is a sine qua non.

- *Complexity.* Many a person has gotten into investments too complex for him to understand. Front pages have reported numerous disasters involving derivatives, some of which can have complexities that are very difficult for mere mortals to fathom.

- *Loss of control.* A portfolio of investments can become so large and diverse that it gets beyond our ability to understand or beyond that which we or our organization are prepared to manage.

- *Illiquidity.* When we have our money tied up in some nonmarketable investment, we may suddenly need to use the money or would like to sell the investment, and can't.

- *Maverick risk.* Making investments that none of our peers is making. Because the investments are off-beat, we might fear that we could be taking a career risk if one of the investments goes sour. We fear being held "imprudent" simply for straying from the pack.

- *Benchmark risk.* Varying too much from a benchmark. If an investment manager has too much variance from his benchmark, how do we know whether or not he is doing a good job? If our overall portfolio strays too far from its benchmark, are we still really in control?

- *Putting too many eggs in one basket.* No matter how confident we are about an investment, there is always some possibility that it will go sour, and we don't want to go with it. The flip side of this is that many of the wealthiest people did just that—focused most of their wealth and energies on a single investment. We don't hear, however, about the large number who followed the same approach but went down the tubes. Bankruptcy courts are full of them.

Volatility

The most widely used definition of risk is *volatility*—how much market values go up and down over time. Volatility is most widely used because it is the most measurable of all risks. Also, over long intervals of time, the volatility of a portfolio encompasses many of the above risks. Volatility measures the uncertainty surrounding an investment, or a portfolio of investments. Because it is measurable, it is more controllable.

How do we measure volatility?

Standard Deviation

The simplest measure is annual *standard deviation* from the asset's (or portfolio's) mean rate of return, the same standard deviation measure we learned to calculate in high school algebra. A low standard deviation of investment returns over time means that we had pretty high certainty of investment results. A high standard deviation means we had a high degree of *un*certainty. Low volatility is good, high is bad.

Standard deviation works well in models of multiple asset classes (such as stocks or bonds) and enables us to calculate how all the asset classes feed into a distribution of expected returns for the aggregate portfolio.

In theory, at least, better measures of risk for the aggregate portfolio, may be (1) *semivariance* (the portion of the standard deviation that's below the mean, or average, return[1]), or better yet, (2) *shortfall risk* (the probability of falling below our target return, or below some other rate of return that we would find painful).

For most of the remainder of this book, when we quantify risk, we shall equate risk with volatility and use the metric of annual standard deviation. That is the most convenient and most broadly useful measure. But it has

---

[1] We might find even greater intuitive appeal in *target semi-variance*—the same as semi-variance (except the *mean* return is replaced by the *target* return). Hypothetically, if an investment manager had very high volatility but in his worst years he never fell below our target return, we could cry about his volatility all the way to the bank!

limitations. Beware of the assumption that historical standard deviations are always good predictors of future standard deviations.[2]

One limitation is that the standard deviation (and many other calculations) force all data into a single mold—that of a bell-shaped curve. While on average, most data relationships may fall into a bell-shaped pattern, many are skewed to the left or to the right, with large asymmetric tails that can get us into trouble. "Tails" refer to the narrow parts of the curve—the probability that a given annual return may be very different from the average annual return (the center of the bell curve). We must be aware of those tails.

Also, while an asset's standard deviation is normally stated as X percentage points *per year,* there are multiple ways of calculating this. We can annualize the asset's daily volatility, or its monthly or quarterly volatility or we can simply take annual readings. These measures often provide different results.

The norm, according to statisticians, is for volatility to increase by the square root of time. For example, a monthly standard deviation of 3 points would be annualized to a 10.4-point standard deviation ($3 \times \sqrt{12}$).

But many assets differ from this norm. Some are mean-reverting; that is, positive performance in one month has a tendency to be offset by negative performance in another month. Hence, the above method to annualize volatility overstates true annual volatility.

The reverse can also occur. Monthly volatility can be serial and therefore compounding. This would be true if *positive* performance should signal a high probability of positive performance in succeeding months (and vice versa). The above algorithm to annualize volatility then understates true annual volatility.

For purposes of assessing volatility, *what interval* is most meaningful to us? Do we care about *daily* or *monthly* volatility? Our managers' traders might care, but why should we? How about *quarterly* volatility? For those funds that must give detailed reports to their boards or committees every three months, quarterly volatility might have some relevance. But I don't favor detailed quarterly reports (they only invite a case of myopia). I am not much concerned about quarterly volatility.

---

[2] Historic standard deviations are considerably better predictors of future standard deviations than historic returns are of future returns. But that is damning with faint praise!

I have a concern about standard deviation that doesn't seem to bother statisticians. We are interested in an asset's *compound* annual return, not its *mean* annual return. (An asset with annual returns of +40%, –20%, and +20% has a compound annual return of 10.4% but a mean annual return of 13.3%.) Yet standard deviation is calculated on *mean* annual return.

To calculate the mean return, we simply add the annual rates of return and divide by the number of years. For example, $(40\% - 20\% + 20\%)/3 = 13.3\%$.

To calculate the compound return, we add 1 to each year's rate of return to derive a wealth index (as $40\% \rightarrow 1.40$), then multiply all of the years' wealth indexes together, raise the product to the power of 1 over the number of years, and subtract 1. For example:

Year	Rate of Return for the Year
1	+40%
2	–20%
3	+20%

Compound return (geometric return):

$$1.40 \times (1 - .20) \times 1.20 = 1.344$$
$$1.344^{1/3} - 1 = 10.4\% \text{ compound annual return}$$

The compound return is what counts for us, because it tells us how our wealth has grown. The compound return is *always less* than the mean return. The higher the standard deviation in annual returns, the greater the disparity between the two rates of return.

An algorithm that approximates the relationship of the two rates of return (provided the volatility is not too horrendous) is:

$$G = A - V^2/2$$

where G = the compound return (the geometric mean)
    A = the mean return (the arithmetic mean)
    V = standard deviation (volatility)

Well, how about *annual* volatility? That *is* relevant because every fund must give a detailed performance report to its board or committee as well as its public at least once a year. The trouble is that, to determine annual volatility, we have so few data points that statisticians tell us we have too low a T-statistic to be meaningful.

Standard deviations have a lot of fuzz around them. But they may be the best measure we have.

Alphas and Betas

A widely used measure of the risk of a stock or of a portfolio of stocks is its *beta*. Every stock (or portfolio) has some correlation with the overall stock market (most commonly measured by the S&P 500). Does Stock A go up more than the market when the market goes up, and down more than the

---

Beta is the result of a regression equation that relates the historical performance of each stock (or our stock portfolio) to the market. A regression is a long, complex computer calculation that solves the following equation:

$$R_x = A + ßR_m \pm SE$$

where: R_x = the return on Stock X (or Portfolio X)
A (alpha) = its risk-adjusted excess return—a positive or negative number that is independent of the movement of the overall market
ß (beta) = its volatility relative to the market
R_m = the return of the overall market (perhaps the S&P 500)

SE = Standard Error, or better, *residual return*. It is that portion of Stock X's performance that is *not* explained by the movement of the overall market. More complex regression equations can then break down residual return further into any number of additional statistics, such as the portion attributed to Stock X's industry exposure, its small-cap exposure, and ultimately *specific risk* that can't be attributed to anything and is therefore unique to Stock X.

market when the market goes down? Or does Stock A tend to move less than the market? Beta is an effort to provide that measure.

A beta of 1.0 means that, other things being equal, Stock A should move up and down with the market. A beta of 1.2 means that when the market is up 10%, Stock A should be up 1.2 times 10%, which is 12%; and when the market is down 10%, Stock A should be down 12%. (Conversely, a beta of 0.8 means that, when the market moves 10%, the stock should be up or down only 8%.)

Of course, the closer to zero the correlation between Stock A and the market, the less meaningful a figure is beta.

Alpha is a particularly important figure because it represents the value a manager is adding to an unmanaged index. It technically stands for *risk-adjusted* excess return. In common parlance, it is often used to denote the simple difference between a manager's return and his benchmark index. When we hear the term *alpha,* we will want to be sure we understand just how it is being used.

Correlation

Correlation is another very important term of investment jargon. Correlation (known statistically as *r*) compares the historical relationship of the returns of Stock A (or Portfolio A) with those of a market index or of any other asset with which we want a comparison. Do returns on the two move together? Or do they march to different drummers?

A correlation of 1.0 between Stocks A and B means they have always moved exactly together. A correlation of −1.0 means they have always moved exactly opposite of one another. A correlation of 0 means there has been no relationship whatsoever between the returns on Stocks A and B.[3]

Correlation is the foundation for the concept of *systematic risk* and *diversifiable risk.*

Systematic Risk and Diversifiable Risk

Most individual U.S. stocks bounce up and down more than the overall U.S. stock market. We can ease that roller coaster ride—reduce that volatility—

---

[3] Correlation squared (r^2) is the portion of Stock A's returns that statisticians say can be explained by the returns of Stock B. For example, if the correlation were .8, then .64 ($.8^2$) of Stock A's returns can be explained by returns on Stock B.

by adding more U.S. stocks, especially ones in different industries that march to a somewhat different drummer. We can strive to eliminate *diversifiable risk*. But after a point, we will still be left with the *systematic risk* of the overall U.S. stock market.

Through statistical methods known as regressions, we can divide the volatility of each U.S. stocks into portions that are:

1.   Systematic with the overall U.S. stock market.
2.   Systematic with its own industry.
3.   Systematic with stocks that have similar price/earnings ratios.
4.   Systematic with stocks that have certain other common characteristics.
5.   Not systematic with any of those characteristics. We call this remaining volatility *residual risk*.

We can easily eliminate residual risk. We can diversify it away by adding more U.S. stocks. Risks (2) through (4) are also diversifiable risks, and we can diversify them away by adding different kinds of U.S. stocks. But we can't diversify away volatility that is systematic with the U.S. stock market by adding more U.S. stocks. We can reduce this volatility only by adding other assets—non-U.S. stocks, bonds, real estate—assets whose volatility has a low correlation with that of U.S. stocks; the lower correlation the better.

Diversifiable risk is a critically important concept that we can put to great advantage, as we shall see later in this book.

What to Do about Risk?

All of the risks we've mentioned are important. We must understand them all and treat them with due respect. But we must place each into proper perspective and not allow ourselves to become traumatized by risk. If we have a good understanding of the risks, then we should be looking for ways to use risk *to our advantage*.

We began this chapter with a truism: The higher the expected return, the higher the expected risk. The job of running an investment fund is not to see how little risk we can take, but to see how *much* risk we can take—*diversifiable* risk, of course. That is, *intelligent* diversifiable risk. As we said at the start of this chapter: Higher risk does not necessarily mean higher return.

This has powerful implications for an investment portfolio. The average stock in a large portfolio of stocks might have an annual volatility of 30 percentage points per year, while the volatility of the *overall portfolio* might be only 14 percentage points. We can reduce risk most productively by investing in multiple asset classes that have a low correlation with one another—domestic stocks, foreign stocks, real estate, bonds. This leads to the critically important concept: *Efficient frontier.*

The Efficient Frontier

Depending on the accuracy of our expectations for future returns, volatility, and correlations of all the assets available to us to invest in, there is theoretically a single portfolio that will give us the highest expected return for any given level of portfolio volatility. For example, point A in Figure 2.1 represents a portfolio that has an expected volatility of 9% per year. At that expected volatility, there is a single discreet portfolio of asset classes that will give us the highest possible expected return. Any other portfolio that has an expected volatility of 9% will have a lower expected return. The most efficient asset allocation at every level of expected volatility forms the line you see, which we call the *efficient frontier.*

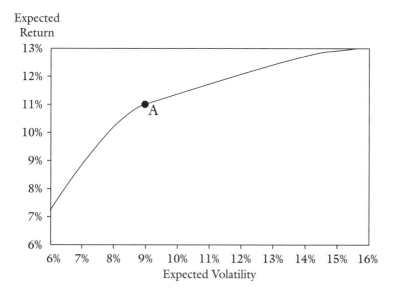

Figure 2.1 Efficient Frontier.

Table 2.1 Sample Input: Assumptions for Efficient Frontier

| | | | Correlations | | | | | | | | | | | | | | |
| | | | Common Stocks | | | | Fixed Income | | | | | | Other Assets | | | | |
	Expected Return	Annual Volatility	U.S. Large	U.S. Small	Non-U.S. Developed	Emerging Markets	U.S. Cash Equiv.	U.S. Bonds	U.S. High Yield	U.S. 25-Year Zeros	Non-U.S. Developed	Emerging Markets	Real Estate Core	Venture	Private Equity*	Oil & Gas, Timber	Arbitrage Programs
Common Stocks:																	
U.S. Large Stocks	9.0%	14.5%															
U.S. Small Stocks	9.5%	16.0%	.7														
Non-U.S., Developed Countries	9.0%	18.0%	.6	.5													
Emerging Markets	11.0%	25.0%	.4	.4	.5												
Fixed Income:																	
U.S. Cash Equivalents	4.5%	3.0%	.0	.0	.0	.0											
U.S. Traditional Bonds	7.0%	8.0%	.4	.4	.3	.3	.2										
U.S. High-Yield Bonds	8.5%	12.0%	.6	.7	.4	.3	.0	.7									
U.S. 25-Year Zeros	7.0%	25.0%	.4	.4	.3	.3	.2	.8	.6								
Non-U.S. Bonds, Developed Countries	7.0%	8.0%	.2	.2	.4	.2	.2	.6	.5	.6							
Emerging Markets Debt	11.0%	18.0%	.4	.5	.2	.6	.2	.5	.5	.5	.5						
Other Assets:																	
Core Real Estate	8.0%	12.0%	.2	.2	.0	.0	.0	.0	.0	.0	.0	.0					
Venture Real Estate	10.0%	18.0%	.2	.2	.0	.0	.0	.0	.0	.0	.0	.0	.8				
Private Equity*	13.0%	29.0%	.6	.8	.5	.3	.0	.2	.2	.2	.1	.1	.2	.2			
Oil & Gas, Timber	10.0%	18.0%	.0	.0	.1	.0	.1	.1	.1	.1	.1	.1	.0	.0	-.1		
Arbitrage Programs	10.0%	7.0%	.2	.2	.1	.0	.1	.1	.0	.1	.0	.0	.0	.0	.0	.0	

*Includes venture capital, LBO funds, buy-in funds, and distressed securities, both U.S. and non-U.S. Some of these sub-classes may not be highly correlated with one another, so it might be advantageous to treat them separately, as well as to treat timber separately from oil & gas.

You can see from this graph that at the lowest level of volatility we can increase the expected rate of return rapidly with little increase in the expected portfolio volatility. But the higher the expected rate of return, the more portfolio volatility we must take on to increase still further our expected rate of return. At some point, we can increase portfolio volatility almost without gaining any incremental expected return.

We can place a dot on this graph to represent any portfolio of assets we might consider. Most such portfolios would fall well below the efficient frontier. Diversifying away diversifiable risk is the way we can move our portfolio toward higher returns, or lower portfolio risk, or both.

The validity of the efficient frontier depends, of course, on the accuracy of our assumptions. Table 2.1 illustrates the kind of assumptions that we must input to our computer. We know these assumptions will be wrong, because no one has that good a crystal ball. But if we calculate efficient frontiers based on a range of assumptions, we will eventually hone in on efficient frontiers that are robust—that are least sensitive to a range of reasonable assumptions.

We'll talk more about the efficient frontier in Chapter 4, where we discuss asset allocation.

Risk-Adjusted Returns: The Sharpe Ratio

We have now talked extensively about investment return and risk. There are multiple ways to bring them together. Perhaps the best-known way is the Sharpe Ratio, named for Dr. William F. Sharpe, a Nobel Prize winner, who devised it.

Conceptually, the Sharpe Ratio is a simple measure—excess return per unit of risk. Specifically, it's an investment's rate of return *in excess* of the riskfree (T-bill[4]) rate, divided by the investment's standard deviation. The Sharpe Ratio answers the question: How much incremental return do we get for the volatility we take on?

We can apply this ratio to a single investment, or to an entire portfolio. The higher the Sharpe Ratio, the more *efficient* an investment it is. That does not necessarily mean that if Investment A has a higher Sharpe Ratio than Investment B, then A is always a preferable addition to our

---

[4] T-Bill stands for Treasury bill, a very short-term loan to the U.S. government, which is considered to have zero risk.

Implicitly, the Sharpe Ratio *leverages* or *de-leverages* actual returns by saying, in effect: What would be the return if we added T-bills to a volatile investment (de-leveraged) until we have reduced its annual standard deviation to our target volatility? Or what would be the return of a low-volatility investment if we borrowed at T-bill interest rates (leveraged) until we have *increased* its annual standard deviation to that of our target volatility?

That's a tough concept. Let's tackle it with a simplistic example. Let's say, with T-bill rates at 6%, we have two investments, A and B, with the following characteristics:

	Return	Volatility	Sharpe Ratio	Calculation
A	12%	15%	.4	$(12-6)/15 = .4$
B	9	5	.6	$(9-6)/5 = .6$

B has a higher Sharpe ratio, .6 to .4. That's preferable. But why should we prefer B when the return on A is 3 points higher? Implicitly, if we wanted to get A down to the 5% volatility of B, we would have to de-leverage—form a portfolio composed of ⅓ A and ⅔ T-bills (whose volatility is assumed to be zero). That portfolio's return would be only 8%—1% less than that of B.

portfolio than B. The correlations of A and B with everything else in our portfolio are also very important. Because of the benefit of diversification, we would almost always have a materially higher Sharpe Ratio for our overall portfolio than the weighted average Sharpe Ratio of our individual investment programs.

Application of Risk-Adjusted Returns

Risk-adjusted returns are viewed by many as the true measure of an investment manager. In the sense that less volatility is almost always better than more, it is intuitively appealing to reward the lower-volatility manager appropriately.

Personally, I have not placed a great deal of value on risk-adjusted returns, for two basic reasons:

1. We can't spend risk-adjusted returns—only actual returns.
2. Our critical measure is not the absolute volatility of *an investment* (or an asset class) but the impact of that investment (or asset class) on the volatility of *our overall portfolio*. Its impact depends on (a) the correlation of that investment (or asset class) with our other assets and (b) the percentage of our overall portfolio we devote to that investment (or asset class).

Those two basic reasons lead to four corollary reasons:

1. Risk-adjusted returns tend to be theoretical and not real world, in the sense that, because of unrelated business income tax (UBIT) and other reasons, it is not usually feasible to borrow in order to leverage up a low-volatility portfolio. Likewise, we would almost never choose to offset a high-volatility manager by adding cash equivalents.
2. While we must be aware that we can afford only so many high-volatility managers in our portfolio, the most productive way to deal with a high-volatility high-return manager is to find another high-return manager in another asset class who has a low correlation with him.
3. While the inclusion of a low-volatility manager in our portfolio does make room for the inclusion of a high-volatility manager, we can benefit from that low-volatility manager only if we do indeed hire a high-volatility, high-return manager.
4. Of course, we should make sure the high-volatility high-return manager doesn't push us beyond the volatility maximum for our overall portfolio. But many pension funds and endowment funds don't take on as much volatility as they should. We don't deserve accolades for reducing overall portfolio volatility below our target at the cost of lowering our overall portfolio return.

Perhaps the best argument against retaining a manager with low risk-adjusted returns is one articulated by Keith Ambachtsheer and Don Ezra: We should "consider the opportunity cost of undertaking risk in a different, perhaps more rewarding way."[5]

---

[5] Keith P. Ambachtsheer and D. Don Ezra, *Pension Fund Excellence,* John Wiley & Sons, Inc., 1998, p. 54.

Risk of Increased Pension Contributions

For much of this chapter we have talked about the risk of a particular invest-ment or a particular asset class. Toward the end we have been talking more about the risk of the aggregate portfolio—where we should ultimately be focused.

Companies must be concerned about the risk of having to make greater contributions if the market value of their pension assets does not increase as fast as the present value of the plan's benefit obligations. If that happens, the companies would also incur higher pension expense—and therefore lower corporate earnings. It is possible for pension plans to achieve strong investment returns but at the same time for declining inter-est rates to jack up the present value of benefit obligations even more, such that pension expense would rise.[6]

A scary risk to some companies would be if they had to report to their plan participants that the market value of their pension assets had fallen below the present value of their benefit obligations—that they were underfunded! Underfunding could also require the pension plan to pay sharply higher insurance premiums to the U.S. Pension Benefit Guar-antee Corporation.[7]

For a pension plan, the most relevant measure of risk may not be *ab-solute volatility,* as it is for endowment funds, but the *volatility of its fund-ing ratio*—the ratio of the plan's assets to the present value of its benefit obligations.

Because the present value of benefit obligations depends on the dis-count rate[8] we apply, and because the discount rate fluctuates up and down with the prevailing interest rates at which the plan could buy bonds

---

[6] Declining interest rates would jack up the present value of benefit obligations be-cause a lower rate of interest would have to be used to calculate how much money a pension plan must have now to meet its benefit obligations in the years ahead. The reason is simple. To accumulate $10,000 ten years from now, we would need more money invested now at 6% than the amount we'd need invested now at 7%.

[7] The PBGC is a U.S. government agency that insures the payment of pension benefits up to a certain benefit level in the event that the pension plan were ter-minated and couldn't come up with the money to fulfill its promises.

[8] The interest rate used to calculate the present value of benefit obligations is called the *discount rate.*

> A pension plan's *benefit obligations* are promises it has made to its employees and retirees. Benefit obligations are the liabilities of the plan. Simplistically, benefit obligations are all the money the plan will have to pay in retirement benefits over the years and decades ahead.
>
> No pension plan has, or should have, that much money in its pension fund now. But the plan doesn't need that much money. It has many years for its investments to earn that much.
>
> This time element introduces the concept of *present value.* How much money at a particular interest rate must a pension plan have now to be able to meet all of its benefit obligations year after year in the future? The answer to that question is the *present value of benefit obligations.*

to immunize its liabilities,[9] the present value of benefit obligations goes up and down like the market value of a long-duration bond. Therefore, relative to the volatility of a plan's funding ratio, cash equivalents are a lot more risky than long-term bonds! Few pension funds have adequately factored this measure—the volatility of its funding ratio—into their definition of risk.

Derivatives—A Boon, or a Different Four-Letter Word?

Derivatives are so often associated with risk in many people's minds that we should deal with them here. Common derivatives include:

- *Futures.* Agreements, usually exchange-traded, to pay or receive, until some future date, the change in a particular price or an index. (Example: S&P 500 index futures.)

---

[9] We can immunize our liabilities if we buy a particular set of bonds which provides interest payments and maturities that precisely match every payment our plan will have to make to retirees in the long years ahead.

- *Forwards (forward contracts).*   Agreements between two parties to buy (or sell) a security at some future date at a price agreed upon today. (Example: Foreign exchange forwards.)
- *Swaps.*   Agreements between two parties to pay or receive, until some future date, the difference in return between our portfolio (or an index) and a counterparty's portfolio (or an index). (Example: We'll pay you the T-bill rate plus 50 basis points,[10] and you pay us the total return on the Financial Times index on U.K. stocks.)
- *Options.*   The right (not the obligation) to buy (or sell) a particular security at a particular price by a particular date. Options are often traded on a stock or commodity exchange. (Example: A "call option" to buy S&P 500 index futures at an index of 1300 by September 15.)
- *Structured notes.*   Agreements between two parties, the nature of which is limited only by the creative imagination of investment bankers.

Derivative securities are extremely valuable tools in managing a portfolio. They enable us to *reduce* risk by hedging out risks we don't want. Through futures, forwards, or options, we can choose to hedge currency risk, or interest-rate risk, or stock-market risk.

They allow us to take *more* risk, such as "equitizing" our cash equivalents by buying S&P 500 index futures.[11]

They can be big cost savers. For example, if we want to invest in an S&P 500 index fund, the purchase of S&P 500 index futures to overlay a portfolio of cash equivalents may be far cheaper (and at least as effective) compared with buying all 500 stocks for our own account. Buying the stocks would entail transaction costs, custodial costs, dividend reinvestment costs, and proxy-voting costs. When it's time to sell, futures are far less cumbersome and costly to sell.

As Nobel laureate Merton Miller has said: "Index futures have been so successful because they are so cheap and efficient a way for institutional investors to adjust their portfolio proportions. As compared to adjusting

---

[10] A basis point equals 0.01%.

[11] An S&P 500 index future is an agreement to pay or receive, until some future date, the change in the S&P 500 index. Our combined cash equivalents and S&P futures would then behave almost exactly like an S&P 500 index fund—a portfolio invested exactly like the S&P 500 index.

the proportions by buying or selling the stocks one by one and buying or selling T-bills, it is cheaper to use futures by a factor of 10."[12]

So why all the fuss about derivatives?

First of all, derivatives can be complex, particularly specially-tailored derivatives that are not exchange-traded. Many people have purchased derivatives without fully understanding all the specific risks involved and have gotten burned badly.

Other investors, through derivatives, have quietly altered their fund's risk/return position substantially without letting their constituents know until suddenly a blowup has occurred. Recent accounting rules changes have helped to lessen this risk through a requirement of sunlight—public reporting.

There is also counterparty risk. What happens if the counterparty to our deal can't uphold its end of the deal? That's a constant risk, but one that fortunately has rarely materialized.

The sheer complexity of certain derivatives—such as those involving options, whose pattern of returns is highly asymmetric—might at times make it difficult for some plan sponsors to assess very accurately their full exposure to the various markets.

A 1994 article in Moody's did a good job of summarizing the situation:

> The financial roadside is littered with the wreckage of poorly run derivatives operations. . . . Even entities with excellent internal controls are not immune from such surprises. . . . Because risk positions can be radically changed in a matter of seconds, derivatives activity has increased the potential for surprise. . . .
>
> [But] derivatives often get a bad rap. A frequent message we hear is that anyone who is involved in derivatives transactions is tempting fate, and that sooner or later major losses will be suffered as derivatives positions inevitably go wrong. Such messages are misleading.
>
> Properly used, derivatives have been and will continue to be a source of risk reduction and enhanced investment performance for many participants. Therefore, any manager who is not looking at how derivatives can be employed to manage financial and economic risks, or to enhance yields, is doing his or her investors a disservice.

Before we use any given derivative, we must be sure we understand how it works and the impact it could have under adverse conditions. If we don't fully understand a particular derivative, we shouldn't use it.

---

[12] *Journal of Applied Corporate Finance.*

Ways to deal with risk when some of our managers are using derivatives for diverse purposes include the following:

1. Ask each manager who uses derivatives:
   —To explain in plain English what he uses and why,
   —To identify any use of derivatives that might expose our account to substantial loss,
   —To provide us with the manager's internal risk management procedures and guidelines and attest to the firm's compliance with them, and
   —To compare the manager's control procedures with the recommendations of the Group of Thirty and the *Risk Standards for Institutional Investment Managers and Institutional Investors,* published in 1996 by the Association for Investment Management and Research (AIMR).
2. For each account that uses derivatives, work with the manager to define the maximum amount of each kind of derivative to be permitted in that account.
3. Establish (or get our custodian to establish) a monitoring mechanism to create a timely flag if any manager should ever exceed its exposure limit or invest in a derivative that we didn't authorize.
4. Isolate each investment account that uses derivatives into a separate limited liability trust fund. That way, if a manager should ever fall into a black hole, he can at worst lose the assets in his account but cannot access our fund's deep pockets.
5. Set maximum aggregate credit limits for both current and potential exposure to any one counterparty, and monitor across our managers to be sure we stay within those limits.

While asset classes that use derivatives (such as some arbitrage programs) require more investor skill to enter, they are well worth consideration by pension and endowment funds. Where an investor can find competent managers and reasonable terms, use of these asset classes can reduce the aggregate volatility of an overall portfolio and also increase its overall expected return. But it pays to be knowledgeable and thoughtful about our exposure.

There is one serious risk that derivatives share with any investment program that our committee members may not understand well: The committee might decide to terminate the program when it hits rough going, which we can be sure it will hit at some point. Selling at the bottom of a market is one of the worst risks. The only antidote is advance education as to what realistically we can expect—the bad as well as the good.

Overall Fund Risk

Stimulated perhaps by special concerns about derivatives, one direction that modern computers are making possible is a quantitative assessment of overall fund risk, through such measures as *value at risk*. Such measures use highly sophisticated computer analyses to identify the greatest risks in our investment portfolio.

We will be hearing a lot more about these measures in the years ahead, because in theory, at least, they can provide useful insights and help avoid disasters. But they will always have some limitations. Their use will require us to forecast the volatilities and correlations of each of the assets in our overall fund. The more diversified our fund, the more difficult and complex this is. On the other hand, the more diversified our fund, the less our fund should be exposed to any one particular risk.

One thing such statistical studies can't do is tell us our potential exposure to specific unexpected events—such as the collapse of some of the Asian markets in the latter part of 1997 and the worldwide liquidity crisis in the summer of 1998. At times like that, historical correlations seem to have less predictive value, and assets with historically low correlations seem to all move down together. Generally, however, such co-variance has been relatively short-lived. Can we count on that?

In Short

An investment portfolio incurs a myriad of risks. We need to understand each of those risks and to assess its potential impact realistically. But we should not be traumatized by risk.

Our challenge is to *take advantage of the risks* that are reflected in the price of each asset by taking sensible actions to control the risks and by mitigating as many of those risks as possible through intelligent diversification.

Chapter 3

Investment Objectives

Now that we know how to keep score, what's our objective? What "wins the game"? Obviously, the higher the rate of return, the better. But this is a *long-term* game. Good returns over short-term intervals aren't very important *except* as they contribute to the long-term rate of return. It's the *long-term annual rate of return* that really counts.

At the end of every game, it's easy to figure out how we've done—what our long-term rate of return was. But no one gets the benefit of 20/20 hindsight when strategizing as to how to play the game. The only thing that counts is tomorrow, and tomorrow is an unknown—anything can happen. So how do we go about deciding how to invest our money today?

We must begin with our objectives. We should write down our objectives—articulate our principles in a way that will serve as criteria against which to weigh both current investment actions and future proposals.

To establish our investment objectives, we must decide mainly on three interrelated elements:

- Return,
- Risk, and
- Time Horizon.

But these are backwards. First, we should decide our time horizon—the average number of years until we need to use our money. That determines how much risk we can take with our investments. If we need our money tomorrow, we can't afford any risk. If we don't need our money for 10 or 20 years, we can put up with a lot of volatility in between.

Time Horizon

There are major reasons why investing money for a pension fund or endowment fund is dramatically different from investing one's personal assets—other than the fact that such institutional funds are taxfree. Their advantage can be summarized in one phrase: *the law of large numbers.*

If I am investing for my family, I have no large numbers. I invest essentially for my spouse and myself and our children. Actuarial tables are of little help in forecasting when we will retire, how likely we will need extended expensive medical care, and how long each of us will live. I really don't know when I will need my savings, and how much I will need, so I must invest conservatively, to prepare for the worst.

A defined-benefit pension fund for a medium-size company, however, knows within a relatively narrow range the timing and amount of its future benefit payments. The laws of large numbers enable the fund to learn from actuarial tables about how many employees will retire each year (barring special retirement incentives) and, more important, about how many plan participants of each age will die each year. An endowment fund, unless its sponsor suddenly invades its principal, has even clearer knowledge of its future payments to its sponsor. A pension fund or endowment fund should make the most of this critical advantage.

This advantage means that a pension fund or endowment fund should invest with a very long time horizon. A pension fund invests money to pay benefits to current retirees, but much of the money is to pay benefits many years from now. The *average duration*[1] of the benefit obligations of a typical pension fund ranges from 10 to 15 years; we shouldn't have to worry very much about the ups and downs in between. Similarly, an endowment fund is money set aside to provide the organization with *perpetual* annual

---

[1] *The average duration of benefit obligations* is the number of years between now and the weighted average date when our pension fund needs to make all payments to retirees. An actuary can tell us about how much our fund will have to pay to all retirees each year, and the weighted average year of all such payments determines the duration of our benefit obligations.

income. A pension fund or endowment fund should thus focus on rates of return over intervals of 10 or 20 years or longer.

Ah, but then there are forces that drive us toward the myopic.

In its annual report to shareholders (and employees) each year, a company must report its pension "expense" and how well the company has funded its pension promises based on Financial Accounting Standard No. 87 (or FAS 87, and more recently, FAS 132). Now I think the advent of FAS 87 in the mid-1980s was a good thing, but both pension expense and funding adequacy[2] are impacted materially by the pension fund's investment results for the latest single year. Company managements take a keen interest in the impact of pension expense on their reported earnings for the year. And companies prefer not to have to show their employees that their pension assets are less than their Accumulated Benefit Obligations (ABO), a measure of funding adequacy in the event that the pension plan were hypothetically terminated.

Of possibly greater concern, a company with a highly volatile pension fund may have to face highly volatile demands on its cash for pension contributions—probably not a happy prospect.[3]

Companies must also be sensitive to their funding adequacy as measured by the Pension Benefit Guarantee Corporation (PBGC), the U.S. government agency that insures pension benefits promised by corporations. The PBGC measures funding adequacy in an extremely conservative way, and if a company's pension funding falls too low relative to its promises, the PBGC will sharply increase that company's annual PBGC insurance premium.

An endowment fund does not have the same problems. But its sponsor—a university, church, or charitable institution—relies heavily on the annual income it receives from its endowment fund, and it needs dependable amounts of income from year to year, not very high income one year and low the next. We shall suggest ways for an endowment fund to deal with this requirement in Chapter 17.

Despite these forces toward the myopic, pension and endowment funds *do* have a long time horizon. And a huge advantage this is, because the

---

[2] Funding adequacy is the ratio of the market value of the plan's assets to the present value of the plan's benefit obligations.

[3] To minimize the chance of unexpected pension contributions being required at an inopportune time, some corporate sponsors seek to invest their pension assets in a way that is least sensitive to the factors to which *the company's* financial performance is most sensitive.

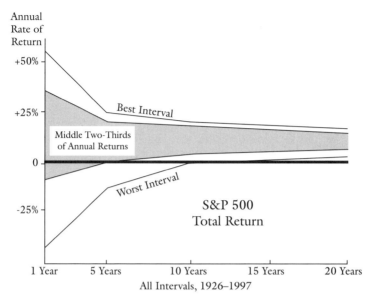

Figure 3.1   The Longer the Time Horizon, the Lower the Risk.
(*Data source:* Ibbotson Associates: *1998 Yearbook.*)

uncertainty of returns narrows with time like a funnel. Figure 3.1 depicts annual rates of return since 1926 on large U.S. stocks for intervals ranging from 1 to 20 years. It shows that one-year returns on common stock have been almost totally unpredictable. Two-thirds of the time, one-year returns have ranged from +35% to −9%. But this range of annual returns has narrowed to +18% to +4% for 10-year intervals, and the range has narrowed further for longer intervals.

Clearly, a pension fund or endowment fund should go for the benefits of being very long-term oriented. But it also has limits in the volatility it can sustain from year to year. This leads to the second element in an investment objective—*risk*.

Risk

With any investment we should recognize up front that no one *knows* what will happen tomorrow. Every investment and every investment approach depends on probabilities. There's a certain probability that over a given

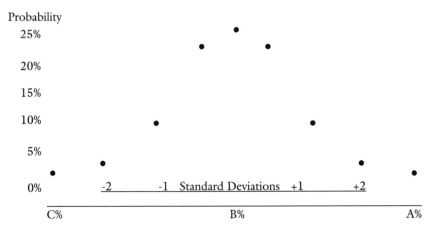

Figure 3.2   Expected Annual Rate of Return. (*Note:* **All probabilities must add up to 100%.**)

time interval the investment will deliver a very high annual rate of return (A%), another probability that it will deliver a most likely rate of return (B%), and another probability that it will deliver a very disappointing rate of return (C%), and lots of probabilities in between. You might think of it something like the bell-shaped curve in Figure 3.2.

The difficulty facing any investor is that the world's investment authorities usually differ over both the probabilities and the values of returns A, B and C. We generally assume the shape is a bell curve, with equal probabilities on each side of the most likely. That assumption simplifies the problem somewhat (because we can use statistical devices like *standard deviations* to measure the uncertainty), but we must remember that a bell curve may often not reflect the probabilities of a given investment. A more accurate curve might be skewed to the left or the right.[4]

The wider the range of probabilities, the more uncertainty. (Or, assuming a bell curve, the larger the standard deviation, the more uncertainty.) And the greater the uncertainty, the greater the likelihood of not achieving our objective over our time horizon. Also, the greater the likelihood of volatile returns over shorter intervals.

---

[4] We should be aware that the distribution of returns on the stock, bond, and currency markets are characterized by high peaks at the mean and fatter tails than the normal distribution, according to Edgar E. Peters of PanAgora Asset Management.

Risk is a hard thing to deal with in setting the investment objectives of a fund. A common way for a fund to quantify its risk tolerance is to establish the maximum *standard deviation of annual returns* it is willing to incur. That's tough to specify.

The lower the volatility we can withstand, the lower long-term rate of return we can rationally aspire to achieve, and vice versa. But what does it mean to say, "We would be willing to incur a standard deviation of X percentage points"? If the financial markets are very placid, we'll have no trouble staying within a standard deviation of X percentage points. But if the markets are turbulent, a standard deviation of X percentage points will be a pipe dream. And we have no control over the financial markets.

Hence, about the only risk measure that's pragmatic is a *relative* risk measure. For example, one could say, "We can withstand the volatility of the U.S. stock market as measured by the S&P 500, but not higher." Historically, the annual standard deviation of the S&P 500 has been about 17 percentage points, but for the past 10 years it has been a lot lower. What we must wrestle with is, can we stand the downside volatility of the S&P 500 when it is two or three standard deviations worse than "normal"?

More concretely, could we stand a 1973–1974 decline, when an S&P 500 index fund would have lost 40% of its value? Or might our decision-making committee lose its nerve at the bottom, decide it should never have been in such a risky investment program, and sell out at precisely the wrong time? At the end of 1974 such a change of direction would have been a disaster, as the market regained in the next two years all it had lost in 1973–1974.

That's the kind of question we should ask ourselves. Conceptually, a pension fund or endowment fund should be able to withstand that level of volatility, but from a pragmatic standpoint, *can its governing body withstand it?*

This is why, as a benchmark for their total fund, many funds set a hypothetical *portfolio* of index funds. Such a Benchmark Portfolio implicitly sets the measure of risk in our objective.

Is that measure of risk appropriate for us? One way to test it is to see what the volatility of the Benchmark Portfolio would have been over various long intervals of years and see if we, our committee, and our sponsoring organization could stand that level of volatility.

I think many institutions set their volatility constraint too low relative to the time horizon that they should establish. As Jack Bogle, founder of the well-known Vanguard Group, has said: "One point of added volatility is meaningless, while one point of added return is priceless."

Return

Many might say: If we set a Benchmark Portfolio for our total fund consisting of X% U.S. stock index, Y% U.S. bond index, that also sets our return objective as well.

Such a benchmark is good because it sets a *relative* objective, not an *absolute* objective. An absolute objective would be something like, "We want to earn 10% per year." Over an extremely long term, like 20 or 30 years, an *absolute* objective—especially in real terms (net of inflation)—might be an appropriate objective. But for intervals of fewer years, *relative* objectives are more appropriate, because we are all prisoners of the market.

Such an investment return objective still seems inadequate, however. I think a more appropriate objective would be "to earn the highest possible rate of return without incurring more risk than *the risk* of our Benchmark Portfolio." We should be greedy, aim for the best possible—as long as we stay within our risk benchmark (set by our Benchmark Portfolio).

We can achieve a rate of return equal to our Benchmark Portfolio if we invest in index funds identical to that Portfolio. Therefore our Benchmark return should be the *minimum* return we should aspire to earn long-term.

We suggested earlier that diversification can help us get more bang for each point of our portfolio's volatility. We should therefore build this diversification into our Benchmark Portfolio. Since we want to be able to calculate returns on our Benchmark Portfolio, we are limited to those asset classes for which relatively valid indexes are available. Which indexes?

The traditional index used as a benchmark for U.S. stocks is the S&P 500. This is *not* an adequate benchmark for our portfolio. The S&P 500 is essentially a large-stock index. Even though it measures more than 85% of the market capitalization of all marketable U.S. stocks, our feet should be held to the fire of *all* U.S. stocks.

Perhaps the best measure of U.S. stocks is the *Russell 3000 index*. The Russell 3000, like the S&P 500, is a capitalization-weighted index,[5] but it consists of the 3,000 largest stocks in the United States and measures more than 98% of the market capitalization of all U.S. stocks. Moreover, it eliminates foreign stocks that happen to be listed on U.S. stock exchanges.

---

[5] A cap-weighted index weights each stock in direct proportion to its capitalization—the number of its shares outstanding times the price of its stock.

Why is that important? Because U.S. stocks account for less than half of the capitalization of all marketable stocks in the world. Therefore, for the purpose of diversification, we should also include non-U.S. stocks in our Benchmark Portfolio. But what index should we use for non-U.S. stocks?

The most widely used index of non-U.S. stocks is the Morgan Stanley Capital International (MSCI) index for Europe, Australia, and the Far East (EAFE). This also is not an adequate benchmark for our portfolio. It fails to include Canadian stocks or those of the emerging markets—Latin America, much of Asia, eastern Europe, and Africa. A better benchmark is the *MSCI World Index, ex U.S.,* especially starting in 1998 when that index began providing Extended Indexes that included small cap stocks in each of the developed markets.

What index or indexes should we use for fixed income? The most broadly based U.S. bond index has for many years been the *Lehman Aggregate Bond Index.* At the start of 1999, Lehman introduced a still broader bond index—*the U.S. Universal Index*—which adds high-yield bonds and a number of smaller and newer bond sectors.

Should we also include a non-U.S. bond index in our Benchmark Portfolio? I am all in favor of allowing bond managers to use non-U.S. bonds—with currency risk either hedged or unhedged, as the managers think best—whenever they believe non-U.S. bonds will add to their portfolio's total return. But since fixed income may form a relatively small percentage of our Benchmark Portfolio, this is a place where I would bow to simplicity, and use just a single bond index.

I tend to favor the Lehman Aggregate for endowment funds. But I question whether a bond index with a longer-duration[6] might not be more appropriate for a pension fund. The Lehman Aggregate has a duration of a little over 4½ years. This modest duration helps to mitigate annual volatility. But a longer-duration benchmark, such as the *Lehman Government/Corporate Long-Term Bond Index,* with its roughly 10-year duration, would be closer to the duration of a pension plan's benefit obligations and therefore

---

[6] Duration is a measure of *when* we receive our returns on an investment—including both interest and principal payments. A 10-year bond with a high interest coupon has a shorter duration than a 10-year bond with a low interest coupon, because we receive more of our total return from the high-interest bond *sooner.* A 10-year zero-coupon bond—one that pays no interest until it matures and then adds all accrued interest to its principal payment—has a duration of 10 years, the same as its maturity.

would do more to minimize the volatility of contributions and the plan's funding adequacy.[7]

Measuring the Benchmark

Once we establish our Benchmark Portfolio, we should then measure the return on that hypothetical portfolio by weighting the total return on each component index by its percentage of our Benchmark Portfolio.[8]

Some funds finesse their investment objectives by using as a benchmark whatever rate of return is earned by their peers (be they other pension funds or other endowment funds), with a target standard deviation of annual investment returns no higher than the average of their peers. I understand the motivations for this, because most institutions are always looking over their

---

[7] Long-term bonds tend to minimize the volatility of a pension plan's funding ratio—the ratio of the market value of its assets to the present value of its benefit obligations—for the following reason: As interest rates rise, the market value of a bond goes down—the longer the duration, the more the market price goes down. Because the discount rate used to calculate the present value of benefit obligations also rises (because it is tied to prevailing interest rates), the present value of benefit obligations goes down also. And if interest rates go down, both values go up.

[8] We should keep an index of our benchmark returns, starting arbitrarily perhaps at 1.0000, and then updating the index each quarter by the return on our hypothetical portfolio. An illustration would be as follows (assuming our benchmark is 50% Index A, 30% Index B, and 20% Index C):

	Total Return On			Benchmark Return (.5a +.3b +.2c)	Index (prior e + (1+d))
	Index A (a)	Index B (b)	Index C (c)	(d)	(e)
12/31/00	—	—	—	—	1.0000
3/31/01	+5%	+10%	+1%	+5.7%	1.0570
6/30/01	+10	−5	+3	+4.1	1.1003
9/30/01	−2	+2	+1	−0.2	1.0981
12/31/01	+6	+9	+4	+6.5	1.1695
3/31/02	−3	+1	−1	−1.4	1.1531

This approach implicitly rebalances our Benchmark Portfolio to its specified weights every quarter. We should be mindful to rebalance our actual portfolio as well, perhaps not as often as every quarter, but with some reasonable frequency.

shoulder to see if they are doing as well as their peers. But I think this is *not* the best kind of investment objective.

Framing our objectives as a function of what our peers are doing makes us a prisoner of their investment objectives and constraints, whether or not their objectives and constraints are appropriate for us. Factors that influence their investment policies may be quite different from those that should influence ours. We should set our investment objectives based on our own independent thinking about the reasons for each part of those objectives. That's because *our peers are not always right,* especially for our situation. Moreover, they are often influenced by herd mentality.

To illustrate the herd mentality: U.K. pension funds have historically invested 80% or more of their portfolio in common stocks, U.S. pension funds more like 60%, Canadian pension funds were at one time more like 40%, and Swiss pension funds closer to zero. (Many Swiss pension plans have been more comfortable financing pensions through annuities.) Those asset allocations are influenced partly by local laws, but in most cases, Company A is following an approach because that's the approach being followed by peers in its country. I would maintain that pension funds worldwide are all trying to accomplish the same thing. Assuming similar liability structures and the ability to hedge currency risk, and subject to local laws, an optimal approach for investing a pension fund in one country is probably pretty close to an optimal approach in another country. Except for the herd mentality.

Hence . . . let's do our own independent thinking, set our own independent investment objectives.

Target Asset Allocation

Our objectives should also specify our *Target Asset Allocation,* which—in order to benefit optimally from diversification—should be more extensive than our Benchmark Portfolio and should include asset classes for which it is not possible to establish a viable index fund. We should build into our Target Asset Allocation any allocation we believe will improve our portfolio's aggregate return without increasing our portfolio's aggregate volatility beyond that of our Benchmark Portfolio.

We should review our Target Asset Allocation periodically for appropriateness—more often than our Benchmark Portfolio—but we should change only with compelling reason. The best theoretical results, of course, would come from reducing the allocation to stocks before stocks enter a bear market and increasing the allocation before stocks enter a bull market. There are few if any professional investors who have been able to do this successfully over time, and probably most would have been better off it they hadn't tried. Therefore, we shouldn't try to time the market but instead generally maintain our Target Asset Allocation over the long term.[9]

Our Target Asset Allocation serves a couple of useful purposes. It can tell us the asset class (or classes) in which we should be looking for a new manager (or managers), and it should help us decide where to apply new contributions to the fund and where to withdraw assets when we need to make payments out of the fund.

Establishing our Target Asset Allocation is a major process that is the subject of Chapter 4.

Rebalancing

Once our fund has reached its Target Asset Allocation, we should rebalance periodically to that Target Allocation. Because the price movements of our various asset classes are less than fully correlated, this periodic rebalancing forces us to do something that is not intuitively comfortable—sell assets out of our recent winning accounts, and add the proceeds to our recent underperforming accounts.

It helps if our committee can agree that this should be done as a routine discipline, as the discipline can cause anguish on a decision-by-decision basis. The effect over time is to force us, on balance, to buy low and sell high.

Quarterly rebalancing to our Target Asset Allocation may increase portfolio return by a few basis points per year (which add up over the years), while it simultaneously reduces portfolio volatility.

An alternative to such "calendar rebalancing" is to rebalance whenever our actual allocation for an asset class strays from its target by some

---

[9] Fidelity Management Company has placed market timing in good perspective with its "Louie the Loser" illustration. Louie invested consistently the same amount of money every year for 20 years, 1978–1997—but, unfortunately, always when the market had hit its high for the year. He still had an average annual return over that 20 years of 15.7%. By comparison, if he had invested each year when the market had hit its low for the year, his average annual return would have been only 1.5 points higher—17.2%.

arbitrary percentage, such as 1% or 5%. This is called "threshold rebalancing." One study has shown that quarterly rebalancing can add several more basis points per year than threshold rebalancing.[10]

But doesn't rebalancing incur trading costs? Of course, but trading costs have been found to be small relative to the benefits of rebalancing. In any case, we can avoid a lot of these small trading costs if we apply contributions and select withdrawals in such a way as to rebalance. It's a good habit to get into.

Preparing a Statement of Investment Policies

Ultimately, every pension plan or endowment fund should prepare a written statement of investment policies. Besides dealing with asset allocation, such a statement might well also establish the criteria for hiring and retaining investment managers. The following is an example of such a statement—recognizing that it would have to be tailored to the particular entity for which it was being prepared.

Investment Policies of XYZ Fund

Overall Objectives: Investment policies and individual decisions are to be made for the exclusive benefit of the Plan's participants [or of the endowment fund's sponsor], and any perception of conflict of interest is to be avoided. Within the relevant laws, the Plan's investment objectives are:

- *Payments.* Without fail, to make every benefit payment [or endowment income payment] on the date it is due.
- *Liquidity.* The plan should maintain liquid assets and other assured sources of cash which in combination will cover projected payouts for at least the next five years.

(continued)

---

[10] See "Rebalancing: Why? How Often? When?" a paper by Robert D. Arnott, president of First Quadrant Corporation, Pasadena, CA, based on a study of the U.S. stock and bond markets, 1968–1991.

(Continued)

- *Aggregate performance.* To achieve the best possible rate of long-term investment return, net of fees, commensurate with our volatility constraint. At a minimum, over intervals of five years and longer, to exceed the total return on a Benchmark Portfolio composed as follows:

  00% U.S. stocks (as measured by the Russell 3000 Index)
  00% Non-U.S. stocks (as measured by the MSCI World Index, ex U.S.)
  00% U.S. bonds (as measured by the Lehman Aggregate Bond Index)
  100%

- *Aggregate volatility.* To experience volatility of the overall portfolio (as measured by the annual standard deviation from average performance over the latest five years) that is no higher than that of the Benchmark Portfolio.

Asset Allocation: In order to achieve the best investment return possible within the above volatility constraint, the Plan will target broad diversification of its investments into many asset classes that have attractive expected returns and low correlation with one another. Currently, the plan's Target Asset Allocation is:

  00% Liquid Investments
  00% Private Investments
  100%

Composition of Liquid Investments:

Common Stocks: U.S. Large Stocks		00%
Small Stocks		00
		00%
Non-U.S. Developed Countries		00
Emerging Markets		00
		00%
Fixed Income: Traditional		00
High-Yield Bonds		00
		100%

(Continued)

The Plan should periodically review its Target Asset Allocation to ensure that it remains appropriate for the needs of the Plan, although it is not expected that changes will need to be made frequently.

Because short-term fixed income securities are the lowest-return asset class over any long-term interval, the Plan should target its holdings of these securities at the lowest possible level commensurate with its immediate cash needs. This generally means selling stocks and bonds "just in time" to meet cash needs.

New contributions to the Plan should be applied to, and payments by the Plan withdrawn from, asset classes in such a way as to bring the Plan's asset allocation back toward its Target Asset Allocation.

Liquid Assets: "Liquid assets" include all investments that the Plan can convert to cash *within a year,* such as marketable securities, both stock and fixed income.

The Plan should consider investments in *all* liquid asset classes in which it can gain competency to invest, and it should base its portfolio weight in each class at any particular time on whatever combination it expects will provide optimal risk/return characteristics for the aggregate portfolio. Where feasible, the Plan should also seek diversification within asset classes. For example, in common stocks, the Plan should normally seek to have managers with different styles, focusing on different sizes of stocks, and with different geographic orientations in the world. The Plan may therefore hire multiple specialist managers in a single asset class.

Illiquid Assets: "Illiquid assets" include any investment that the Plan cannot convert to cash at fair market value within a year, such as partnerships invested in real estate, venture capital, oil & gas, and timberland.

Each new illiquid investment should be selected on an opportunistic basis and have an expected internal rate of return, net of all costs, that is at least 2% per year higher than the expected return on common stocks. The purpose of this higher expected return is to compensate for the risk and inconvenience that is inherent in

(continued)

(Continued)

illiquidity. Still higher expected return should be required of an illiquid investment to the extent that its underlying risk is greater than that of common stocks.

The attractiveness of a prospective illiquid investment will be enhanced by its expected diversification benefit to the Plan's overall portfolio, that is, the extent to which the key factors affecting its investment returns differ from those that affect the Plan's other investments.

No single commitment to an illiquid investment should normally exceed _____%* of the Plan's total assets. Such commitments are much smaller than commitments typically made to managers of liquid assets. This is because a great diversity of private asset classes and managers, including time diversification, is desirable due to the illiquid and often specialized nature of private investments.

Manager Selection and Retention: In every asset class, the Plan's goal is to have its investments managed by the world's best investors that the Plan can access in that asset class. Until such time (if ever) that the Plan's investment staff can prove itself world class in managing any particular asset class (at least equal, net of all costs, to the best we can get outside), the day-to-day portfolio management of all of the Plan's investments shall be performed outside the company.

To achieve superior investment returns, the Plan should seek investment managers and investment opportunities that either (a) have expected rates of return higher than those expected from existing investment programs, provided these opportunities would keep the Fund's aggregate volatility within its benchmark, or (b) would reduce the Fund's aggregate volatility without reducing its aggregate expected rate of return.

All managers—both prospective and existing—should be evaluated under the following criteria:

---

* I'd suggest inserting perhaps 0.5% for a very large fund and 2% for a very small fund.

(Continued)

- *Character.* Integrity, reliability, worthy of our trust.
- *Investment approach.* Do the assumptions and principles underlying the manager's investment approach make sense to us?
- *Expected return.* Historic return, net of fees, overlayed by an evaluation of the predictive value of that historic return, as well as other factors that may seem relevant in that instance and may have predictive value.
- *Expected impact on the plan's overall volatility.* This criterion has two facets:

  (1) The expected volatility of the manager's investments is the historic volatility of its investments overlayed by an evaluation of the predictive value of that historic volatility, as well as a recognition of the historic volatility of that manager's asset class in general.

  (2) The expected correlation of the manager's volatility with that of the Plan's other assets.

- *Liquidity.* How readily in the future can the account be converted to cash, and how satisfactory is that in relation to the Plan's projected needs for cash?
- *Control.* Can our organization, with the help of outside consultants, adequately monitor this investment manager and its investment program?
- *Legal.* Have all legal concerns been dealt with satisfactorily?

Managers should be selected without regard to the geographic location of their offices and without regard to the nature of their ownership except as those factors may impact the above considerations.

Unless it is viable for the Plan to select active managers who can, with high confidence, be expected to add meaningful excess value, net of all fees and expenses, above their benchmark, the Plan should invest its assets in index funds.

Criteria applicable to the selection of an index fund manager include that of character and integrity and the manager's historic performance (net of fees, taxes, and transaction costs) relative to the respective index.

This sample statement of investment policies contains a number of concepts we have not discussed heretofore. Let's address them now.

The opening statement about "exclusive benefit" is right out of ERISA.[11] The "exclusive benefit" concept should be as applicable for an endowment fund as for a pension plan. That statement and the next—of making all benefit payments without fail—are a bit of motherhood and apple pie, but I think they are so basic that any policy statement should begin with something like them.

Liquidity requirements are necessary to meet the first objective. That statement, however, serves best to remind us that we have great flexibility. The minimum-liquidity requirement, if taken by itself, permits vastly more illiquid investments than is held by any pension plan or endowment fund I've ever heard of.

The goal of broad diversification, and its rationale, is important to state. The sample asset classes listed are for a relatively simple plan. For a more sophisticated plan we should probably include additional asset classes in its Target Allocation.

Certainly the Target Allocation should be reviewed periodically, but it is helpful to say that reviewing it does not necessarily mean changing it. If the Target Allocation has been developed thoughtfully, it probably should *not* be changed often.

The target of minimizing short-term fixed income assets is worth defining, as most pension and endowment funds tend to retain more cash equivalents than they should.

The sentence about using contributions and withdrawals to rebalance toward the Target Allocation implies that this might be done more or less mechanically, without judging what asset classes are attractive or unattractive at the time. That's exactly what I mean to imply! There are few if any mortals who can time asset classes. The sentence takes judgment out of a decision where judgment isn't likely to add value. Also, as mentioned before, it is the lowest-transaction-cost method of rebalancing.

Further defining diversification objectives under Liquid and Illiquid Assets provides useful additional focus. It is important to establish return and diversification criteria for Illiquid Assets. We should certainly require higher returns from private investments than from liquid assets. And when

---

[11] ERISA is the Employee Retirement Income Security Act of 1974, which governs all private pension plans in the United States.

we find a private opportunity that strikes us as the greatest thing we've ever seen, we need, in order to control our own enthusiasm, a constraint on the maximum percentage of assets we should commit to that opportunity.

Criteria for manager selection and retention are helpful as guideposts against which future manager recommendations should be evaluated. As part of these criteria, we should aim to use the world's best managers that we can access in each asset class. That is obviously an unreachable target, but that's the direction in which we should always be striving. More about this in Chapter 5 on selecting investment managers.

I also think we should include a statement about in-house management and its rationale, and also about the role of index funds.

In Short

Every pension or endowment plan should have a written statement of investment objectives. The statement sets up directions and criteria that will help to focus everyone who will be involved in subsequent decisions. The value of the statement will be proportional to the wisdom and thought that goes into preparing it.

Chapter 4

Asset Allocation

B y far, the most important single investment decision a pension fund or endowment fund makes is not the particular managers it selects, but its *asset allocation*. That's the proportion of its assets it puts into each asset class, such as large U.S. stocks, long-term bonds, or real estate equity.

If we think first of manager selection, we are implicitly making allocations to asset classes, perhaps without fully realizing we are doing so. It's the cart before the horse.

Why? Because investment results within an asset class are so dominated by the wind behind that asset class,[1] *any* manager's results will be highly impacted by that wind. If large U.S. stocks achieve high returns, so will nearly all managers of large U.S. stocks; and those managers will not be able to escape the slaughter if large U.S. stocks should crash.

Historically, many U.S. pension and endowment funds have drifted toward an asset allocation something like 60/30/10—60% in stocks, 30% in bonds, and 10% in cash equivalents, all U.S. based. Is there something inherently ideal in that asset mix? If there is, it isn't apparent in other countries. As mentioned in Chapter 3, typical Canadian pension funds for many years held only about 40% stocks and 60% fixed income. Many pension plans in continental Europe were more likely to fund their pensions

---

[1] The "wind," as I call it, means the things that tend to affect the returns of *all* investments in any particular asset class at any given time.

66

through annuities with an insurance company, or with a managed fund overwhelmingly oriented to fixed income. On the other hand, most British pension funds had an asset mix consisting of 80% or more stocks (not exclusively British). Meanwhile, Australian pension funds have tended toward the selection of "balanced managers"—investment managers who invest in both stocks and bonds, with each manager deciding on the mix.

Which nation's "conventional investment wisdom" is best?

Let's start with the reasons for such differences. Laws in some countries limit investment choices. But the overwhelming reason for each fund's asset allocation is . . . *that's how it's always done here.* Fund sponsors feel safety in numbers and many are timid about investing their money differently.

Let's obey all laws diligently. But I suggest that a fund does well to ignore how its peers are investing their money. Instead, asset allocation should be set on the basis of (1) one's objectives, as discussed in Chapter 3, and (2) after careful study of available information about the financial markets, one's independent application of logic and common sense.

If we can for a moment ignore laws in some countries that limit investment options, as well as currency considerations, I would contend that to a very large extent pension funds in the United States, Germany, and Hong Kong that have the same liability structure and the same investment objectives might rationally decide on *the same* global asset allocation.

Characteristics of an Asset Class

The trouble is, the very names of asset classes—foreign stocks, small stocks, emerging markets, venture capital—evoke varying emotions that get in the way of rational evaluation by investors. A helpful starting point with *any* asset class is to describe it quantitatively in order to move as far as possible from the emotional to the intellectual.

As suggested in Chapter 2, there are three critically important characteristics of every asset class that need to be quantified:

1. Expected return,
2. Expected risk, and
3. Expected correlation with other asset classes.

Why are these characteristics so important? Because of what they enable the investor to achieve through diversification. This takes us back to our basic investment objective: To achieve the highest investment return we can within whatever limit of year-to-year volatility we can accept.

The problem is that essentially riskless assets—like U.S. Treasury bills—provide the lowest returns. And assets with the highest expected returns—such as start-up venture capital—are the most risky. It is generally quite true that the higher an asset class's expected return, the riskier it is.

Diversification offers a way for the investor, to some extent, to have his cake and eat it, too. By assembling a portfolio of asset classes that march to somewhat different drummers (that have a low correlation with one another), we can increase our portfolio's expected return at any given level of expected volatility.

Why? Because what counts is the portfolio's *aggregate* volatility, not the volatility of each asset. To illustrate, let's look at an imaginary portfolio of only two assets, both having a high expected return of X%, both extremely volatile, but with returns that move exactly opposite to one another—that is, with a correlation of −1. That means when asset A goes up by X + Y%, asset B returns X − Y%, and vice versa. Although each asset is extremely volatile, the aggregate volatility of the portfolio would be nil—and we would essentially have a very high-returning portfolio with no volatility.

Oh, if only two such assets existed! We can't achieve this, but we can get part way by combining asset classes whose annual returns are only partly correlated.

How do we go about quantifying the three key characteristics of each asset class? It's a tough assignment. But if we don't do this *ex*plicitly, we will end up doing it *im*plicitly, without as much direct thought. So let's try to be as explicit as we can.

Expected Investment Return

To consider expected return, let's use as an example the asset class of *large U.S. stocks*. A logical place to start is historical returns, and large U.S. stocks have about the most reliable historical data of any asset class. Ibbotson Associates' *Yearbook*[2] provides the total investment returns (including

---

[2] Historical returns on the S&P 500 and other U.S. asset classes shown subsequently in this chapter are taken or calculated from Ibbotson Associates' *Stocks, Bonds, Bills and Inflation Yearbook.*

reinvested dividends) on Standard & Poor's 500 Index—a good index of the performance of large U.S. stocks—starting in 1926.

From the beginning of 1926 through year-end 1998, the S&P 500 compounded about 11% per year. That's an impressive figure, considering it includes the Great Depression, World War II, and the terrible investment climate of the 1970s. Does that mean we should expect 11% per year going forward?

Well, let's say we have a 20-year time horizon. What is the range of the S&P's total annual returns over all 20-year intervals? We find it varies from a low of 3.1% per year for the 1929–1948 interval to a high of 17.7% per year for the latest interval, 1979–1998. On a real (inflation-adjusted) basis,[3] the range is from a low of 1.6% to a high of 13.6%.

A key question: Should we attribute equal predictive value to all years of available historical data? Or should we say the world has changed materially since 19XX, and we should rely mainly on data since then? Remember, historical data for an asset class (or for a particular investment manager) is no more useful than its *predictive value*, and that's a *judgment* we each must make.

Also, we should consider adjusting our expectations relative to historical returns based on our view of whether stocks are expensively priced or cheap today. We should recognize, for example, that the phenomenal returns on U.S. stocks for the 20 years 1979–1998 reflect (1) the fact that corporate earnings grew exceptionally fast over that interval while (2) stock valuations zoomed from a price/earnings ratio of about 8 at year-end 1978 to about 32 by year-end 1998.

So what should we select as our return expectation for large U.S. stocks? No, we can't look to the gurus of Wall Street to tell us, because we will find an impressive guru who will support any expectation we select. Recognize from the start that any return expectation we select will almost surely be wrong! A bullseye forecast would be phenomenal luck.

---

[3] We calculate a *real* return by subtracting the inflation rate for an interval of years from the annual investment return for that same interval. (The proper way to derive inflation-adjusted returns, of course, is to calculate the change in buying power of our wealth—a process of division instead of subtraction. We can illustrate best with an extreme example, using 500% inflation. If we earn 510%, then $100 would grow in a year to a value of $610. But something priced at $100 would now cost $600. Our *real,* inflation-adjusted return would not be 10% (510% – 500%) but 1.7% (610/600 – 1)!)

Should we therefore give up? No, because a well-thought-out expectation should get us in the ballpark. This is true of all asset classes, some of which do not have clean historical data going back very far. We should examine whatever data exists and apply our common sense in projecting that data into the future.

Our purpose in this book is not to provide all the historical data and try to apply it but rather to suggest the kinds of questions we should ask about the relevance of that historical data to our expectations for the future.

Expected Risk

As discussed in Chapter 2, risk could be defined as the probability of losing money—or in the extreme, losing all our money, through bankruptcy or expropriation. Relative to any single investment, we can usefully assess the probability of losing all our money. But in discussing an *asset class,* within which we will be forming a portfolio of investments, there's a more helpful way to look at risk.

That's the *uncertainty* of returns, or the *volatility* of returns, of that asset class. One can measure that historically by the *standard deviation* of annual returns. For example, over the last 70+ years the total return on the S&P 500 has had a standard deviation of some 20 percentage points.

That means if the average year's return (not *compound* average but *simple* average annual return[4]) was 13%, and if future returns should be the same, then in roughly two-thirds of the years the S&P 500's return should be about 13% ±20 percentage points, or between −7% and +33%, and about one-sixth of the years it should be below −7%, and one-sixth of the years above +33%.

It also suggests that in some 95% of the years, its return should be within two standard deviations—13% ±40 percentage points, or between −27% and +53%.

That's history. But how do we *forecast* volatility? Do we assume historic volatility over the last 70+ years (20 percentage points), or over the last 20 years (about 13 percentage points), or over some other interval?

---

[4] Remember, compound annual return is always lower than the simple average. For example, if our investment earns successive annual returns of 5%, −10%, and 30%, its simple average return is $(5 - 10 + 30) / 3 = 8.3\%/\text{year}$, while its compound return is $(1.05 \times .90 \times 1.30)^{1/3} - 1 = 7.1\%/\text{year}$.

Again, no one can give us the answer. We must apply our own common sense . . . and run a few sensitivity tests to see how serious it will be if we are wrong.

As might be predictable, cash equivalents have very little volatility. Bonds have next least volatility, although volatility of bond returns has been increasing at the same time as the volatility of stock returns has been declining. But stocks are still materially more volatile than bonds.

As to other asset classes, how does one assess expected volatility where there is no reliable historic information? It is not easy. But it is still worth doing, then challenging our results through a series of sensitivity tests.[5]

Reminder: The most useful measure of volatility is *annual* standard deviation. As we annualize weekly, monthly, or quarterly volatility data, let's be mindful of the caveats discussed in Chapter 2, p. 32, and make adjustments if appropriate.

Expected Correlation

Few investors will settle for a 3-stock portfolio. They are properly taught to diversify to reduce the volatility of returns. Within large U.S. stocks, however, we can diversify only so much. "Common factors" of the overall stock market account for over half of an individual stock's return. No matter how many large U.S. stocks we hold, we can't diversify away those common factors (the systematic risk referred to in Chapter 2, p. 36).

We can, however, hold other asset classes. Small U.S. stocks are affected by many of the same common factors, but not all. Adding a certain percentage of small stocks—say, 20%—can give us a slightly lower aggregate volatility than large stocks alone, even though small stocks by themselves are more volatile. Non-U.S. stocks are less correlated and add further diversification. Ditto emerging markets stocks.

As we diversify, each additional asset class does incrementally less to lower our aggregate volatility. One student of investing, Ray Dalio of Bridgewater Associates, has shown that after we have 5 to 10 investments (depending on the correlation among them), it is essentially pointless to

---

[5] Sensitivity tests are additional what-if calculations, based on different assumptions. What different asset allocations do those sensitivity tests favor? We would like an asset allocation that may not be the best under any one set of assumptions but looks as if it will be reasonably good under a fairly wide range of assumptions.

add any more, although the ideal would be 10 to 15 investments with totally uncorrelated returns (see Figure 4.1).

Given that fact, then why do I advocate using as many asset classes as
possible that have high expected returns? Mainly because I don't believe
my own correlation estimates. I suspect that some asset classes that we expect to be highly uncorrelated will become more closely correlated over
time, and vice versa. The more diverse asset classes we invest in, and the
less correlated their returns, the more protected we are.

Our task, of course, is to identify an appropriate assumption of what
correlation each asset class will have with every other asset class. For example, if we work with 15 asset classes, we will need a matrix of 105 correlations. Where do we get them?

Historical correlation data is available for some asset classes, mainly
through consulting firms at present. The challenge with correlations is
much the same as with volatility—we are interested in the correlation of
annual returns, not monthly and quarterly returns, and there can be a big
difference.

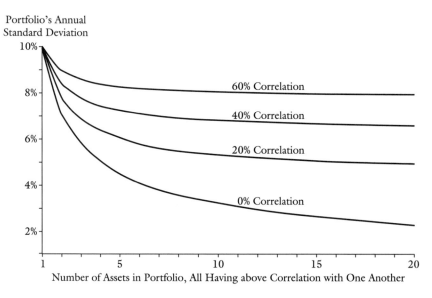

Figure 4.1 **Incremental Benefits of Diversification. (Courtesy of
Bridgewater Associates, Inc.)**

As an illustration, consider the correlation of the Lehman Government/Corporate Bond Index with that of the S&P 500 stock index for the following intervals:[6]

	Correlations		
	Annual	*Quarterly*	*Monthly*
1994–1998	.88	.38	.53
1985–1998	.63	.22	.38
1979–1998	.36	.33	.35
1973–1998	.51	.39	.37

For many intervals of 5 years or longer, the correlation actually has been *negative!* Which correlation do you think we should build into our expectations?

For certain asset classes, I don't know of any historical correlations. We must simply guess at these correlations, as we relate those asset classes to others for which correlation data is available. Illustrated in Table 2.1 on page 38 is a sample table of input assumptions for an efficient frontier, including a correlation matrix—not necessarily with as good assumptions as you can come up with.

Do you get the idea we are dealing with some soft projections? You are right. But if selected with proper research and thought, those projections can be good enough to help us develop reasonably optimal asset allocations. The key is to try enough sensitivity tests based on different expectations for return, risk, and correlation and see how much impact those different expectations have upon the model's optimal asset allocation. We are likely to find some optimal asset allocations that are robust[7] and don't rely on a small difference in key assumptions.

We shouldn't get discouraged, especially when we need to go through this taxing exercise with each individual asset class. With effort, the exercise can be highly rewarding.

---

[6] Per Bridgewater Associates.

[7] Robust, in this context, means that a particular asset allocation looks good under a relatively wide range of different assumptions.

Asset Classes

Well, what asset classes should we consider? *All of them*. Or at least all asset classes that we are competent—or can gain competency—to invest in. Some of the more obvious asset classes include:

Cash Equivalents

Cash equivalents (which, for short, we shall call "cash") includes Treasury bills, short-term certificates of deposit, money market mutual funds, and short-term investment funds (STIF's)—investments that are usually thought of as *riskless*, in that their maturity is so short that we can hardly lose any of our principal. If we venture outside of U.S. government securities, we may take some credit risk, but for our purposes here let's consider cash as riskless.

If cash is riskless, then we should expect that cash has the lowest expected return—and this has been true through the years. Over the 70+ years, cash hasn't even returned 1 percentage point more than the inflation rate. For certain periods of years cash hasn't even returned the inflation rate, but over the past 10 years or more its return has been more like 2 percentage points higher than inflation.

We might start our expectations with an estimate of the inflation rate going forward and then decide what increment over that inflation rate cash is likely to return.

And then ask ourselves: If over any long-term interval cash is likely to provide the lowest return, why should we target any portion of our portfolio to cash? Well, cash is a great tool for market timing, but I feel safe assuming we are not blessed with the gift of prescience.

Many investors keep a portion in cash so that whenever they must withdraw some money from their fund they can do so without having to sell a longer-term security at a possibly inopportune time. Withdrawals, however, occur repeatedly over time. Over the long term a fund is undoubtedly better off keeping cash to zero and selling other securities whenever a withdrawal is needed—selling "just in time." Sometimes we'll sell at the bottom of the market and other times at the top. But over the long term, we should be well ahead.

No matter how hard we try, it is difficult to keep cash down to zero. Over the long term, any amount of cash is a drag on portfolio return. One way to deal with this if our cash balances are not too volatile is to overlay our cash balances with very liquid index futures, such as S&P 500 futures. Such futures "equitize" our cash, effectively converting it into an S&P 500 index fund.

In any case, I favor a target allocation of 0% to cash.

Longer Term Fixed Income

Traditional Bonds. Traditional investment-grade U.S. bonds come in various maturities, typically from one year to 30 years, and various levels of credit risk, each having somewhat different long-term risk and return characteristics. When talking of this asset class, we often talk in terms of the Lehman Aggregate Bond Index, which attempts to include all investment-grade U.S. fixed income securities that are longer in maturity than cash equivalents. In recent years this index had an *average* maturity between 5 and 10 years and an average duration of 4½ to 5 years.[8]

Bonds clearly have more risk than cash equivalents, so we would expect a higher long-term return from them. Over the 73 years through 1998 U.S. bonds provided a return averaging 1½ to 2 percentage points higher than cash equivalents. Real returns on bonds during these 73 years averaged some 2½%, but many people believe something like 3½% is closer to a norm today.

Historically, bonds have had a modest annual correlation with stocks, and that correlation has been increasing in recent years. Over longer holding periods, like 5 to 10 years, that correlation has been lower than over shorter intervals, sometimes negative. Will the correlation continue to be lower over longer intervals? And if so, how should we work that fact into our asset allocation equation? I don't know the answer to those questions, but I have tended to work with one-year correlations and keep the longer-term correlations in mind.

---

[8] Duration is a measure of *when* we receive our returns on an investment—including both interest and principal payments. A 10-year bond with a high interest coupon would have a shorter duration than a 10-year bond with a low interest coupon, because we receive more of our total return from the high-interest bond *sooner*. A 10-year zero-coupon bond—one that pays no interest until it matures and then adds all accrued interest to its principal payment—has a duration of 10 years, the same as its maturity.

Many investors consider only traditional U.S. bonds. Yet there are at least five distinct *additional* classes of bonds, and we should consider including each.

It is difficult to find an active manager of traditional investment-grade U.S. bonds who can add as much as 1 percentage point of excess net return above his benchmark. The other classes of bonds offer active managers the opportunity to add a little more excess net return above their benchmarks—if the managers are among the best.

High-Yield Bonds.   During the 1980s, high-yield bonds were introduced to finance less creditworthy companies. Known for some years as junk bonds, they are bonds with a high interest rate, with interest rates 1% to 4% higher than investment-grade bonds. The higher interest rates were designed to compensate investors for a small percentage of the issuers who statistically could be predicted to default.

High-yield bonds have provided investors with moderately higher long-term returns than investment-grade bonds, and at least during the seven years 1992–1998 they did it with roughly the same volatility. These, however, were good economic times. During harder economic times, as in 1990, more issuers of high-yield bonds default, and prices of high-yield bonds tumble. First Boston's high-yield bond index in 1990 provided a total return of –6%.

Emerging Markets Debt.   Some people consider debt issued in the developing countries of the world simply another facet of high-yield bonds. I believe emerging markets debt is driven by somewhat different factors, and therefore I tend to view it separately.

After the world's banks in the 1970s and early 1980s experienced a fiasco in loans to many Latin American and other developing economies, the U.S. government developed "Brady bonds" to provide a U.S.-guaranteed floor beneath much Latin American dollar-denominated debt. Prices of Brady bonds were still volatile, but at least investors knew they couldn't lose their principal if they retained the loan long enough.

Brady bonds were subsequently extended to a number of eastern European countries. A number of countries have redeemed many of their Brady bonds, because the bonds were expensive for the issuing countries. Now investors can choose among Brady bonds, regular sovereign government debt denominated either in dollars or local currency, or bonds issued by large corporations in those countries.

Until 1998 emerging markets debt tended to provide total returns that seemed more in the range of common stocks, with commensurately high volatility. Then defaults on Russian bonds in August 1998 triggered a collapse in prices of all emerging markets debt and left high volatility as the only remaining indisputable truth.

If we can stand the volatility with a small portion of our portfolio, I still like emerging markets debt. I think it will provide good returns long term, and returns that have a low correlation with more traditional assets.

Non-U.S. Bonds (Developed Countries). While the U.S. government and U.S. corporations are the world's largest issuers of public debt, government and corporate bonds are sold to the public in all developed countries of the world. That spells additional opportunity.

When fully hedged for foreign exchange risk, foreign bonds tend to have a fairly high correlation with U.S. bonds. Knowledgeable global investors, however, can find ways to add value, because interest rate movements across countries are certainly not in perfect synch.

A global bond portfolio that is *not* hedged provides more diversification benefit. The difference is volatility in foreign exchange values, which is largely uncorrelated with the volatility in bonds and stocks.

Long-Duration Bonds. Unless we think interest rates are going to decline (usually a gambler's bet), why would we want to consider long-duration bonds, with their high volatility, as a staple asset class for our portfolio? I can think of two good reasons:

1. As mentioned in Chapter 3, the duration of the benefit obligations of a pension plan is usually much longer than 10 years, and the present value of those obligations rises as interest rates go down and falls as interest rates rise—just like the market value of bonds. Therefore a bond with a substantially longer duration than the usual 5 years does a far better job of hedging those obligations. Its value goes up or down by a percentage change more similar to the present value of our obligations.
2. The volatility of a long-duration bond account can give us much more protection against declining interest rates than a traditional bond account, especially in a climate such as occurred in the third quarter of 1998, when stock prices collapsed at the same time interest rates declined. Long-duration bonds reduce our need to

allocate as large a percentage of our portfolio to fixed income, which historically has provided a lower long-term rate of return than equity investments.

We could establish a bond account that has a normal duration of about 10 years that is benchmarked against the Lehman Government/Corporate Long-Term Bond Index. My preference, however, is one that is benchmarked against the 25-year zero-coupon U.S. Treasury bond (a Zero account). Also, while a Zero account can be invested in real, honest-to-goodness U.S. government zero-coupon bonds, it can be more effectively kept in cash and overlayed with interest-rate futures.[9] This reduces transaction costs and should result in a higher return long-term.

Why would the use of futures increase expected return? Because it takes five interest-rate futures, each with 5-year duration, to equal one 25-year zero-coupon bond. Now think about the yield curve, which normally is positive (Figure 4.2).

Interest rates are *usually* lowest at short maturities, rise quite sharply out to, say, 2-year maturities, and continue to rise out to 5 or 10-year maturities. Interest rates for longer-maturity bonds are rarely much higher than for 10-year maturities. A 10-year interest rate future will pick up value little by little over time as it rides down the yield curve.[10] Hence, under normal circumstances, a Zero account invested through futures, is, in effect, leveraging the steep portion of a positive yield curve—giving greater weight to the short end of the yield curve, which it can ride down over time.

Ray Dalio of Bridgewater Associates has calculated that for the 11 years starting June, 1986, when Salomon Brothers' 25-year strips first

---

[9] An interest-rate future works the same as an S&P 500 index future. When we buy an interest-rate future, we agree to pay or receive, until some future date, the change in the price typically of a U.S. Treasury bond. If the U.S. Treasury bond has a 5-year duration and we buy futures equivalent to five times the amount of cash we have in a money market account, we have created a *synthetic* 25-year zero-coupon U.S. Treasury bond. The combination of our futures and cash operate very much like a real, honest-to-goodness 25-year zero-coupon U.S. Treasury bond.

[10] Riding down the yield curve is a matter of *time*. Let's say we buy a 2-year bond with an interest-rate of 6.8%. Six months later, it's only a 1½-year bond (with 1½ years to maturity). Assuming no change in the yield curve, we can see from the chart on the prior page that the market would pay a price based on an interest rate of 6.7%—a higher price than we paid for the bond. If we sold the bond at that point we would have earned our 6.8% rate of interest *plus* a small capital gain.

Interest
Rate

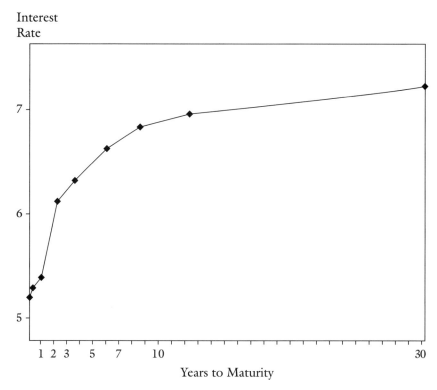

Years to Maturity

**Figure 4.2 Average Yields on U.S. Treasuries, 1989–1998.
(Courtesy of Bridgewater Associates, Inc.)**

became available, actual zeros returned 12.0% per year with a 22.5-point standard deviation, while synthetic zeros returned 13.5% per year with a 24.0-point standard deviation.

As a further consideration, a highly competent active manager can add further value (without incurring currency risk) by also investing in inter-est-rate futures on government bonds of other major countries, such as the United Kingdom, Germany, Japan, and Canada.

Inflation-Linked Bonds.   These are mainly government bonds that promise a *real* return (above the inflation rate) until their maturity. Inflation-linked bonds were first introduced in the United Kingdom in the early 1980s. The United States introduced them in 1997, and they are known here as Treasury Inflation-Protected Securities (TIPS). Other countries that have issued inflation-linked bonds include Sweden, Canada, France, Australia, and New Zealand.

Investors who hold the bonds to maturity have a locked-in real return of typically 3% to 4%. In the meantime the bonds fluctuate in value but not normally as much as traditional bonds. Inflation-linked bonds may play a role in asset allocation as investors become more comfortable with them and as they gain more liquidity. One advantage is that their volatility may tend to be slightly *negatively* correlated with that of traditional bonds—that is, when regular bond prices go up, prices of inflation-linked bonds may tend to go down, and vice versa.

Equities

Large U.S. Stocks. Large U.S. stocks have been the least volatile stocks in the world. We've talked a bit about large U.S. stocks earlier in this chapter, but now let's compare their returns with those of bonds.

There hasn't been a 20-year interval in the last 65 years when bonds provided a higher rate of return than stocks. Such historical results also square with good old common sense. After all, unless we had a rational expectation that stocks would give us a materially higher return, why would we buy a stock whose future price could be anything, high or low, when we could buy a bond we know we can redeem at par value (usually $1,000) X years from now? For the long-term, unless investors en masse are irrational, we have to expect a materially higher return from stocks than from bonds. The key question is—how much higher?

Over the 73 years through 1998, the S&P 500—a measure mainly of the largest stocks—has returned some 5½ percentage points per year more than bonds and about 8 points more than inflation.[11] My guess

---

[11] These figures overstate the advantage of stocks to some extent. In 1926, at the beginning of the 73-year interval, stocks sold at prices that provided an average dividend yield of more than 5%. Today, prices have risen so high that the average dividend yield has dipped below 1½%. That decline couldn't happen again from today's dividend yield. If the dividend yield had remained unchanged over the 73 years (and that might be the best we can expect from today), and if the interest rate on bonds had remained at 4½%, where it was in 1926, then the 73-year annual return on the S&P 500 would have been less than 10%—only about 3½% more than the return on bonds and little more than 6% above inflation.

is that, in the years ahead, both the real return on stocks and the return differential between stocks and bonds will be distinctly smaller than they have been heretofore, partly because volatility has diminished. Even so, the return differential over the long-term should still be material.

Stocks of any size are often arbitrarily divided between growth stock and value stock categories. No one quite agrees on the precise quantitative definitions of *growth* and *value,* but in general, stocks with higher EPS growth rates clearly are categorized as *growth* and those with low price-to-book-value ratios are categorized as *value.*

There are multiple indexes of growth and value stocks, and while each is a little different, all show that growth and value tend to move in different cycles. Unless we recognize this, we might regard all managers of growth stocks as brilliant during some intervals, and as dunces during other intervals (and vice versa for value managers). Obviously, we must understand a manager's style to evaluate him properly.

From a standpoint of asset allocation, the moral is that we should, for the sake of diversification, probably have both growth and value managers.

Small U.S. Stocks. Step one is to define small stocks. The Russell 2000 Index defines them by market capitalization, as the 2,000 largest U.S. stocks *after* eliminating the largest 1,000 stocks, rebalanced annually. As of May 31, 1999, for example, the Russell organization reconstituted the Russell 2000 index to include companies with market caps between $178 million and $1.3 billion. But, of course, by the time the reconstituted index was put in place on June 30, market price changes had materially widened the range of market caps.

At that time, the country's largest 1,000 stocks accounted for some 91% of the total market capitalization of U.S. stocks; the Russell 2000 for another 7%; and some 8,000 tinier stocks (which we might refer to as micro-caps) accounted for the final 2%.

Small U.S. stocks are often treated as a separate asset class, because over the years they have at times had quite different returns than large stocks. Over the 73 years through 1998, Ibbotson data shows that small stocks (defined differently from and smaller than the Russell 2000) have returned roughly 1¼ percentage points per year more than the S&P 500— but not in any dependable way.

Witness these cycles:

No. of Years	Interval	S & P 500	Small Stocks	Advantage of Small Stocks
		Annual Rates of Return		
34	1926–59	10.3%	10.5%	+0.2 points
8	1960–67	9.6	19.5	+9.9
5	1968–72	7.5	0.5	−7.0
10	1973–83	8.0	21.4	+13.4
13	1984–98	17.9	11.4	−6.5

What expectation is most rational for us to make going forward?

Individual small stocks have been a lot more volatile than large stocks, and even a broad portfolio of small stocks like the Russell 2000 has averaged several percentage points more in annual volatility than large stocks. The correlation has been low enough, however, such that a mixture of, say, 20% small stocks with the balance in large stocks has had a slightly *lower* volatility than a portfolio of large stocks alone.

Because investment analysts don't follow small stocks as widely as larger stocks, a good manager of small stocks should be able to add more value to an index of small stocks than a good manager of large stocks can add to an index of large stocks. The flip side, of course, is that a below-average manager of small stocks is more likely to get bagged!

As with large stocks, the use of both growth and value small-stock managers can add useful diversification.

Possibly a separate category is micro-cap stocks—stocks smaller than those in the Russell 2000 index. It is hard to get much money into micro-cap stocks because they are simply too small. To the extent it is possible, however, micro-cap stocks act as a further diversifying element, as they behave somewhat differently from Russell 2000 stocks. They have much higher volatility and transaction costs, but if we can stand the volatility, a strong manager can earn good returns from them.

By the way, Richard Brignoli has shown that the average compound return on *individual* micro-cap stocks is lower than for larger stocks, and their returns are far more volatile. Yet micro-cap stocks are so uncorrelated with one another—they provide so much diversification benefit—that a large portfolio of them can actually provide very good returns.

Non-U.S. Stocks.   Unlike Scottish investors, who have been global investors for nearly 200 years, U.S. investors have until relatively recent years been among the more provincial. They implicitly assumed that appropriate investment opportunities began and ended in the United States even though the total value of U.S. stocks has for much of the last 20 years been well below half of the total value of all stocks in the world (although by year-end 1998 U.S. stocks had again risen close to 50% of world market cap).

Some U.S. investors have now moved 20% or more of their equity portfolios outside the United States—and for good long-term reasons. It is hard to argue that expected returns from stocks in the developed countries of the world should be materially different from those in the United States. From the beginning to the end of the 26-year interval 1973–1998, there was only a little difference in their total returns (Table 4.1). But the difference over shorter intervals has been phenomenal!

This triangle shows, for example, that during the four years 1985–1988 non-U.S. stocks of the developed countries outperformed U.S. stocks by 26 percentage points per year, and in the four years 1995–1998 U.S. stocks outperformed non-U.S. stocks by 21. For the 16 years 1973–1988, non-U.S. stocks outperformed U.S. stocks by 6 percentage points per year, and in the 10 years since, U.S. stocks have outperformed by 13. We don't need to calculate a correlation coefficient to see that U.S. and non-U.S. stocks provide real diversification for one another.

U.S. investors often worry that foreign currencies will lose value relative to the dollar. Of course, foreign currencies can be an opportunity as well as a risk. But from the beginning to the end of the 25 years 1974–1998, changes in foreign exchange values had very little impact on investment returns—despite substantial impact during shorter intervening intervals.

If U.S. investors are unduly worried about foreign exchange risk, they can always hedge that risk through the purchase of foreign exchange futures, although I am not much inclined to spend my money on such an "insurance policy" unless a very large percentage of our portfolio is at foreign-exchange risk. In any case, foreign exchange risk is not a reason to avoid considering non-U.S. investments.

While non-U.S. stocks have historically been more volatile than U.S. stocks, and emerging markets stocks substantially more volatile yet, the volatility of our overall stock portfolio would historically have been actually *reduced* by the inclusion of a portion of non-U.S. and emerging markets stocks. It has been estimated that we could place over 20% of our

Table 4.1 MSCI Stock Index for Europe, Australia, and the Far East (EAFE) vs. S&P 500 Index

To End of	_____ From Start of _____																										
	73	74	75	76	77	78	79	80	81	82	83	84	85	86	87	88	89	90	91	92	93	94	95	96	97	98
98	2	2	2	2	1	3	4	4	4	4	3	3	4	5	9	12	(13)	13	12	11	0	15	(21)	19	21	10
97	1	1	2	2	2	3	4	3	3	4	2	3	3	5	9	12	14	13	12	11	9	16	25	24	31	
96	0	0	0	0	1	1	2	2	2	1	0	1	1	3	7	10	12	11	9	7	3	11	21	17		
95	1	0	0	0	1	0	2	2	1	1	1	1	1	3	5	9	11	10	7	5	1	9	26			
94	2	2	2	3	3	1	1	2	1	3	3	3	3	1	3	7	9	7	3	2	14	6				
93	2	2	1	1	0	1	1	1	0	1	3	3	3	1	5	9	12	11	6	1	22					
92	1	1	0	2	1	2	1	1	1	1	1	1	0	2	9	15	20	20	19	20						
91	2	2	2	3	5	1	1	1	3	4	4	4	4	1	7	13	21	20	18							
90	3	3	3	5	7	3	1	1	3	6	7	8	8	5	4	11	21	20								
89	5	5	5	7	10	5	3	2	6	12	13	16	14	16	4	5	21									
88	(6)	7	7	9	8	8	6	8	10	11	17	20	26	26	16	12										
87	6	6	6	8	7	7	5	8	10	11	18	23	31	34	19											
86	5	5	5	6	6	6	3	6	8	9	18	24	38	51												
85	2	2	2	5	1	1	6	4	1	6	8	12	25													
84	1	1	0	3	3	1	7	6	5	11	2	2														
83	1	0	0	3	3	3	6	8	8	22	2															
82	0	0	0	3	8	2	9	1	4	22																
81	3	3	3	8	10	3	5	8	4																	
80	3	3	3	9	14	2	10	8																		
79	4	5	5	6	14	7	12																			
78	6	8	9	12	27	28																				
77	3	3	3	4	27																					
76	3	4	11	20																						
75	2	3	0																							
74	3	4																								
73	1																									
Actual	-14	-22	37	4	19	34	6	23	-1	-1	25	8	57	70	25	28	11	-23	12	-12	33	8	11	6	2	19

White = outperformed benchmark
Gray = underperformed benchmark

Note: The numbers on the left and at the top reference the year.

stock portfolio in non-U.S. stocks, and perhaps 5 of these percentage points in emerging markets stocks, without increasing the volatility of our overall stock portfolio.

The comments earlier in this chapter about growth and value relative to U.S. stocks apply equally to non-U.S. stocks.

Emerging Markets Stocks. With the rapid spread of private enterprise among the less-developed countries of the world, especially since the end of the Cold War, a new asset class has come about. Stocks of Singapore, Hong Kong, and the less-developed countries now account for some 10% of the value of the world's common stocks. Because, until 1998, the GNP of many of those countries was growing at a rate of 5% to 10% per year, compared with 2% to 3% per year for the developed economies—and in time this disparity should emerge again—there is reason to expect companies in the emerging markets to grow faster and their stocks to provide a greater return than in the developed world.

Let's digress a moment to consider the volatility of emerging markets stocks. It is not at all unusual to see the aggregate return on stocks in a particular developing country go up by 100% in a year or down by 50%—or more. If we could invest only in a single developing country, the risk would be tremendous. But today we can invest in some 60 developing countries, and—except during times of crisis in a few key countries as in 1998—their returns have had a relatively low *correlation* with one another. Stocks in one country may be way up when those in another country go into a tailspin. Indexes of emerging markets stocks are composed of 25 to 30 different countries, and these diversified indexes—while still a lot more volatile than those of the developed countries—are still low enough to be fruitfully considered by institutional investors.

A good example of the importance of correlation is the previously mentioned emerging markets stock indexes. The volatility of the stock market of the average developing country may be well over 40 percentage points per year, but taking all countries together, the volatility of the emerging markets is in the range of 25 to 30 points.

Tactical Asset Allocation (TAA)

In the mid-1980s, a number of managers developed highly sophisticated computer programs that move assets back and forth between stock and bond index funds, depending on which seemed most attractively valued at the time. These Tactical Asset Allocation programs are now sometimes invested entirely through index futures, because futures are most cost-efficient. And many such programs are global, which makes great sense to me, because TAA managers now have 15 or more futures to work with instead of only the few index futures that are available in the United States. That should allow the law of large numbers to help TAA managers achieve a higher probability of success.

Well, how have they done? Most TAA managers added a lot of value in 1987 and 1990, when the markets were hard hit. In other years they have tended to add little or no value and in some years did not do as well as their benchmark. Their benchmark can readily be tailored to the individual client—such as 60% stocks/40% bonds, or 80%/20%, or 100% stocks. The volatility of TAA managers has tended to be only slightly less than that of their benchmark.

If we want at least one account that will vary its asset allocation tactically, a TAA manager may well be our best choice. It is hard to get excited about the value added by TAA managers since their inception, but this has been an era of an exceptionally strong U.S. stock market. A TAA manager might be one of our best anchors to windward when the going gets rough, although that was not widely demonstrated during the brief but sharp collapse of stock prices in the third quarter of 1998.

Alternative Asset Classes

The concept of asset allocation ends in the minds of many investors with traditional marketable securities. Perhaps they might identify real estate as another viable asset class. But we can strengthen our portfolio materially with additional asset classes, such as:

Oil and gas properties

Timberland

Farmland

Start-up venture capital funds

Leveraged buyout funds

Corporate buy-in funds

Distressed securities

Commodity funds (including foreign exchange funds)

Merger and acquisition arbitrage

Convertible arbitrage

Hedge funds (funds that are both long and short common stocks, for example)

We shall discuss these asset classes in some detail in Chapter 8. But for now, let's just consider how we go about estimating future returns, volatility, and correlations.

With arbitrage programs or hedge funds,[12] where skill of the manager may be more important than the asset class itself, an analysis of the particular manager's historic returns may be the best method. Asset classes that add great value to a portfolio are those that are *market neutral*—whose correlation with the stock market is close to zero. Many arbitrage strategies get down to correlations of 0.3 or less. Also close to zero correlation are many hedge funds whose short positions are equal in value to their long positions.

When it comes to illiquid investments, such as real estate or venture capital, estimating their volatility and correlation with other asset classes is harder yet. The values at which we carry these assets on our books are much less meaningful because each asset is unique. No identical asset is being bought and sold every day in the marketplace. Valuations are established by (1) judgmental appraisals, as with real estate, or (2) the price at which the last shares of a stock were sold, even if that was two years ago, or (3) the book value of the investment, which is the usual valuation of an investment in which there have been no transactions, perhaps for years, or (4) a written-down value if the manager has strong evidence that an investment's value has been impaired.

Given these approaches to valuation, illiquid investments often *appear* to have materially less volatility than common stocks. But note the emphasis on the word "appear." The price at which a particular investment could be sold certainly goes up and down each quarter—undoubtedly with great volatility for a start-up venture—even though its reported value is kept unchanged quarter after quarter.

---

[12] See pages 174–177 for discussion of arbitrage programs and page 181 for hedge funds.

Which volatility of an illiquid investment should one assess—the volatility of its *reported* returns, or the estimated volatility of its *underlying* returns?

In the reports we make on our investment fund, we have to base our returns on *reported* valuations. But let's stop and consider two investments—a marketable stock, and a start-up venture capital stock. Let's say each is sold after seven years and each returned 16% per year over that interval. Which was more volatile?

The marketable stock had lots of up and downs, whereas the venture capital stock was kept at book value most of the time. Was the marketable stock more volatile? If our time horizon for measuring volatility is seven years, we could say they had the same volatility. But we know there was obviously a lot greater uncertainty as to the seven-year return on the venture capital stock than the marketable stock. The underlying annual volatility of the venture capital stock had to have been a lot higher.

We could make a good case that our expected volatility of an illiquid investment should reflect the innate uncertainty in its return—that is, its *underlying* volatility.

How does one assess correlations between liquid and illiquid investments? We should study whatever data we have, but ultimately we'll have to go with an educated guess—and again do some meaningful sensitivity tests.

Putting It All Together

Perhaps with the help of a consultant, we have developed our return, volatility, and correlation assumptions for each of the asset classes we are going to consider: What do we do now?

Why Not 100% Equities?

A question that has long bugged me, and continues to do so, is *why not 100% equities?* If we agree that we should be very long-term oriented, and if we are convinced that over any 20-year interval stocks should outperform bonds, then why not target 100% stocks?

Well, the roller coaster ride of the stock market could be very upsetting. The worst eventuality would be if, at the bottom of a bear market, the investment committee's stomach weakened and it reduced the allocation to common stocks. So how can we ease the roller coaster ride a little but not impair expected returns unduly?

At this point, I would like to introduce *my* definition of the term *equities*. By equities I mean *all investments whose expected returns are generally as high as, or higher than, common stocks.* I am big on diversification and believe in reducing the volatility of our aggregate portfolio through diversification. But I am convinced that strong diversification can be achieved without resorting to assets whose expected returns we really believe are materially below that of equities—such as traditional fixed income.

Some judicious use of fixed income might enable us to increase our aggregate return *per unit of risk,* but unless we can leverage our overall portfolio (and that's tough to do), we can't spend risk-adjusted returns. If we are truly long-term oriented, why not accept slightly higher volatility in exchange for higher returns?

Before relegating fixed income to oblivion, let's ask what purpose fixed income should serve in a portfolio, and how best we can fulfill that purpose. Traditional fixed income serves three key purposes:

1. Traditional fixed income lowers the expected volatility of the portfolio. This is the most common purpose of fixed income, and the purpose I would hope to achieve instead with diverse asset classes that have materially higher expected returns than fixed income.

2. Fixed income gives the portfolio needed strength whenever interest rates decline and stock prices decline at the same time, as in a recession—or heaven forbid, in a depression. No asset class serves this function as well as fixed income.

3. For a pension fund, fixed income serves a related function. Because the present value of pension liabilities goes up as interest rates go down, and vice versa, just like the market value of bonds, fixed income serves as a good hedge to the pension plan's funding ratio. Particularly for benefit obligations to retirees—liabilities that are normally not so sensitive to inflation—nothing serves as a better hedge than fixed income.

So maybe there is a bona fide rationale for fixed income, after all. If we must use fixed income with a lower expected return to fulfill purposes 2 and 3 above, how can we do it most efficiently? The answer, it seems to me, is in long-duration high-quality bonds—such as a Zero account, the kind we described earlier in this chapter. This approach will give us (1) the maximum protection for the economic scenarios where we need protection most, for (2) the lowest allocation to lower-expected-return assets.

Another approach is to use interest rate futures as overlays for absolute-return programs—programs that have little or no correlation to other investments in our portfolio. This kind of approach is covered in Chapter 8 under the headings of Arbitrage Accounts and Portable Alpha.

A superficial but simple way to measure how well our portfolio serves purposes 2 and 3 above is to measure our portfolio's *duration-equivalent allocation to traditional fixed income*. If a traditional bond portfolio has about the same duration as the Lehman Aggregate—say, 5 years (actually, a little less)—then 1% of our portfolio allocated to a 25-year Zero account would be duration-equivalent to a 5% allocation (25/5). Another 1% with a 10-year duration would be equivalent to a 2% allocation. We could fairly readily reach a 30% *duration-equivalent allocation* to fixed income with a relatively small *actual allocation*.

This discussion, however, focuses only on one aspect of asset allocation. Let's now describe two related tools that will suggest the kinds of asset allocations we might consider for our aggregate portfolio.

The Efficient Frontier

We enter our assumptions on returns, volatility, and correlation into an Efficient Frontier Optimizer. The concept of the Efficient Frontier was introduced in Chapter 2. It's a computer program that will develop a range of most efficient portfolios—portfolios that have the highest expected return for any level of expected portfolio volatility. Figure 4.3 is a repeat look at an Efficient Frontier.

Every point on the line represents an efficient portfolio. We should have two objectives:

1. To move the Efficient Frontier line as high as possible. The larger the number of diverse asset classes that we include in the optimizer the higher the Efficient Frontier line is likely to be—and the higher-expected-return portfolio we can achieve at any given volatility level.
2. To develop at our chosen volatility constraint a Target Asset Allocation that will be as close to the Efficient Frontier line as possible.

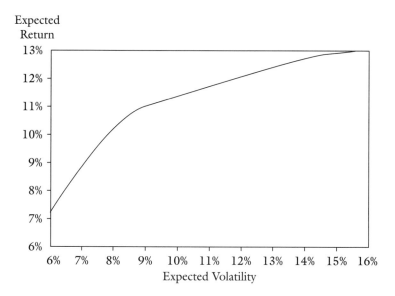

Expected Return (y-axis): 13%, 12%, 11%, 10%, 9%, 8%, 7%, 6%

Expected Volatility (x-axis): 6%, 7%, 8%, 9%, 10%, 11%, 12%, 13%, 14%, 15%, 16%

Figure 4.3   Efficient Frontier.

As we input our assumptions for the return, volatility, and correlation of each asset class (see illustration of input assumptions in Table 2.1 on page 38), we should also enter certain constraints. With no constraints, the optimizer might hypothetically tell us the most efficient portfolio consists of only emerging markets stocks, emerging markets debt, and arbitrage programs!

Notwithstanding our assumptions, we wouldn't want more than X% of our portfolio subject to the common factors that periodically infect prices in the emerging markets. And we doubt that we could get more than Y% of our portfolio into quality arbitrage programs. We should go through each of our asset classes and ask ourselves if we need a constraint for it or for any combination of asset classes. We also might enter a requirement to have *at least* Z% of the portfolio in a particular asset class, such as U.S. stocks. We should limit such constraints and requirements, however, to only those cases where we have a compelling reason. Each such constraint will lower the Efficient Frontier line.

An Efficient Frontier Optimizer provides captivating output. But it's all dependent on our assumptions, and we must remember GIGO (garbage in, garbage out). So how can we gain comfort in using the output? That's where sensitivity tests come in. If there is one portfolio that seems optimal, what changes in which assumptions will make the portfolio sub-optimal? What alternative portfolios are just about as good but are not as sensitive to changes in assumptions?

The Efficient Frontier is a great tool, but it is no substitute for common sense. Dick Michaud gives a stronger warning: "Mean/variance optimization presents an illusion of precision that is seductive and generally fallacious and even dangerous. . . . Managers should seldom take portfolio optimizations literally and should often feel free to include valid judgment in the portfolio management process."[13]

The best portfolio we can develop through the Efficient Frontier exercises will probably be the best portfolio for an endowment fund. But it may *not* be the best portfolio for a pension fund.

Optimal Pension Portfolio

As indicated in Chapter 2, the optimal portfolio for a pension fund may be different because perhaps we should not be as concerned with the *absolute volatility* of the portfolio as with the *volatility of its funding ratio*. Our funding ratio ultimately determines the amount of contributions we must make to our pension fund. Also, our funding ratio must be published in our annual report for all employees and the investment community to see.

Rationally, we should target a portfolio that will give us *the lowest probabilistic present value of future contributions to our pension fund*. Or the lowest present value that will also *minimize the probability of extremely large contributions*.

To determine this, we need more than asset information. We need an analysis of the pension plan's benefit obligations and a projection of its payments of pension benefits. For any given asset allocation, the computer

---

[13] Richard O. Michaud, *Efficient Asset Management,* Harvard Business School Press, 1998, pages 77 and 79. See Michaud's book for an in-depth analysis of the limitations of the Efficient Frontier and ways to minimize these limitations.

can be programmed to run 500 simulations to develop a probability curve of the present value of future contributions, and to project the range of funding ratios and contributions going out for many years.

Some typical insights that may come from such a study include:

- The optimal portfolio will usually have relatively high weighting toward equities.
- The optimal amount of fixed income will be higher for a pension plan that has a lot of retired lives than for a pension plan that has only a small percentage of retired lives.
- The optimal average duration of the fixed income allocation will be 15 to 20 years (more in synch with the duration of the pension plan's liabilities).
- The optimal portfolio will shun cash equivalents, as relative to the present value of liabilities, cash is more risky than long-term bonds.

Not many pension funds are using this kind of analysis today to help them set their Target Asset Allocation, but I suspect more will do so in the future.

A Secondary Benefit of Diversification

Gaining the benefits of diversification is what this chapter is all about. Everyone understands that diversification reduces the aggregate volatility of our portfolio. Fewer people recognize that, in addition, diversification actually adds a little to our expected return! How?

Let's say we invest $100 each in Asset A and Asset B, so we have a portfolio of just those two assets, and we hold those two assets for 10 years. Then let's say over that 10-year interval that Asset A earns 20% per year and Asset B loses 20% per year. The value of the portfolio after 10 years would be about $630. Rates of return never occur in a straight line, but if they did, this is what would have resulted:

Year	Market Value Asset A	Total Asset B	Market Value
0	$100.00	$100.00	$200.00
1	120.00	80.00	200.00
2	144.00	64.00	208.00
3	172.80	51.20	224.00
4	207.36	40.96	248.32
5	248.83	32.77	281.50
6	298.60	26.21	324.81
7	358.31	20.97	379.28
8	429.98	16.78	446.76
9	515.98	13.42	529.40
10	619.17	10.74	629.91

Our portfolio's compound annual return for the 10 years would not be zero (the average of +20% and −20%) but 12.2%:

$$(\$629.91 / \$200.00)^{1/10} = (3.14955)^{0.1} = 1.122, \text{ or } +12.2\%$$

This is an extreme case (or I wouldn't have picked it!), but we can test the value-added ourselves on any well-diversified portfolio. Assuming a buy-and-hold portfolio—no rebalancing—we'll use our expected returns, standard deviations, and correlations for each asset class to project the *portfolio's* expected return and standard deviation over the next 10 years. We'll then compare those measures with the weighted-average return and weighted-average standard deviation of each of our asset classes.

Figure 4.4 shows a hypothetical expected *real* return (net of inflation) for each asset class (for example, 2.3% for U.S. stocks) and a *10-year* standard deviation[14] for that asset class (3.7% for U.S. stocks, for which the graph shows 6% as the *expected return plus one standard deviation,* and −1.4% as the *expected return minus one standard* deviation).

---

[14] A 10-year standard deviation is derived from an expected *annual* standard deviation. For the above example, we assumed the annual standard deviation of real returns on U.S. stocks was 11.7 percentage points. We divided this annual standard deviation by the square root of the number of years—10 years in this case—and we got a 10-year standard deviation of 3.7 percentage points $(11.7 / \sqrt{10} = 11.7 / 3.16 = 3.7)$.

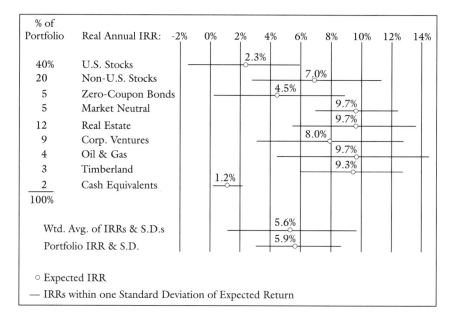

Figure 4.4   Probable 10-Year Returns on Fund.

Don't get hung up on what you might think of the particular return and volatility assumptions. Note instead that the bottom of the graph shows that the weighted average expected real return is 5.6%, with a one-standard-deviation range from 1.4% to 9.8%. After factoring in correlation assumptions, however, the *portfolio's* expected real return is 5.9%, and its one-standard-deviation range is much narrower, from 3.2% to 8.6%.

Not only has diversification narrowed the standard deviation from 3.2 percentage points down to 2.7, but it has also increased the expected real return by 0.3%. That's what I call diversification benefit!

In Short

The range of asset classes that we can include in our portfolio far exceeds traditional ones of domestic stocks, bonds, and cash. To the extent we make use of all the attractive asset classes that we can access, the additional diversification can meaningfully reduce our portfolio's volatility and can even ratchet up our expected return.

Chapter 5

Selecting Investment Managers

O nce we have developed our fund's objectives and its asset allocation, we must decide who will manage the investments in each asset class.

Our Goal

What should be our overriding goal? We should be striving for the *world's best* managers in each asset class—the managers who are most likely to produce the best future performance.

Such perfection is obviously unattainable. First of all, no one can realistically evaluate all managers in the world. And simply chasing managers with the best track record is a losing game, because all managers have hot and cold streaks. Also, some of the best managers won't accept our money. Finally, no one can come even close to being a perfect judge of the future performance of investment managers. But the *world's best* managers should still be our *goal*.

That goal implies a couple of things:

- No constraints or preferences as to geography or kind of manager (small, large, here, there, bank, independent firm, etc.).
- A commitment to objectivity, to gather information as meticulously as we can and make decisions as dispassionately as possible. That does not mean relying entirely on numbers and ascertainable facts. Ultimately, these decisions come down to judgments. But we

should arrive at those judgments after examining all of the data, interrelationships, and ramifications. We must make a determined effort to maintain our objectivity.

Three Basic Approaches

There are three basic approaches to investment management:

1. Index funds
2. In-house (do it ourselves)
3. Outside managers

Index Funds

For stocks or bonds, an index fund should not only be our benchmark. It should also be our *investment vehicle of choice* unless we can find a manager in that asset class who we are confident will do better—net of all fees and expenses. The case for index funds is persuasively articulated by Jack Bogle in his book *Common Sense on Mutual Funds* (John Wiley & Sons, Inc., 1999).

Let's consider the Wilshire 5000 Index initially. This is a capitalization-weighted index of all stocks traded in the United States. It is a truism that the average active investor *has to* underperform the Wilshire 5000 in his U.S. investments. The investor has trading costs and investment management fees that in combination can amount to 0.5% to upwards of 1% per year, whereas a large investor can invest in an index fund that closely matches the Wilshire 5000 Index for no more than a few basis points.[1] So the odds are *against* active investing.

The most widely used index fund is one that replicates Standard & Poor's 500 Index, which is very heavily weighted toward the largest U.S. stocks. These are widely researched stocks. It is difficult for any investor to get an information advantage over other investors. As a result, the pricing of large U.S. stocks is often thought to be very *efficient*. That means that if a good active investor stays within the S&P's 500-stock universe, it is difficult to produce *net* returns that outperform the index over the long term. If we don't use an index fund for these stocks, we must be arrogant

---

[1] A basis point equals 0.01%.

about our ability to choose active managers—and then must prove our right to be arrogant.

So what's wrong with an index fund like the S&P 500? Well, intuitively, does it make a lot of sense to increase the weighting of a stock in our portfolio as its price goes up, and vice versa (as an index fund implicitly does)? That would make sense if the change in this year's price was a good predictor of next year's price, but we know that isn't true. In fact, contrarian investors have long known that a pervasive general trend in the investment world is *reversion to the mean*.[2]

Is it possible to minimize this drawback with an index fund? I have not seen it done widely, but I believe it is possible. We could run an equal-weighted index fund, where each stock is the same percentage of the portfolio, regardless of its size. This would provide more diversification benefit, but there are two problems:

1. Periodically—such as every six months or every year—we would have to rebalance the portfolio to equal weighting. Such broad rebalancing would probably incur an unreasonable amount of transaction costs.
2. Buying the same dollar value of a smaller stock as of a large stock would probably be expensive, if not impossible.

We've been talking mainly about large U.S. stocks. One can also invest in a smaller stock index fund such as a Russell 2000 index fund. Would that make just as much sense?

Because smaller stocks are not as widely researched, it is possible for a good investor who digs hard enough to gain an information advantage on other investors and therefore outperform a small-stock index by a wider margin than a good large-stock investor can outperform the S&P 500. But if the opportunity is greater with small stocks, the reverse is true as well.

---

[2] *Reversion to the mean* is the tendency for the price of an asset (or an asset class) that has greatly outperformed or underperformed the average of other assets (or asset classes) to revert over time toward the average. That tendency, which in general has been well documented, also makes some intuitive sense.

For example, if a company is earning a particularly high rate of return in a line of business, its high earnings will attract competitors to that line of business. The competitors will challenge the pricing flexibility of the company and limit its subsequent returns. Conversely, a company that is performing poorly attracts takeover bids from other managements who believe they can squeeze more value out of the company.

One can really get bagged with small stocks. In short, if we are careful in selecting managers, I believe for most investors active management of small stocks can make more sense than a Russell 2000 index fund.

The active investor has another advantage: He is able to invest *outside* the index being used for his benchmark. For instance, from a practical standpoint, a large-stock investor may be able to invest in a 700-stock universe—not just the 500 stocks included in the S&P 500. In fact, most active investors periodically do go outside their benchmark universe. That is undoubtedly why active investors as a group will outperform the S&P 500 for a period of years, and then underperform it for another period of years.

How about index funds for *non-U.S. stocks?* Viable index funds have become available for large stocks in the developed countries and are now beginning to become available for some of the emerging markets. Since there are so many countries with so many different dynamics, it would intuitively seem as if an active investor should be able to add a lot of value through his country allocation alone. This has proved hard to accomplish—unless the manager was smart (or lucky) enough to underweight Japanese stocks starting in 1990, and to fully weight them in the 1980's, when Japanese stocks accounted for more than 60% of the non-U.S. index.

Reliable index funds for U.S. bonds are also available and compete very well with many active bond managers. In selecting an active fixed income manager, it is equally important to ask ourselves—do we really have sound reason to believe that, net of fees and expenses, this manager can meaningfully outperform an index fund? In short, index funds are a very viable alternative. Yes, it is entirely possible to do better. But do we have the resources to expect realistically to do better?

In-House

Index funds can be managed inexpensively in-house, but fees are so low for outside-managed index funds, it is hard to justify in-house management. Hence, in our discussion of in-house management, we will focus on *active* management.

Many large sponsors of pension plans and endowment funds actively manage all or a portion of their assets in-house. They avoid the high fees charged by active outside managers by hiring a staff to buy and sell the assets themselves. If we are large enough, is this the way to go?

Let's go back to our original goal—to have the world's best managers in each asset class. With respect to whatever asset class (or classes) we are talking about, can we objectively convince ourselves that *we* can put together a management team that, net of all costs, can match or exceed the net results of the best managers we could hire outside? If so, then in-house is the way to go.

In-house management, however, faces serious challenges. For example, does our compensation schedule enable us to attract some of the world's best investment managers? And if we hire some smart young people and are lucky enough to grow them into the world's best, can we keep them? The best managers tend to be entrepreneurial people who want ownership in their own firm. Even if we insulate our investment management team from the rest of our bureaucratic organization, can we realistically aspire to hire and retain the best?

And if our in-house hires don't ultimately challenge the best we can hire outside, we have the unpleasant task of putting them out on the street. That's a lot tougher than terminating an outside manager.

Outside Managers

To make a sound decision about the best management approach for us, we should see what is available in outside managers. Given that there are literally thousands of outside managers, that is a large and challenging exercise. How should we go about it?

Developing a Universe.   The most effective way to develop the universe of candidates to assess is, over time, to get to know as many investment managers as we can. We can help to minimize the degree to which we are a prisoner of our own prejudices by returning all phone calls in a timely manner and never turning down a manager who seriously wants to visit us. Also, I like to meet with each visiting manager myself, together with other members of our staff. That's a key part of our research and development. I recognize, however, that if our office were as conveniently located as Manhattan (instead of Rochester, NY) we might have to be more selective about whom we meet with.

Another way is to obtain from a consultant a short list of managers he considers best in a given asset class.

A third way is to go through directories, such as *Morningstar* for mutual funds and *Investworks* for pension fund managers, select those with the best past performance, and invite them to visit us. This approach, however, can be a trap, because for intervals of 3 to 5 years and longer, the correlation between a manager's *past* and *future* absolute performance is so low as to make a grown man cry.

We can minimize this problem if we try to compare apples with apples— that is, compare like universes of managers. For example, we should compare managers of large growth stocks only with other managers of large growth stocks, managers of small value stocks only with other managers of small value stocks, etc. Unfortunately not all managers fit into nice neat pigeon-holes. But by making an attempt to do this, and by looking not only at 5-year performance but also performance for longer intervals as well—even 10 and 15 years or longer if valid data is available—we can assemble a universe of managers that is viable to look into.

Suggestions from our peers can also be worth considering, but we should keep in mind the breadth of the perspective from which any particular peer is making suggestions.

For each candidate we consider, we find it useful to prepare performance triangles similar to Triangle C (Table 1.5 on page 18), which compares the candidate's historic performance against one or two indexes that we believe may be the best-fitting benchmarks.

Criteria for Selection. Our criteria should be the same for both new and existing managers, and our process should flow from those criteria. The six criteria we listed in Chapter 3 on Investment Objectives can be applied to managers in any asset class:

1. *Investment approach.* Do the assumptions and principles underlying the manager's investment approach make sense to us?
2. *Expected return.* Historic return overlaid by an evaluation of the predictive value of that historic return, as well as other factors that may seem relevant in that instance and may have predictive value. (We'll touch on these factors in the next couple of pages.)
3. *Expected impact on the overall volatility of our aggregate portfolio—* Two considerations are:
   (a) The expected volatility of the manager's investments. The historic volatility of his investments overlaid by an evaluation of the predictive value of that historic volatility, as well as a recognition of the historic volatility of that manager's asset class in general.
   (b) The expected correlation of the manager's volatility with that of our aggregate portfolio.

4. *Liquidity.* How readily in the future can the account be converted to cash, and how satisfactory is that in relation to the overall portfolio and our needs for cash?
5. *Legal issues.* Are there any legal concerns?
6. *Trust.* After considering the above five criteria, does the selection or retention of the manager seem appropriate? Can we give this manager our wholehearted trust?

Relative to the second criterion, what do we mean by "predictive value of historic return"? The whole selection process has to do with predicting future performance. Past performance is irrelevant unless it has predictive value. How can we judge whether it has predictive value?

Ultimately, it is a judgment. My judgment has tended to be influenced by the following factors:

- *Decision makers.* Who is the individual or individuals responsible for the performance record (they may not necessarily be the heads of the firm). Have the same individuals been responsible throughout? If so, are they still in the saddle? If not, the predictive value is essentially nil, because the past performance reflects somebody else's work. Of all considerations, this is probably the most important.
- *Support staff.* To the extent that there has been material turnover in the research or other support staff, that may impair predictive value of past performance.
- *Process.* In investment approaches where the investment *process* is equally as important as the individual decision makers—a rarity, in my judgment—I *may* attribute some predictive value to past performance even though there has been turnover in key people. Continuity of methodology is particularly important with quantitative managers, whose decisions are driven by mathematical algorithms[3]—where the *product* of human judgment is the algorithm rather than the individual investment decision. With such managers, I am also interested in their commitment to continuing quantitative research.
- *Size of assets managed.* If, adjusted for the growth in market capitalization of the overall stock market, a manager is managing a much larger value of assets today than he did X years ago, his

---

[3] Mathematical equations that transform raw data about companies and the economy into specific buy and sell decisions.

performance of X years ago may carry very little predictive value. Managing $5 to $50 million would seem to have little predictive value for a manager who is now managing over $5 *billion*.

> A classic example concerns managers of *small* stocks. The case is a matter of simple arithmetic. If a manager of a 50-stock portfolio was managing $150 million, he could typically compose his portfolio with stocks that had market caps as small as $100 to $200 million. To retain some element of liquidity in his portfolio, he probably wouldn't want to own more than, say, 3% of a stock's outstanding shares. Hence, he could own a full $3 million position (1/50th of $150 million) in a stock with a market cap of only $100 million.
>
> Let's say that manager is now managing $750 million. A full position is now $15 million (1/50th of $750 million). That would be 3% of a $500-million market-cap stock. Unless the manager increases the number of stocks in his portfolio (changes his management approach) or increases the percentage of a stock's outstanding shares that he will hold (reduces his liquidity), the manager can no longer give serious consideration to stocks much smaller than $500 million market cap.
>
> He has eliminated some 1,000 stocks from the universe he can viably consider. What impact do you think that should have on the predictive value of his past performance?
>
> Of course, the manager could buy a smaller position in those smaller stocks, but those holdings would not have the impact on the portfolio that they once did.

- *Number of decisions.* Performance that is the result of a thousand small decisions should have a much higher T-statistic (confidence level) than performance dominated by only a handful of decisions, as might be the case with a manager whose past performance hinges on several key market-timing calls. The smaller the number of data points, the more difficult it is to distinguish skill from luck.

> I have found it challenging to evaluate international equity managers because their record is often dominated by a few key decisions. The most common benchmark for such managers is Morgan Stanley's index for Europe, Australia, and the Far East (EAFE). There are other international indexes I like better, but they all present a common problem. As cap-weighted indexes, they properly give Japan a dominant weighting in the index— some 25% in recent years, and as great as 65% back in the 1980s.
>
> Why is this a problem? Because the performance of managers of non-U.S. stocks is so dominated by a single decision: How much of the portfolio should they allocate to Japanese stocks?

The Japanese market is one of the least correlated with the rest of the world and has gone to extremes. Back in the 1980s when Japanese stocks were priced in the stratosphere, clearly too high, any investor who greatly underweighted (or avoided) Japanese stocks looked like a dunce compared with the EAFE index. And vice versa in the 1990s: When Japanese stocks fell on hard times, investors who avoided them looked like geniuses compared with EAFE. They were neither. Assessing predictive value when performance is impacted heavily by a key decision can be a real challenge.

- *Consistency.*   Performance that is consistently strong relative to a valid benchmark would seem to have a lot more predictive value than performance that is all over the place.
- *Proper benchmark.*   Performance that is compared with a tight-fitting benchmark should have much higher predictive value than performance that is simply compared with the market in general, especially over intervals as short as 3 to 5 years. Comparisons with the market in general can lead us astray, as the dominant influence may be a manager's *style* (which can go in and out of vogue) rather than the manager's *skill.*
- *Time.*   How many years of a manager's past performance do we think has predictive value? Three years of performance may reflect mainly noise. I am particularly impressed when I see a manager with 15 years of strong performance that also meets other criteria of good predictive value.

Another yardstick is intuitive. What implicit assumptions about how the world works are built into the manager's approach? Do those assumptions make sense to us? If the logic underlying the manager's basic strategy doesn't seem to be one that can win over the long term, we better try another manager. If the basic strategy is overly simplistic, such as *just buy the lowest P/E stocks,* the strategy may be on the right track, but a manager that follows that approach as part of a more sophisticated strategy should do better yet.

Some quantitative managers who don't have long track records will show extensive simulations of how they *would* have performed if they had been using their quantitative method. Beware! Let's understand how the manager developed his algorithm in order to evaluate how much data-mining[4] the manager has done. It's almost impossible to completely

---

[4] The extent to which 20/20 hindsight has influenced the manager's algorithm.

eliminate data-mining, but let's make a hard judgment about how academically honest and objective the manager has been. Then if he passes both these tests, let's discount his results by several percentage points per year and see if the manager is still worth considering.

Assessing the predictive value of a manager's past performance is not easy. But it's *critical*. Assessing the likely impact of the manager's volatility and correlation on the rest of our portfolio is likewise not easy, but it's also important. An understanding of the volatility and correlation of the manager's particular *asset class* can be helpful here.

Evaluating Candidates.   A traditional way of selecting managers is to send candidates a long questionnaire called an RFP (request for proposal), use their responses to prune the universe, then invite the finalists to make one-hour presentations to us and our committee, one after the other in what is sometimes called a "beauty contest." My language here suggests I am less than enamored of this approach.

The idea of a questionnaire is a good one. In fact, it is a must for every manager. A sample questionnaire is enclosed as Appendix 5A. But I wouldn't suggest sending all managers the identical questionnaire. We should obtain a manager's marketing materials, and after learning as much from those materials as we reasonably can, tailor a questionnaire for that manager—focusing on those questions that are particularly relevant to that manager and which are likely to elicit responses that will help us answer, "so what?" Preparing a tailored questionnaire is more work, but the manager's responses to it are generally more helpful.

A meeting with the manager, at his office if at all possible, allows the manager (not his marketing man) to tell his story more completely than he can through a questionnaire. Having studied his questionnaire responses, we can go into the meeting with a set of follow-up questions we want to pursue. A key challenge is cutting to the *substance* of what a manager has to say. Some managers are extremely articulate; some others could never begin to earn their living as communicators. And I've found there is little correlation between articulateness and good investing.

That's why I believe the "beauty contest" is a poor approach. Those of us who have participated in the full, painstaking evaluation of all the managers we are considering, are the ones best equipped to conclude who should be hired. Committee members who spend only a relatively few hours per year on our fund's investments can't hope to make any meaningful evaluation on the basis of a 20- or 30-minute presentation.

In coming to our conclusions, the challenge is to remain as objective as possible. I find it helps to write out our recommendation and explain the rationale of our conclusions in detail—even if we never show the recommendation to anyone. If we can't do a convincing job of articulating *why* to ourselves, and then to our committee, we haven't done the job.

Categorizing Managers by Style

It is helpful to categorize managers by *style*. For example, common categories of styles of U.S. equity managers are large, medium, or small cap, and growth or value. But simply placing such labels on a manager is a lazy-man's way of understanding them and is likely to be costly to us.

These style categories can only be very gross. There are great differences of style *among* large-cap value managers and *among* small-cap growth managers, for example. Hence, this label is only the beginning of understanding a manager's investment approach. We must devote serious effort if we are to understand the individual style of a particular large-cap growth manager and what differentiates him from other large-cap growth managers.

Applying a large-cap value *benchmark* against a manager we have labeled large-cap value may or may not be appropriate. First of all, which large-cap value benchmark should we choose? Several are available. Any particular benchmark may relate to the manager's style in only a very coarse way. Where the benchmark doesn't fit very well, we should not downgrade the manager because of benchmark risk.[5] Many of the best managers don't manage to a benchmark, and shouldn't. That means we just have to work a little harder to understand and interpret their performance.

There are other managers who don't fit neatly into any one style—either because they are so eclectic or because they change styles from time to time. Let's not try to shoehorn them into a cubbyhole they don't fit.

Benchmark Risk

The more valid a benchmark is for a particular manager, and the more he invests within the universe of that benchmark, the narrower his deviations

---

[5] *Benchmark risk* is the risk that the manager's performance will deviate greatly (up and down) from his benchmark.

from that benchmark—and superficially, at least—the easier it is for us to evaluate his performance. We should never, however, confuse benchmark risk with absolute risk, or forget that our objective is to *make money.*

Some of the best managers are ones for whom there isn't a very good benchmark. They are managers who will invest our portfolio however they think it will make the most money. Their benchmark risk is gigantic. Categorizing such a manager in our asset allocation is fuzzy at best.

Should we include such a manager on our team? By all means, *if* he is good enough. We should use benchmarks as tools, not as crutches.

We once found a manager of international equities who had a strong, consistent record. Upon investigation, we found that the manager followed a discipline of never letting his portfolio stray very far from his benchmark, the EAFE index.[6] In one sense, he was managing an index-plus fund.[7] Our pension fund was so diversified, we didn't feel we needed the index portion, so we asked him if he could manage a portfolio for us that included just the "plus." He said no one had ever asked him to do that, but he thought he could do a great job. And he did indeed (while continuing to do reasonably well on his index-plus accounts for other clients).

Several years later as the manager was trying to capitalize on his great performance for us by recruiting additional clients for similar accounts, he found he was not having great recruitment success. We asked why. "It's like this," he explained. "A large pension fund considered us recently and liked our performance but passed us up because we have too much benchmark risk! I don't understand that," he said. And neither do I!

Accentuating the Positive

We always want to find what a manager can do best and take advantage of his key strength. Sometimes that means probing a manager to find where his greatest strength actually lies. Two examples:

- A quantitative manager is managing an account benchmarked against the Russell 3000 index. His performance is above benchmark, but

---

[6] The Morgan Stanley Capital International Index for Europe, Australia, and the Far East.

[7] An index-plus fund is a portfolio that can take only limited deviations from the composition of the benchmark index and is therefore targeted to achieve a modest return in excess of the index without varying very much from the index's return in any one year.

analysis shows that virtually all of his value-added is coming from small and midcap stocks.

Why not continue to use the market-cap-weighted Russell 3000 as benchmark but tailor the index by truncating the market cap of every stock larger than $10 billion to exactly $10 billion? That would sharply reduce the benchmark's heavy weighting to the largest stocks, which compose the lion's share of the regular index, and would "accentuate the positive" by allowing our manager to emphasize what he does best—invest in smaller and midcap stocks.

Another alternative would be to change his benchmark to the Russell 2500—which is the Russell 3000 *minus* the 500 stocks that compose the S&P 500.

- One theory says that, at equilibrium, all asset classes have the same risk-adjusted returns. Hence, the reason why fixed income has lower returns than equities is that its risk is a lot lower. If we believe that, how do we take advantage of it?

  We go to a manager who appears strong in all aspects of fixed income, and we say: "How would you like to manage a fixed income portfolio with no constraints other than maintaining your long-term volatility at a level no higher than the S&P 500?" A typical reply might be: "No one has ever asked us that before. But that's the way fixed income should be managed!"

  Settling on an appropriate benchmark for such an account would be challenging, but again, why not trade higher expected return for benchmark risk and for volatility in an asset class that has a relatively low correlation with common stock?

Arrogant Managers

I like arrogant investment managers *whose performance history has earned them the right to be arrogant.* By arrogant, I don't mean rude or insensitive. There is no excuse for that kind of behavior. By arrogant, I mean, "I'm going to manage portfolios my way, and if you like it, I'll be glad to manage your portfolio too. But I'm not interested in modifying my approach for any client."

Not many investment managers are so good that they have been able to adopt that approach. Many managers say, "Tell us what your specifications are, and we'll be glad to manage to those specs." And indeed, especially with quantitative managers, some are prepared to do it well. But I don't think managers can be all things to all clients. Managers have particular areas of strength, and it seems to me that the job of us clients is to find out what are those areas of greatest strength, and then how can we make the most of them.

It is a big advantage to managers if they can be so arrogant as to focus on managing only one kind of portfolio.

A Passion to Be Best

My highest admiration is reserved for those investment managers (and those athletes) whose aspiration for the highest possible compensation is greatly exceeded by their passion to be the best in their class.

The two motivations are not always compatible. A manager's fees from incremental money he manages drop quickly to his bottom line, whereas the additional money may mean fewer investment opportunities that he can realistically choose from (because some attractive opportunities have become too small for him to bother with). Also, more clients mean more demands on his time.

There are some managers who are sufficiently wealthy that they have no financial need to work but still do so for the sheer fun of playing the game and striving to be the best. Their greatest compensation is the high rate of return they produce over the long term.

Such managers rank at the top of my list.

Strategic Partners

Seeking managers asset-class-by-asset-class adds a lot of complexity to our investment program. Some plan sponsors seek large investment organizations that have strength in most asset classes globally, and they report good success the last several years in forming "strategic partnerships" with these managers. They have three reasons:

1. The managers should be able to add material value by shifting their tactical asset allocation within fairly broad limits.
2. With such a large account, the sponsors can negotiate extremely favorable fees with the manager.
3. Such "strategic partners" reduce the complexity of the sponsor's program and give the sponsor strong sources of investment advice.

The hiring of "balanced managers" 25 years ago faded away as those managers were generally unable to add value through their shifts in asset allocation. But that was in the days when the investment paradigm was largely limited to U.S. stocks and bonds. With certain well-chosen managers, the "strategic partner" concept may work far better this time.

I have yet to subscribe to the concept for the following reasons: (1) Few if any managers are among the world's best in multiple asset classes, even net of low management fees; (2) we should be staffed in such a way as to be able to deal efficiently with the complexity of numerous managers; and (3) we should consider *each* of our managers a potentially valuable consulting resource, and we should opportunistically pick their brains on issues about which they have particular expertise.

How Much Excess Return to Expect

When we find a manager we think is about the world's best in his asset class, how much excess return[8] above his benchmark, net of fees, might we expect long-term in the years ahead?

Depending on the asset class, I would be well pleased with 3 percentage points per year, net of fees. That would be within the range of my experience and would also be consistent with a little study I did some years ago.

As of the end of 1984, I looked at the performance of all 63 common stock mutual funds that had been in existence over the prior 30 years. That universe had much survivor bias, as it excluded all mutual funds that had been terminated or merged out of existence—almost surely for less-than-stellar performance. Anyhow, the results for that 30-year interval were as follows:

35 Funds underperformed the S&P 500, twelve of them by more than 1½ percentage points per year, three of them by nearly 3 points per year
 4 Equaled the S&P 500
<u>24</u> Outperformed the S&P 500, twelve by less than 1 percentage point per year, nine by about 2 points per year
63

Only two mutual funds exceeded the S&P 500 by more than 4 points per year—the Templeton Growth Fund and the Mutual Shares Fund. And both invested far outside the universe of the S&P 500. The Templeton

---

[8] Sometimes, imprecisely, called "alpha."

fund invested heavily outside the United States, and Mutual Shares invested heavily in bankrupt companies.

It would be interesting to see such a study updated, especially one without survivor bias. But I doubt whether the dimensions would be much changed.

Considering the fact that we will inevitably choose some managers who are destined to underperform their benchmarks, I think we will be doing very well indeed if, in the aggregate over the long term, all of our active equity managers combined can succeed, net of fees, in beating their benchmarks by 1½ percentage points per year.

Commingled Funds

Sometimes we have a choice between a commingled fund or a separate account.[9] Which route should we take? Some investors like their own separate account whenever they can get it. My preference, however, would be whichever approach is likely to achieve the best rate of return net of all costs, and that depends on the facts of the matter.

If we want something other than what the commingled fund is offering, the decision is easy: we can get it only with a separate account. But what if the manager invests the commingled fund and separate accounts in a similar manner?

A commingled fund can often be preferable to a small separate account because the commingled fund is more diversified and is usually given more "showcase" management attention.

Does the manager charge extra for the commingled fund? Many managers do not charge extra, because they find it is more economical to manage one commingled fund than multiple separate accounts. We could save custodial costs with such a commingled fund.

Does the commingled fund permit investors to withdraw their money on very short notice? If so, the manager of the commingled fund may maintain more cash than for a separate account in order to be able readily

---

[9] A commingled fund is one in which two or more parties invest. Group trusts and most limited partnerships are common examples. A mutual fund is an extreme example of a commingled fund. On the other hand, a separate account (except when the term is used by insurance companies) is an account held only for a single investor.

to cash out investors who wish to make withdrawals. Such cash is a drag on performance, and a mark against the commingled fund.

Does the manager require an entrance or exit charge for the commingled fund? If the manager doesn't, he probably should, provided the proceeds go back into the fund to offset transaction costs (rather than into the manager's pocket). If there is *no* entrance or exit charge, as with a mutual fund, that's an enticement, because we can avoid transaction costs when we contribute our cash. But the savings might be ephemeral, as the fund subsequently will pay transaction costs for all future contributions and withdrawals by other investors. (There should be no charge if a contribution and withdrawal of the same magnitude cross at the same time.)

A fairer way is for the manager, in lieu of an entrance charge, to invest new contributions briefly in a separate account and then move the assets into the commingled fund *in kind*. That way the investor shoulders precisely its own transaction costs. Conversely, a withdrawal is also made in kind and moved briefly into a separate account, from which the assets are then sold.

Some investors prefer a separate account because they then always know precisely what is in their account and can gain composition analyses periodically on their account and on their aggregate assets. One doesn't need a separate account for that, however, as our trustee, or whoever is doing our composition analyses, can usually obtain a computer disk from the custodian of the commingled fund showing our beneficial holdings in each of that fund's underlying investments.

In short, neither a separate account nor a commingled fund is necessarily more advantageous than the other. It all depends.

How Many Managers?

To gain optimal diversification in common stocks, we have already discussed the importance of selecting outstanding managers in large stocks and small stocks, "growth" stocks and "value" stocks, managers of U.S. stocks, stocks from the developed countries abroad, and stocks from the emerging markets. Such diversification is the way to get the best long-term investment return with the lowest aggregate volatility.

A single manager would be most convenient for us—if he were among the world's best in *each* of those specialties. But we have seldom seen managers who are considered among the world's best in more than one or two of those specialties.

If we are a multibillion dollar fund, we should have the resources to select outstanding managers in each of these areas. There is no magic number that's optimal. An extremely large fund can add further specialties to the above list—as long as the managers on its team are complementary to one another.

Upon finding two outstanding managers who ply the same turf, we may have a hard time deciding which to hire. Should we ease our problem by hiring both? If it's that close a call, flip a coin. Adding both might well add more complexity than value.

There is, however, a reason other than diversification for having multiple managers. No matter how diligent the selection process, and how confident we are of our ultimate selection, every selection is a probability. If two-thirds of our selections are above-average performers, we'll be doing well. But let's not kid ourselves about our selections being error-free. If we have only one or two managers, the odds of below-average future performance are higher than if we have, say, ten of them. With multiple managers, the probability of a home run declines, but (assuming a sound selection process) so do the odds of striking out.

What if we are only a $100,000 endowment fund? How can we gain such diversification? It's easy—use mutual funds. With thousands of mutual funds to choose from, we can gain broad diversification with, say, 10 mutual funds, investing $10,000 in each fund. But which ones? How can we know which are among the world's best? If we're large enough to afford it, we can hire a consultant to advise us. If not, we probably should add someone to the investment committee who follows mutual funds professionally.

In selecting mutual funds, we should have a sufficiently broad universe if we limit our choice to *no-load* mutual funds—funds that do not charge any brokerage commission for either buying or making withdrawals from the fund.[10] Some brokers might tell us their consulting services are free, as the commissions cover their compensation. Their motivations can never be

---

[10] In the selection of mutual funds, I also recommend sticking with funds that do *not* charge 12(b)(1) fees. These fees amount to up to 0.25%/year of assets and are used by a mutual fund for advertising and promotional purposes. The fees are permitted by the SEC in what I consider an inappropriate action by the SEC, because the fees clearly do not promote the interests of mutual fund investors. The fees enable a mutual fund to become larger, which in due course reduces the flexibility of its fund manager to perform. There is an ample supply of good mutual funds with the integrity not to charge 12(b)(1) fees, and I would stick with them.

congruent with ours, however, as brokers are compensated on turnover—the amount of buying and selling in our portfolio—which by itself is irrelevant to us. Consultant remuneration based solely on a percentage of total assets managed would seem to align their motivations more closely with ours.

Fees

When hiring a manager, we never know what his future performance will be. But we *do* know his fees. The manager must add value at least equal to his fees just to equal an index fund. So we must take fees seriously.

Let's recall a few facts of life. Great investment managers command high compensation—perhaps higher than warranted by their contribution to society. That's true also of star athletes, popular actors, and top corporate executives. Compensation is controlled by supply and demand, which means charging what the market will bear. If we place a low limit on our fee schedules for active management, we are likely to get no more than what we're paying for.

On the other hand, it doesn't work the other way. Just because we are paying high fees does not assure us of better long-term performance. *Caveat emptor.* The only thing besides luck that can increase the probability of good future performance is thorough research and rigorous analysis in the selection process. In the end, what counts is only what we can spend—performance *net* of fees.

A typical fee schedule is based on a percentage of the account's market value, payable quarterly. A particular percentage applies to the first few million dollars of market value, with declining percentages applied to incremental amounts of market value. Such break points, for example, may occur at $5 million, $20 million, $50 million, and $100 million. Fee schedules of managers differ widely in both fee percentages and these break points.

Can we negotiate fees? Perhaps, if our account is large enough. As part of negotiations, I like to insist on a "most-favored nation" provision[11] in the management agreement.

---

[11] Such a provision might go something like the following: "The Manager represents and warrants that the fees and expenses charged to the Plan are the most favorable terms available to any client for whom the Manager performs similar services. In the event that any current or future client of the Manager negotiates more favorable terms, the Manager will promptly notify the Plan and extend to it terms that are at least as favorable."

Some plan sponsors favor performance fees. Performance fees come in multiple flavors, but an example might call for a fixed annual fee of 0.2% of market value, plus 15% of the past year's return in excess of a benchmark index, often with a maximum percentage the manager can earn in any one year. Any such performance fee should include a high-water mark. That is, it should provide that if the manager fails to qualify for a performance fee in year 1, he must earn an excess return in the following year equal to the shortfall in year 1 before he can begin to accrue a performance fee in year 2.[12]

Such a "high-water mark" should perhaps work the other way as well. If the manager earns more than his maximum performance fee for any one year, the excess can be carried over to year 2. Otherwise, the manager would lack incentive to add value once he has reached his yearly maximum.

Proponents believe performance fees are fairer—they compensate a manager according to the results he achieves. And proponents take comfort knowing they will not be paying high fees for poor performance. Plan sponsors should not, however, use performance fees with the expectation of reducing their overall fees. That would mean they expect their managers, as a group, to underperform their benchmarks. If that's true, the plan sponsors should be using index funds instead.

Those who oppose performance fees are fearful that such fees motivate managers to shoot the moon—especially if a manager's performance has fallen behind and he has a large shortfall to make up. In practice, I have not observed managers acting that way as a result of performance fees. Managers are restrained by fear of losing their reputation for integrity. But

---

[12] An example of a more complex high-water mark provision is as follows: "The Performance Fee shall equal (i) 15 percent of any amount by which (a) is greater than (b), less (ii) the sum of all prior Performance Fees paid, where:

a = the Account's value as of the end of the latest Fiscal Period, net of all Expenses, Base Fees, and any Unrelated Business Income Tax payable as a result of the Account's investments through the end of that Fiscal Period, and increased by cumulative performance fees paid out of the account since inception, and

b = the hypothetical cumulative dollar return on the Account if it had earned a net 9 percent internal rate of return compounded annually from the inception of the Account, adjusted for any subsequent contributions or withdrawals."

This language assumes that all fees, including performance fees, are paid out of assets in the account, which I view as an appropriate standard procedure.

viewed in a vacuum, performance fees can provide an incentive to take greater risk.

Another drawback to performance fees is the complexity they add to the administration of an account. The plan sponsor is responsible for auditing fees thoroughly, and that can be complicated work.

Performance fees are essential in private investments (such as real estate), but unless an outstanding manager of regular marketable securities insists on a performance fee, I generally prefer the typical fee schedule. It's simpler. And most common stock managers don't need incentive fees to motivate them to work hard; beyond a certain point, their working harder doesn't generally improve their performance.

By the way, on an ongoing basis we should check the computation of *every* fee before we authorize its payment.

In Short

To select investment management for any asset class, we must first decide whether to use an index fund or active management, then whether to manage in-house or to hire outside managers.

Hiring outside active managers is a very challenging assignment. Numbers help, but they are only the beginning. The task requires lot of hard research and, ultimately, judgment as to a series of criteria.

Appendix A

Typical Questionnaire for a Prospective Equity Manager

1. What was the market value of all funds for which your firm is responsible on a fully discretionary basis?

	Number of Accounts	Total Assets	Non-U.S. Equities*
Equity accounts with same objectives as the one we are considering	_____	_____	_____
Other institutional taxfree accounts:			
Other equity accounts			
Fixed income accounts			
Balanced accounts	_____	_____	_____
Total			
Taxable accounts:			
Equity accounts			
Fixed income accounts			
Balanced accounts	_____	_____	_____
Total			
Mutual funds:			
Equity accounts			
Fixed income accounts			
Balanced accounts	_____	_____	_____
Total			
All accounts:			
Equity accounts			
Fixed income accounts			
Balanced accounts	_____	_____	_____
Total			

* Non-U.S. equities not listed on U.S. exchanges, except please include ADRs.

2. For how much in nondiscretionary assets was your firm also responsible?
3. How much more in assets will you accept in accounts with the same objectives as the one we are considering? How much more in all equity accounts?
4. How many taxfree accounts of $5 million or more did your firm lose in the past three years? Would you care to comment on the circumstances?
5. a. For each calendar year (or quarter), what was the performance of (i) your investment approach we are considering, net of fees, and (ii) its benchmark? [*This will enable us to develop a performance triangle such as Triangle C (Table 1.5 on page 18).*]
   b. How much money did you manage under this investment approach as of the start of each year?
   c. What has been the volatility of your investment approach vs. that of its benchmark?
   d. For intervals of the past 1, 3, 5, and 10 years, what has been the standard deviation among all your accounts that use this investment approach?
6. Do these performance figures conform to AIMR standards?[13] If not, how do they differ, and why?
7. To what do you attribute any performance differences among accounts?
8. What benchmark do you consider most appropriate, and why?
9. Would you please comment qualitatively on your performance?
10. Who has been the person (or persons) most responsible for the above performance?
11. Would you please provide a list of all your portfolio managers and research analysts, together with their current responsibility, whether they are a principal in the firm, their year of birth, the year they started in the investment business, and the year they joined your firm?
12. How is compensation handled in your firm? What percent of compensation is in bonuses? On what basis is the distribution of bonuses decided? Who shares in the profits of the firm, and in what proportion?
13. When are your key people planning to reduce their current level of activity or retire?
14. Would you please provide the names and positions of all persons who have left your research and portfolio management staff in the last three years? In each case, please indicate the person's responsibility and length of service with your firm. Also, either in your reply or verbally when we meet, would you care to comment on the circumstances of the person's departure?

---

[13] Performance measurement and reporting standards established by the Association for Investment Management and Research.

15. During the past five years what changes have taken place in the key decision-making positions within your staff?

16. Who would be our account manager and his or her backup. For how many accounts and how much money is each responsible? What additional responsibilities, if any, does each have?

17. How much more in assets will each accept?

18. Please provide a description of your investment approach and your decision-making process for accounts such as the one we are considering.

19. Has the investment approach and process changed in any way since inception, and if so, how?

20. How is research handled in your firm? To what extent is it done in-house?

21. How many securities are typically included in your portfolio?

22. What are the composition measures (weighted medians, preferably) of your current portfolio—such as market cap, P/E, price/book, EPS growth rate, EPS volatility, etc.? How have they changed over time relative to the portfolio's benchmark?

23. May we see a current portfolio that is managed with the same objectives we are considering?

24. How important is market timing to your investment approach? To what extent do you use cash equivalents?

25. What economic situations are best and worst for your particular investment approach?

26. May we have the names of clients for whom you manage accounts larger than $X million? Please identify those for whom you manage accounts with the same objectives we are considering.

27. Have you used (or would you use) any derivatives in managing these accounts? If so, what kind, and to what extent?

28. Please describe your policies or procedures to mitigate the risk of unauthorized trading by members of your staff? How do your policies and procedures stack up against those recommended by the "Group of Thirty" and AIMR standards?

29. To what extent do you rely upon derivative valuations that are provided by your counterparties?

30. What has been the average turnover on accounts such as the one we are considering, as a percent of the account's average assets? What percent of assets is typically paid for brokerage commissions?

31. What is the range and average of commissions paid for trades on these accounts?

32. What percent of commissions, if any, is paid to affiliated broker/dealers? On what basis do you pay such commissions?

33. Relative to brokerage commissions, do you meet both the requirements and the recommendations of AIMR Soft Dollar Standards? If not, how do you vary from those standards?

34. What amount of commissions did you do with brokers that rebate a portion of the commission to clients' trust funds?

35. For all other soft-dollar brokerage you do for these accounts, what is the average percent of total commissions used for soft dollars?

36. Please list the services you receive through soft dollars, a description of the service, the cost in soft dollars, and the conversion ratio (or alternative cost in hard dollars).

37. What are your internal policies with respect to employees trading for their own accounts?

38. What provisions have you made for disaster preparedness in the case of fire, earthquake, or whatever?

39. What is the fee structure for the kind of account we are considering?

40. Is any client (including public funds and eleemosynary clients) paying a lower fee structure, net of any discounts in the form of contributions to eleemosynary clients, for essentially a similar investment management approach?

41. Do you have any investment services that are not the same as the one we are considering but are still somewhat similar, which operate with a lower fee schedule (net of any rebates)?

42. If any client has a performance fee arrangement, please describe the arrangement.

43. Who is the owner of your firm? Who owns the parent company? Have there been any changes in ownership in the past year? What companies are affiliates of yours?

44. What is the net worth of your firm?

45. Would you please comment on the profitability of your firm?

46. Is your firm bonded as required under ERISA? Aside from this bonding, does your firm carry any fiduciary liability insurance?

47. Are any litigation or enforcement actions (including enforcement actions initiated by the DOL or SEC) outstanding against your firm, any of its affiliates, or any of its investment professionals? If so, would you please comment on these actions?

48. Have you had any additional such litigation or enforcement actions in the past five years?

49. Are you qualified as an Investment Manager under Section 3(38) of ERISA?

50. Do you know of any conflicts of interest—actual or potential—that could conceivably affect our account?

Chapter 6

Managing Investment Managers

M anaging investment managers is easy," asserted a chief financial officer I met back in the 1970s. "Each year we simply fire the managers with the worst two records over the last three years."

Oh, if only it were that simple! Let's start this subject with the mundane and work our way up to the hard decisions.

The Management Agreement

If we hire multiple managers we will find it helpful to have a standard investment management agreement with all of our managers—at least the boilerplate (the main body of each agreement). We can then put everything special applying to a particular manager into the exhibits. Exhibits may include:

- The objectives of the account.
- The fee schedule.
- Information the manager needs to know about our plan (such as its tax ID number, date of its tax determination letter, type of plan, members of its fiduciary committee, authorized signatories, and the names and addresses of the trustee-custodian and actuary).
- Names and addresses of the manager and plan sponsor to whom official notices should be addressed.

Objectives of the Account

Our first exhibit, which we label Objectives, is something of a catch-all where we spell out the goals, benchmarks, and constraints for the account as well as anything about the account that differs from the agreement's boilerplate. An example of a simple statement of objectives for an active equity account might read as follows:

> Our objective for your account is that you build the highest long-term rate of total return that you can relative to that of the Russell 3000 [or whatever official benchmark is more appropriate].
>
> The account you manage will at all times constitute a small percentage of our plan assets. For this reason, you will not be subject to any diversification requirement in managing the account. The only reason you should buy additional common stocks for this account should be your belief that they will add to its total return. The only reason you should hold securities other than common stocks should be your expectation that they will earn a better return than common stocks. The account should be composed only of securities that are relatively marketable. Beyond these constraints, there is no limit to the kinds of securities you may hold.

Why include something about our manager not needing to have a diversified portfolio? Doesn't ERISA require diversification? It does, but that very sound requirement applies to the plan's *overall* assets, not to any individual account. Unless a manager is aware that he is managing only a small percentage of our overall portfolio, he may feel compelled to diversify his particular portfolio more than necessary. He may add investments for the sake of diversification that aren't ones he necessarily expects can add the most value. Relieving the manager of the need for diversification frees him to focus on what we really want him to do—make money for us.

What constraints should we establish for the account? We should define the maximum amount of each kind of derivative to be permitted in that account (as indicated in Chapter 2 on page 46). However, the fewer constraints the better. This places me at variance with plan sponsors who feel they should develop an explicit list of constraints for each manager. But if we have done a careful job of selecting the manager, we should trust him enough to give him all the rope he wants. We *want* his creativity, so let's not limit it.

Just by establishing the manager's benchmark—a necessary step—we may be applying greater constraint than we realize, even assuming it is a benchmark with which the manager feels completely comfortable. In managing an account, many managers are fearful of wandering too far from the benchmark portfolio for fear of having a large negative variance some year and losing the account. Many managers are more constrained by *their* risk tolerance than by ours.

Of course, then, we have a keen responsibility to monitor each manager carefully on an ongoing basis.

Monitoring Managers

As suggested earlier, I am not a believer in micromanaging investment managers. We can only get in their hair if we watch their every trade and try to second-guess them. We should stay out of their way. I much prefer a manager to spend his time and resources making money for us than holding our hand.

Once we hire a manager, there are only five constructive actions we can take. We can:

1.   Give the manager more money.
2.   Take some money away.
3.   Change his objectives, benchmark, or constraints.
4.   Terminate him.
5.   Accept the status quo.

Everything we do should be relevant to one or more of these actions. Because it is relevant to every one of these five actions, we must understand what the manager is doing. How do we go about gaining this understanding?

We should expect managers to send us periodic reports (usually quarterly) on their performance and why they performed as they did, what principal changes they made in the portfolio, and what their current investment strategy is. When we become aware of actions we don't understand or which don't seem consistent with the account's objectives, we should phone the manager and try to understand why—but not reprimand him unless he has violated his word.

The manager's quarterly and ad hoc reports, however, are only the beginning of our monitoring. In addition, we should independently monitor the manager's performance and his portfolio composition, and we should be aware of changes in his organization.

Performance

I have heretofore preferred to calculate each manager's performance in-house because I believe we understand better what the numbers mean when we put them together ourselves. Also, we can group managers any way we think best and obtain aggregate performance data for each group.

Most plan sponsors, however, have their trustee calculate performance and provide benchmark figures of indexes and other taxfree funds. This is a logical choice because the trustee has all the data in its computer. Moreover, the sophistication of performance measurement systems of the best trustees is rapidly outstripping anything we can do in-house.

We rely heavily on performance triangles vs. benchmark such as Triangle C illustrated on page 14 of Chapter 1. One of the good things about these triangles is that they prevent us from looking at the last quarter's or even the last year's performance without looking at performance in the context of multiple years. Trying to dissect each quarter's performance in great detail invites a heady case of myopia, as most of what happens in intervals as short as a quarter or even a year can be attributed to the noise of the market. *Our job is to sift out evidence of skill (or lack thereof).*

Where a manager's benchmark is not a tight fit with his investment approach (a not infrequent occurrence), we find it helpful to prepare performance triangles against multiple benchmarks.

Portfolio Composition

I like our trustee to provide a monthly summary of all trades by each manager, plus key aggregate characteristics of those trades. With this, we can see at a glance if the manager is, for example, going more heavily into growth stocks, or smaller stocks, or some different industry.

Most of all, however, I like a quarterly analysis of each manager's portfolio by such things as:

- Industry
- Dividend yield
- Earnings growth
- Earnings volatility
- P/E
- Price/book

- Market cap
- Turnover (usually value of sales as percent of portfolio value)
- Number of stocks

A "motion picture" of these measures and industry composition, such as shown in Table 6.1 on pages 126–129, can help us understand how the manager has modified his portfolio over time.

A standard of the industry is the group of more scientifically developed portfolio composition measures—called BARRA factors (after Barr Rosenberg, who developed them). These factors include:

- Variability in markets
- Success
- Size
- Trading activity
- Growth

- Earnings to price
- Book to price
- Earnings variability
- Yield

Few of these factors have definitions simple enough that I could explain them cogently to a lay person, or to my committee members. They are nonetheless sophisticated measures, and we should become familiar with them. Table 6.2 on page 130 provides a motion picture of the BARRA factors for the same manager depicted in Table 6.1.

Analyses of this nature help us develop the kind of questions we can ask our manager to fill out our understanding of how he goes about managing our account. The purpose of our questions is to get inside his head—to learn what differentiates him from other managers, and why he performs as he does. This understanding is key in helping us assess the predictive value of his track record.

And this understanding is particularly crucial with a manager for whom we can't find a tight benchmark—a manager where there is a lot of benchmark risk: frequent and wide variances of his performance from his benchmark. This situation places extra pressure on us to understand the manager and make well-informed qualitative judgments.

Organization

Evaluating the predictive value of past performance is as important with our current managers as with prospective managers. As indicated in the previous chapter, a key factor in evaluating predictive value is stability of the management organization. In the standard boiler plate of our management agreement, we should require the manager to report to us in a timely manner any change in the key persons managing our account or the departure of any senior investment person in the firm.

Table 6.1   Portfolio Composition Analysis and Industry Composition

	Div. Yield	P/E Ratio			Price/Book Ratio			5-Yr. EPS Growth*		
	Mean	*75th*	*Median*	*25th*	*75th*	*Median*	*25th*	*75th*	*Median*	*25th*
01Q1	.64	1.02	.97	1.03	.77	.98	.97	1.06	1.45	2.70
01Q2	.61	.99	1.00	.84	.82	.96	.97	1.23	1.83	2.85
01Q3	.62	.87	.99	.89	.82	.97	1.01	1.19	1.58	3.27
01Q4	.62	.88	.84	.81	.78	.91	.92	1.25	1.38	2.41
02Q1	.59	.84	.80	.77	.78	.84	.91	1.22	1.68	2.66
02Q2	.63	.83	.71	.75	.71	.82	.85	1.23	1.60	2.09
02Q3	.62	.91	.89	.82	.73	.87	.85	1.38	1.35	2.70
02Q4	.59	1.01	.94	.88	.80	.97	.89	1.57	1.40	3.29
03Q1	.56	1.00	.87	.77	.82	.88	.84	1.62	1.24	3.78
03Q2	.59	.93	.82	.85	.87	.92	.79	1.36	1.21	3.67
03Q3	.63	.99	.93	.91	.82	1.04	.96	1.32	1.47	4.57
03Q4	.62	.86	.94	.88	.91	1.03	.95	1.15	1.33	3.05
04Q1	.60	.87	.95	.91	.91	.90	.99	1.38	1.53	2.40
04Q2	.59	.86	.91	.91	.80	.92	.91	1.45	1.53	3.08
04Q3	.55	.87	.99	.81	.87	1.02	1.09	1.21	1.64	.88
04Q4	.55	.83	.85	.76	.95	.94	.90	1.13	1.81	1.05
05Q1	.55	.81	.85	.75	.90	.87	.85	1.17	2.00	.88
05Q2	.53	.85	.89	.92	.96	.94	.90	1.13	1.66	.60
05Q3	.54	.87	.95	.84	1.00	.93	.96	1.10	1.84	.72
05Q4	.61	.92	.90	.88	.84	.91	.90	1.17	1.61	1.00

Notes: All figures except under "Market Cap" are relative to the values of the Russell 3000 index.

A relative dividend yield of .64 means that the portfolio's average dividend yield is 36% less than the Russell 3000's average dividend yield.

Median P/E, for example, means that half the value of the portfolio has a higher P/E, half has a lower P/E. A median EPS growth rate of 1.45 means that the portfolio's weighted median EPS growth rate is 45% greater than that of the Russell 3000.

The 75th percentile P/E means that 75% of the value of the portfolio has a lower P/E, 25% has a higher P/E. A 75th percentile EPS growth rate of 1.06 means that the portfolio's weighted 75th percentile EPS growth rate is 6% greater than that of the Russell 3000.

The 25th percentile P/E means that 25% of the value of the portfolio has a lower P/E, 75% has a higher P/E. A 25th percentile EPS growth rate of 2.70 means that the portfolio's weighted 25th percentile EPS growth rate is 170% greater than that of the Russell 3000.

* Least squares growth rate. Volatility is standard deviation of EPS growth rate.

Weighted Percentiles, Relative to Russell 3000								
5-Yr. EPS Volatility*			5-Yr. Return on Equity			Actual Market Cap ($B)		
75th	Median	25th	75th	Median	25th	75th	Median	25th
1.26	1.43	1.40	1.07	.98	.83	10,802	4,664	1,865
1.45	1.50	1.58	1.01	.99	.84	10,825	4,290	1,522
1.00	1.21	1.38	1.01	.99	.94	10,458	4,788	1,983
1.06	1.09	1.62	1.00	.97	.87	11,012	4,785	2,002
1.30	1.24	1.54	.92	.98	.77	9,449	4,703	1,748
1.57	1.54	1.74	.90	.95	.94	10,011	4,056	1,551
1.50	1.33	1.74	.90	.96	.96	7,653	3,952	1,283
1.47	1.45	1.59	.91	.94	.88	8,335	3,818	1,882
1.17	1.24	1.46	.95	.98	.97	6,490	3,745	1,431
.99	1.27	1.67	.97	.98	.94	7,963	4,441	1,574
1.24	1.32	1.88	.99	.98	.91	12,355	4,974	1,662
.92	1.33	1.75	1.11	1.08	.98	11,815	4,833	1,697
1.39	1.48	1.51	1.09	1.15	.99	12,500	5,464	2,511
1.68	1.58	1.86	1.01	1.13	.79	10,481	6,477	2,542
1.49	1.26	1.13	1.07	1.11	.86	14,988	5,963	2,488
1.01	1.12	1.10	1.00	1.11	.84	15,965	6,180	2,673
1.06	1.17	1.10	1.11	1.09	.84	12,467	5,675	2,093
1.01	1.03	1.16	1.09	1.01	.66	15,458	6,137	2,155
1.14	1.01	.97	1.18	1.06	.78	16,398	6,018	1,886
1.58	1.08	1.13	1.25	1.04	.81	13,595	4,371	1,174

Many of the measures in this figure are my own idiosyncratic preference—weighted medians (and 75th and 25th percentiles), most of them relative to the weighted medians (and weighted percentiles) of a benchmark index. Why weighted medians? Because (using price/earnings ratios as an example) one or a few stocks with outlier P/Es aren't going to have a material effect on weighted medians. I want to know that half the portfolio's value is above what P/E, a quarter is above another P/E, and a quarter is below a third P/E, all relative to the benchmark index. Is the manager focusing on stocks with a narrow range of P/Es, or a broad range?

The issue is clearest with respect to the market cap. A portfolio's mean market cap may be highly misleading. Let's assume a portfolio has 10 equally weighted stocks—nine of them at $100 million cap, plus a company like GE at $300 *billion* cap. The portfolio's mean cap would be over $30 billion (large cap), whereas 90% of the portfolio would be exposed to the *micro-cap* sector. Where is the manager investing most of our money?

(continued)

Table 6.1   (Continued)

	Finance	Health	Consumer Durable	Consumer Non-Dur.	Services	Energy	Transp.
			Percent of All Stocks in the Portfolio				
01Q1	12.5	12.6	6.2	0.4	13.1	4.8	7.5
01Q2	15.9	15.4	5.9	1.2	11.2	3.8	3.7
01Q3	21.0	14.4	4.1	1.3	11.4	2.6	2.1
01Q4	22.4	13.0	1.6	1.3	10.2	2.7	3.2
02Q1	22.7	9.0	1.6	1.3	12.2	4.4	1.9
02Q2	20.8	7.6	1.3	1.3	16.6	5.7	2.4
02Q3	20.5	10.2	1.5	1.2	19.9	5.9	0.0
02Q4	22.5	14.1	1.4	1.2	20.6	4.7	1.1
03Q1	21.2	10.7	1.5	1.7	22.8	4.0	3.5
03Q2	28.3	10.3	1.2	3.2	21.2	3.1	2.8
03Q3	31.5	8.6	0.0	3.4	21.6	5.7	2.8
03Q4	33.5	7.9	0.0	6.8	22.6	3.1	4.3
04Q1	35.1	6.2	0.0	8.1	21.4	3.2	3.3
04Q2	37.4	2.9	0.0	6.7	21.3	3.0	2.0
04Q3	34.6	5.8	0.0	5.6	21.2	4.2	2.1
04Q4	35.1	6.1	0.0	5.8	21.3	4.3	0.0
05Q1	37.7	7.9	0.0	8.1	17.6	4.7	0.0
05Q2	37.8	7.4	0.0	8.4	17.4	4.6	0.0
05Q3	37.1	9.7	0.0	10.5	14.0	6.3	0.0
05Q4	36.2	11.5	0.0	12.6	14.0	7.1	0.0

In years past, it was common for the plan sponsor to meet with each of its investment managers once each quarter. The manager would provide his insights on the economy and market and comment on his investment strategy. I quickly concluded that, for me, such meetings were a waste of the manager's and my time, as I did not know how to integrate any new information into a judgment about the above five actions we might take. Moreover, such frequent meetings simply invited a severe case of myopia. I believe less frequent meetings are now the industry norm.

My own preference is for an annual meeting, typically during the first quarter of a year, as soon as year end performance figures and other analytic data are available—plus ad hoc meetings during the course of the year, any time either the manager or we feel there is a special reason to get together. I feel, however, it is important to do a lot of planning around our annual meeting. For example, while our managers send out Christmas cards, I (the grinch) have made it a practice to send them an extensive questionnaire

Tech.	Basic Industry	Capital Goods	Utilities	Percent Cash	Number of Stocks	Percent Turnover
Percent of All Stocks in the Portfolio						
15.8	12.6	9.1	5.3	9%	63	62%
18.1	15.0	5.6	4.3	12%	65	21%
17.3	12.4	10.5	2.8	9%	64	19%
17.3	15.1	9.7	3.5	11%	71	10%
18.1	15.0	10.9	2.8	22%	62	26%
16.0	17.0	7.0	3.8	12%	68	13%
16.5	12.1	7.4	4.8	7%	69	11%
14.9	10.8	3.9	4.8	4%	71	16%
11.5	12.2	6.7	4.0	4%	70	19%
10.5	12.1	4.1	3.2	7%	69	13%
10.1	8.4	3.6	4.3	8%	67	16%
10.2	6.9	3.7	1.0	10%	73	22%
8.0	5.7	5.8	3.3	5%	71	19%
8.1	6.8	6.1	5.8	2%	61	17%
6.8	6.7	6.4	6.5	3%	58	15%
7.7	5.5	8.8	5.4	1%	59	13%
7.0	5.2	9.3	2.4	2%	62	8%
7.2	5.9	8.3	2.9	5%	63	14%
7.2	6.5	5.0	2.9	2%	63	17%
8.5	6.0	2.6	1.5	2%	64	13%

under the belief that we should know as much about our current managers as we would if we were hiring a new manager. (In a sense, if we haven't terminated a manager, we have, of course, implicitly rehired him.)

The questionnaire (to which I would request a response by the end of January) should cover amounts of assets the manager is responsible for, information on personnel, and so on. A sample questionnaire is included as Appendix A at the end of this chapter. Managers, however, routinely receive carloads of questionnaires, and if the questionnaires sound as if they are canned, I would expect answers that seem canned. For this reason, we tailor each question to the particular manager. Is the question relevant to that manager? Should it be asked in a different way? Does it reflect our awareness of what the manager wrote in his response to last year's questionnaire and in subsequent communications? Are there special questions we want to probe with this manager? Preparing such tailored questionnaires for a sizable number of managers requires a lot of time and effort, but I have always felt it is worth it.

Table 6.2 Portfolio Composition—BARRA Factors vs. Russell 3000

	Variability in Markets	Success	Trading Activity	Growth	Earnings to Price	Book Value to Price	Earnings Variability	Yield
03Q1	0.27	-0.25	0.39	0.30	0.17	0.09	0.21	-0.38
03Q2	0.39	-0.19	0.31	0.27	0.15	0.12	0.17	-0.41
03Q3	0.33	-0.08	0.30	0.21	0.22	0.10	0.19	-0.38
03Q4	0.34	-0.19	0.32	0.19	0.24	0.10	0.12	-0.36
04Q1	0.35	-0.02	0.31	0.19	0.19	0.08	0.15	-0.39
04Q2	0.26	-0.11	0.37	0.21	0.19	0.13	0.16	-0.39
04Q3	0.21	-0.08	0.29	0.25	0.13	0.04	0.19	-0.43
04Q4	0.29	0.02	0.32	0.26	0.24	0.12	0.17	-0.40
05Q1	0.32	0.06	0.31	0.26	0.24	0.12	0.19	-0.44
05Q2	0.24	0.09	0.22	0.27	0.19	0.11	0.19	-0.44
05Q3	0.29	-0.04	0.23	0.24	0.20	0.06	0.10	-0.43
05Q4	0.28	-0.01	0.37	0.23	0.25	0.12	0.09	-0.45
Mean	0.30	-0.07	0.21	0.24	0.20	0.10	0.16	-0.41
Std. Dev.	0.05	0.10	0.05	0.03	0.04	0.03	0.04	0.03
Minimum	0.24	-0.25	0.22	0.19	0.13	0.06	0.09	-0.45
Median	0.29	-0.06	0.31	0.25	0.20	0.11	0.17	-0.41
Maximum	0.39	0.09	0.39	0.30	0.25	0.13	0.21	-0.36

Note: Positive figures in this table indicate that the portfolio has higher growth (for example) than the benchmark index. The higher the figure, the higher the growth relative to the index. Negative figures indicate the portfolio has lower growth than the index. All figure are decimals of one standard deviation.

We want to study each manager's response carefully, note in the margin of the questionnaire trends that become apparent as we compare it with the manager's prior questionnaire responses, and jot down questions we would like to pursue at our meeting.

Also prior to the meeting I like to have performance triangles through year end relative to whatever benchmarks seem relevant for that manager, plus analyses of the year end composition of the manager's portfolio.

The purpose of all this preparation is to obtain as much *objective* information as possible in advance of our annual meeting so we can devote our meeting to more subjective matters and can probe any concerns raised by the data we have collected. A meeting of an hour and a half is usually sufficient for the purpose. If the meeting should occur during a noon hour, I find that a working lunch in the office is more conducive to productive discussion than going to a restaurant.

Where should the meeting be held? I think at least once every two years it is important to meet at the manager's office—to meet other key people in the firm and to absorb the ambiance of the office. With some managers where there are multiple people who are key to our account, I prefer always to meet at the manager's office.

Immediately after our meeting, we write notes about the significant things that were discussed. We find these notes helpful at least in planning for next year's meeting, and the sheer act of writing the notes impresses on us salient information we might subsequently lose with the ephemeral spoken word.

These visits are not something for the chief staff person to delegate to other members of the staff. I believe all senior staff members should meet with every manager *together,* share their observations, and probe their reasons for any diverse points of view.

Finally, I recommend a critical discipline: After having made our annual visits to each of our managers, we should write, separately from our meeting notes, a concise evaluation of each manager—*why* we should retain that manager (or why not) and what concerns have we about that manager. This discipline forces us to think hard about each manager, even if we don't show the evaluation to anyone else (we generally have not). As we re-read our rationale for retaining a manager, if it isn't persuasive to us or wouldn't be persuasive to our committee, we probably should consider terminating the manager's account.

Incidentally, the possibility of termination should not be a once-a-year consideration, even if we discuss individual managers' performance with our committee only once a year. The staff should initiate such a recommendation any time during the year when it concludes that reasons warrant such action. We'll discuss what those reasons might be later in this chapter.

The Meaning of Control

Every investment committee rightly expects its staff to have its investment portfolio under control. Let's look at what we mean by *control,* and what we don't mean.

Control means that we have a solid management information system that tells us what our managers are doing, and that we know pretty much what each portfolio looks like and what variances our overall portfolio may have from its target asset allocation. Control means we have guidelines for each manager, as broad as they may be, and we are alert to any occasion when a manager might be investing outside of those guidelines. It means we are aware of each manager who is performing below expectations and alert to any action we should take—even if that action is no more than to commiserate with that manager and assure him he continues to have our confidence (a worthwhile action, occasionally).

Control does not mean looking over a manager's shoulder and second-guessing. We can mainly get in his way. I never want to have a discussion with a manager about who is accountable for any action or inaction he may have taken. The manager should be 100% accountable. As mentioned before, if he doesn't warrant our trust, he shouldn't be one of our managers.

When we are considering any particular step in control, we should ask ourselves: Can this step really add value, or preserve value? And if so, at what cost?

Some plan sponsors feel that a key element of control is making sure their managers don't invest outside the universe of securities in their respective benchmarks. The sponsors fear that such lack of control will mess up the carefully orchestrated asset allocation of their overall fund.

I certainly don't want a manager investing in an area where he has no demonstrated competence, and especially where he may be trying to climb a learning curve in a new asset class at *our* expense. But our carefully orchestrated overall asset allocation is not that sacred. I am glad to have our managers bend our asset allocation in an opportunistic way, knowing that they will still be held to the respective benchmark we have agreed upon with them.

In so doing, however, we take on a key responsibility. We must monitor our *actual* overall asset allocation to make sure it has not slipped further from our target than we and our committee feel is appropriate and prudent. But in practice, I have rarely if ever felt that our opportunistic managers have bent our actual overall asset allocation seriously out of shape.

When to Take Action

Adding or withdrawing assets to or from a manager's account may reflect a positive or negative evaluation about a manager, but more often such actions simply reflect efforts to adjust the allocation of total plan assets closer to the target allocation. We may increase an account's assets as the result of a new contribution to the plan or of a transfer of assets from another account that had become overweighted relative to its target. We may periodically have to withdraw assets from an account to raise money to pay pension benefits (or for an endowment fund to make payments to its sponsor).

I do not advocate withdrawing money from a manager's account solely because we have given him a poor evaluation. Investment managers do not need a wakeup call. Any manager worth his salt is going all-out continuously and knows when he is not performing well. He cannot perform better simply by working harder. If he's performing poorly, he is probably hurting even more than we are. We can't possibly flagellate him into better performance. If we have lost confidence in a manager, we should terminate his account.

On one or two occasions I have heard sponsors consider giving a manager a warning, something like, "We'll give you X quarters to straighten out your performance, or we'll have to terminate the account." While it's essential to be honest with our managers, I believe such a warning is never appropriate. First of all, we can never know whether his (short-term) performance during the warning period has any predictive value. And second, the manager gets an absolutely wrong motivation: "We must do something, anything, because if we do nothing we will lose the account. And if we do something, maybe we'll get lucky." We never want to motivate the manager to roll the dice.

We should be honest with a manager about what we think of his performance (which should come as no surprise to him) and about anything else we like or don't like about what he is doing. But I view that as very different from giving a manager a warning notice to shape up.

Another action we should periodically consider: Should we change the manager's benchmark, or his constraints? Is our official benchmark motivating the manager to run our account as we want him to, or would a different benchmark take better advantage of the manager's strengths? As an example, if we are using EAFE[1] as the benchmark for a manager of non-U.S. stocks, and if the manager hesitates to allow his portfolio to stray too far from EAFE's country allocation, even though he believes EAFE's asset allocation is strategically suboptimal, then why not modify his benchmark? We could discuss with him EAFE-GDP weighted, or EAFE with a 15% maximum weighting to any one country—or he might have a better idea. The point is, why let a standard benchmark get in the way of making money?

---

[1] Morgan Stanley Capital International's equity index for Europe, Australia, and the Far East.

Another question we might ask ourselves: If we eliminate a constraint we previously placed on his account, would the manager be able to add more value to our account, long-term?

When to Terminate a Manager's Account

This is one of the toughest recommendations to decide on, especially if the manager is one whom we ourselves had previously recommended for hire. Reasons for termination may fit under five overlapping headings:

1. We lose trust in the manager. If we believe a manager is being less than honest with us, or if he fails to honor agreements with us, it is time to part company. Trust is a *sine qua non* of our relationship with any manager.
2. Three reasons related to our diversification needs:
   - We perceive that two of our managers in the same asset class are pursuing the same investment style.
   - We have reduced the target allocation to an asset class to an extent where we no longer find it as important to have as many managers in that asset class.
   - We perceive that a particular asset class no longer adds useful value and diversification to our plan's total portfolio.
3. When we find an alternative manager who we believe would add materially more value than an existing manager in the same niche.
4. When we lose confidence that a manager can add material value to his benchmark. What would cause us to lose such confidence?
   - Performance is below benchmark
       for a meaningful interval,
       by a sufficient magnitude, and
       for reasons not explainable by investment style (for example, market cap, or growth vs. value),
     such that we can no longer objectively expect that the manager is likely to exceed his benchmark materially in the future.
   - The manager's performance has become inexplicably erratic.
5. Even though a manager's performance remains satisfactory, its predictive value declines materially. This judgment is rarely based on a single factor. It is influenced by factors such as the following:
   - A key person (or persons) left the firm or has lost his burning interest in managing our account.

- Personnel turnover caused a deterioration in the quality of the research staff on which the manager relies.
- The manager embarked on a different management approach than that on which his track record is based.
- The manager is now managing materially more money than that on which his track record is based, and we believe this added money will impair his future performance.

Judging predictive value requires tough objectivity of all relevant facts. The key word is *relevant*. Figuring out what's relevant and what's not relevant for a particular manager is a major challenge, and if we get it wrong, we're likely to make the wrong recommendation.

Then What?

After terminating a manager, what do we do with the money? Transfer it to another existing manager, or appoint a successor manager.

If, as suggested in Chapter 5, we are continuously becoming acquainted with alternative managers in all asset classes to see if there are any we think are better than our current managers, we should normally have a short list of prime candidates in each asset class. By the time we terminate a manager, we should know who the successor is.

If the terminated manager is managing a separate account, what do we do with the assets in that account? We should offer the successor manager any assets he would like to keep, although usually he chooses few. We might also give the successor manager all remaining assets to sell, or even sell them all simultaneously through an investment banker/broker. I am not fond, however, of such fire sales. I prefer to have a special manager who follows virtually all marketable stocks and has low transaction costs, to serve as our liquidation manager. He can then sell the unwanted assets opportunistically over time and turn the cash over to the successor manager.

Case Study

The best example I can give is how *not* to do go about terminating a manager. When I first got into this business in 1971, our plan had an investment in Mutual Fund X, which I understood to be outstanding but conservative, one that should provide strength in a weak market. Fund X returned 8% in

1971 when the S&P 500 total return was 15%, and 10% in 1972 when the S&P returned 19%. Those were fairly strong years in the stock market, but we thought Fund X would pick up relative performance in a down market.

The next year, 1973, gave us the down market, with the S&P down 15%. And our conservative fund? Down 25%! Look at the performance triangle of Fund X in Table 6.3.

It was obvious: Out with Fund X!

We studied the performance of other major mutual funds and came upon one—Mutual Fund Y—which had a superior track record for the same eight years, with strong performance also predating 1966. Table 6.4 shows its performance triangle.

What an obvious swap! So that's exactly what we did.

How did this work out? Well, Fund X was about the best performing mutual fund over the next four years. And Fund Y was among the poorest (see Tables 6.5 and 6.6).

During the years 1974 to 1977, Fund X outperformed Fund Y by 20 percentage points per year! And it didn't stop there. During the next seven years, 1978–1984, Fund X outperformed Fund Y by 8 percentage points per year.

What happened? The early 1970s were the period of the two-tier market, "The Nifty Fifty." Some 50 of the larger stocks that had consistent growth in earnings—such as IBM, Kodak, and Avon—were bid up to price-earnings ratios of 40 or 50. Meanwhile investors shunned small stocks, cyclical stocks, and higher yielding but slower growing stocks.

Table 6.3   Mutual Fund X vs. S&P 500 Index

To End of	*From Start of*							
	66	*67*	*68*	*69*	*70*	*71*	*72*	*73*
73	0	1	2	4	6	9	10	10
72	2	1	0	2	4	8	9	
71	4	3	3	0	2	7		
70	6	6	6	4	2			
69	7	7	7	5				
68	8	9	10					
67	7	8		White = outperformed benchmark				
66	7			Gray = underperformed benchmark				
Actual for Year	−3	31	21	−4	6	8	10	−25

Note: The numbers on the left and at the top reference the year.

77 *When to Take Action* **137**

Table 6.4 **Mutual Fund Y vs. S&P 500 Index**

To End of	From Start of							
	66	67	68	69	70	71	72	73
73	4	3	3	4	1	5	5	0
72	4	4	3	5	2	9	12	
71	3	2	1	3	3	7		
70	3	1	0	2	10			
69	6	6	5	14				
68	3	1	5					
67	7	7		White = outperformed benchmark				
66	7			Gray = underperformed benchmark				
Actual for Year	−4	31	6	6	−6	21	31	−15

Note: The numbers on the left and at the top reference the year.

Both Funds X and Y tended to invest in larger stocks, but different kinds. Fund Y targeted mainly the kinds of stocks characterized by the Nifty Fifty, while Fund X focused on stocks whose prices were lower than the present value of their discounted dividends and earnings. The stocks Fund X invested in, however, became cheaper and cheaper. No one was

Table 6.5 **Mutual Fund X vs. S&P 500 Index**

To End of	From Start of											
	66	67	68	69	70	71	72	73	74	75	76	77
77	5	4	4	4	3	4	5	8	14	15	15	8
76	4	4	4	3	3	3	4	7	16	20	23	
75	3	2	2	1	0	0	1	4	13	17		
74	2	1	0	1	2	3	2	0	10			
73	0	1	2	4	6	9	10	10				
72	2	1	0	2	4	8	9					
71	4	3	3	0	2	7						
70	6	6	6	4	2							
69	7	7	7	5								
68	8	9	10									
67	7	8										
66	7			White = outperformed benchmark								
				Gray = underperformed benchmark								
Actual for Year	−3	31	21	−4	6	8	10	−25	−17	54	46	1

Note: The numbers on the left and at the top reference the year.

Table 6.6   Mutual Fund Y vs. S&P 500 Index

To End of	From Start of											
	66	67	68	69	70	71	72	73	74	75	76	77
77	0	0	1	1	3	1	2	5	6	10	7	1
76	0	0	1	1	3	1	3	6	8	15	15	
75	2	1	1	1	1	1	0	3	5	16		
74	3	3	2	3	1	4	4	1	1			
73	4	3	3	4	1	5	5	0				
72	4	4	3	5	2	9	12					
71	3	2	1	3	3	7						
70	3	1	0	2	10							
69	6	6	5	14								
68	3	1	5		White = outperformed benchmark							
67	7	7			Gray = underperformed benchmark							
66	7											
Actual for Year	−4	31	6	6	−6	21	31	−15	−25	21	9	−8

Note: The numbers on the left and at the top reference the year.

more perplexed or frustrated than the manager of Fund X, but he maintained his discipline in the face of continuously disappointing price movements and continued to do so through the years.

The "Nifty Fifty" stocks would have had to maintain both their historical earnings growth rates *and* their lofty P/E's to provide strong future long-term returns. But over time the growth rates of many of these stocks began to "revert to the mean," and their price/earnings ratios plummeted accordingly. Market favorites moved toward smaller stocks and cyclical stocks.

So what did we learn from this school of hard knocks?

1. A manager's performance relative to the S&P 500 (or any measure of the overall market) is not sufficient to judge a manager. (At the time, that was about our only criterion.)
2. We must understand thoroughly the manager's style of investing. We should try to find a better-fitting benchmark than the S&P 500, if available, but we should recognize that probably no benchmark can substitute completely for a subjective understanding of how the manager is performing relative to his style.

3. We must judge whether the manager's style makes intuitive sense. (We had never visited the manager of either Fund X or Fund Y, and we certainly didn't understand the investment style of Fund X. If we had, we would have had to agree that its style made intuitive sense.)
4. We must assess each fund's manager and the organization behind the manager. (If we had, we would have known that Fund X was essentially the result of the same single, dedicated manager, supported by but not really dependent upon a broad research group. Fund Y was more of a group effort, with all managers and analysts pursuing the same investment approach. Continuity of management of Fund X had been as solid as it gets, and the continuity of management people at Fund Y had also been good, except for the departure of a key person some years before.)

If we had applied all these lessons in a sophisticated manner at that time, would we have made the right decisions? We'll never know, but I trust we would have known enough at least to keep Fund X.

For the record: Fund X was the Windsor Fund, managed by the renowned John Neff. Fund Y was the Chemical Fund, managed by the Eberstadt organization, which was merged out of existence in 1984.

Another Case Study

Here's another classic example of why the evaluation of managers is so difficult to do simply by the numbers. Table 6.7 is a triangle of the Templeton World mutual fund, compared with the Morgan Stanley Capital International World Index, an appropriate benchmark.
As shown by this triangle:

- By the end of 1983, the Templeton World Fund looked brilliant, having outperformed its benchmark by 7 points per year for the last six years.
- By the end of 1988, the fund looked like a dunce, having underperformed its benchmark by 10 points per year for five years.
- As of the end of 1997, the fund looks like a remarkably consistent solid performer, having outperformed its benchmark by 4 points per year for nine years.

Table 6.7 Templeton World Fund vs. MSCI World Index[a]

From Start of

To End of	78	79	80	81	82	83	84	85	86	87	88	89	90	91	92	93	94	95	96	97
97	1	1	1	1	0	0	1	1	0	2	3	4	4	5	4	3	1	4	5	3
96	1	1	1	1	0	0	1	1	0	2	4	4	4	5	4	3	1	4	7	
95	1	1	0	1	0	1	2	2	1	1	3	4	4	5	3	1	2	0		
94	1	1	0	0	0	1	2	2	1	1	3	5	4	6	4	2	5			
93	2	1	0	1	0	1	2	2	1	1	5	7	7	10	9	10				
92	1	0	1	0	1	2	3	3	2	1	4	6	6	9	8					
91	0	0	0	1	1	3	4	5	4	0	3	6	5	11						
90	0	1	1	2	2	4	6	7	7	3	1	5	1							
89	0	1	2	2	3	5	8	9	9	3	1	5								
88	1	1	3	3	5	7	10	13	14	9	4									
87	1	1	3	3	5	8	12	16	18	13										
86	1	1	2	1	3	6	11	18	24											
85	4	4	2	4	2	0	6	11												
84	6	6	4	7	6	4	1													
83	7	8	6	9	9	11														
82	6	7	4	9	8															
81	6	6	2	9																
80	4	4	7																	
79	9	15																		
78	3																			
Actual	21	28	21	6	19	34	5	30	18	3	20	23	−16	30	3	34	1	22	21	19

White = outperformed benchmark
Gray = underperformed benchmark

Note: The numbers on the left and at the top reference the year.
[a] Morgan Stanley Capital International's equity index for Europe, Australia, and the Far East.

140

The fund was managed neither as brilliantly nor as poorly as the numbers would suggest. There was reasonably good continuity in the management approach throughout. The overwhelming factor that explains most of the anomalous performance is a single decision. Through 1983, Templeton was overweighted in Japan at a time when the Japanese market was doing spectacularly well. During 1984, the Templeton fund exited Japan because it felt Japanese stocks were overvalued, and it has basically stayed out of Japan since. Because the Japanese market continued to do spectacularly well through 1988, Templeton had terrible *relative* performance for the next five years. And because the Japanese market has been a disaster since 1988, Templeton looks very good relative to its benchmark.

Few managers have records that have such a dominant explanation as Templeton. But our challenge is always to search hard for explanations.

Dollar-Cost Averaging

When we are investing in a new program (such as buying into a commingled fund or funding a new investment manager), should we give the program all the money we intend to give it up front, or feed the money little by little—in a manner called dollar-cost averaging? Dollar-cost averaging literally means investing equal dollar amounts at different times, which is theoretically advantageous, because we will buy more shares when the price is lower and fewer when the price is higher.

Dollar-cost averaging is a prudent way to fund a new program, but if we are talking about perhaps funding multiple programs like that over time, I tend to think we will be ahead of the game long-term if we make it a practice generally to fund with our lump sum up front. The analysis that leads me to this conclusion is included as Appendix B.

Rebalancing

Once we have gotten the actual asset allocation of our portfolio to be the same as our target asset allocation, it won't stay that way. One asset class will perform better than another, and we'll soon be off target. Should that bother us?

Many plan sponsors set ranges for their target asset allocations—such as 20% plus or minus 5%. The market could drive such an asset class mighty far from its 20% target before the plan sponsor would be motivated to take some action.

My preference is for a pinpoint target—such as 20%. No range. And if the market drives the asset class away from that target, let's rebalance to bring it back. Why?

- If the outperformance of a particular asset class gave any valid prediction that the same asset class would outperform in the next interval of time, that would be a valid reason for utilizing a range. But that is not the case. Outperformance by Asset Class A in Interval 1 gives almost zero information about its performance in Interval 2—with one exception. One of the pervasive dynamics in investments is *reversion to the mean,* and sooner or later Asset Class A will begin to *underperform.*

  Hence, over the long-term, rebalancing to a target can add a tiny increment of return by forcing us, on average, to buy low and sell high. That can be a counterintuitive discipline, of course—adding money to an asset class (and therefore to managers) who have been less successful lately, and taking it away from stellar performers. But it makes sense, provided we retain high confidence in our managers.

- If we were confident we could predict with reasonable accuracy which asset class would outperform or underperform others in Interval 2, then we should take advantage of tactical asset allocation insights. I, for one, have no such confidence, and I don't tend to have much confidence in such insights of others. Unless we justifiably have that confidence, rebalancing makes sense.

  We can spend a lot of time agonizing over where to take that withdrawal we need, or where to place our latest contribution. A rebalancing discipline removes a good deal of the agonizing and also makes good sense.

- Presumably we established our target asset allocation in order to earn the best expected return for a given level of aggregate portfolio risk. To the extent we stray from our target asset allocation, we are probably straying from the efficient frontier.

Doesn't rebalancing incur unnecessary transaction costs? It doesn't have to. If we have sizable amounts of contributions to or withdrawals from our fund, we can probably rebalance without any incremental costs—

simply by using those cash flows to rebalance. Or, if we invest in no-load mutual funds or commingled funds, we can usually rebalance without cost to us. But what if rebalancing will necessitate additional transactions by some of our investment managers?

Such transactions can actually be done with little incremental cost if we give our manager enough notice. If we tell a manager, "we will need $10 million from your $100 million account any time in the next three months, as soon as you want to send it to us," he can typically raise much of that $10 million through his normal transactions in the course of that quarter, simply by not reinvesting proceeds from his routine sales.

Even if we can rebalance entirely from the withdrawals we must make from our fund to pay benefits or endowment income, we should still forecast our cash needs well in advance and try to give our managers a few months, if possible, to raise the cash. All for the purpose of minimizing transaction costs.

How often should we rebalance?

There have been some good scholarly studies on rebalancing. Some suggest we might be ahead by adopting a quarterly discipline. Others seem to suggest that there is little difference between doing it once a quarter or once a year. I favor doing it continuously with cash flow and then taking action once a year if we are still materially off our target allocation.

How about rebalancing managers within the same asset class? If two managers are in two different sub-classes, such as large-cap growth and large-cap value, I think rebalancing makes sense. If two managers are in the very same asset class, well, I haven't seen scholarly studies on that, and I think that's up to our qualitative judgment on a case by case basis.

In Short

We need a well-disciplined process for monitoring our investment managers. We should know at least as much about them as about managers we are considering to hire.

We should carefully evaluate each manager in writing at least annually and terminate any who we no longer believe is the best manager we can get for his asset class. Termination, however, is not a decision to be made simply by the numbers. It requires a thoughtful review of all relevant facts.

Appendix A

Typical Annual Questionnaire for an Existing Equity Manager

1. What was the market value of all funds for which your firm was responsible as of year end?

	Number of Accounts	Total Assets	Non-U.S. Equities*
Equity accounts with same objectives as ours	_____	_____	_____
Other institutional taxfree accounts:			
Other equity accounts			
Fixed income accounts			
Balanced accounts	_____	_____	_____
Total			
Taxable accounts:			
Equity accounts			
Fixed income accounts			
Balanced accounts	_____	_____	_____
Total			
Mutual funds:			
Equity accounts			
Fixed income accounts			
Balanced accounts	_____	_____	_____
Total			
All accounts:			
Equity accounts			
Fixed income accounts			
Balanced accounts	_____	_____	_____
Total			

---

* Non-U.S. equities not listed on U.S. exchanges, except please include ADRs.

[It is helpful to make marginal notes on the questionnaire response showing how key figures—such as the value of assets managed with the same objectives as ours, and total equity assets—have changed in each of the last five years.]

2. For what nondiscretionary assets, if any, was your firm also responsible?

3. How much more in assets will you accept in equity accounts with the same objectives as ours? How much more in all equity accounts?

4. How many taxfree accounts of $5 million or more did your firm lose from the beginning of last year to date? Would you care to comment on the circumstances?

5. What has been your firm's annualized after-fee performance on equity accounts with the same objectives as ours?

	Average for All Accounts	Standard Deviation Among Accounts	Our Account	Benchmark
Latest year				
Latest 3 years				
Latest 5 years				
Latest 10 years				

6. To what do you attribute any difference in performance?

7. Would you please comment qualitatively on your performance over the past one and five years?

8. We have been using the [name of index] as the benchmark for your account. Would any alternative benchmark seem more appropriate to you?

9. Would you please provide a list of all your portfolio managers and research analysts, together with their current responsibility, whether they are a principal in the firm, their year of birth, the year they started in the investment business, and the year they joined your firm?

10. Would you please provide the names and positions of all persons added to or deleted from your research and portfolio management staff since the beginning of last year? In the case of each addition, please provide brief biographical background. In the case of each deletion, please indicate the person's responsibility and length of service with your firm. Also, either in your reply or verbally when we meet, would you care to comment on the circumstances of the person's departure?

    [It is helpful to make marginal notes on the questionnaire response showing who left the firm in each of the last five years and what their responsibilities and length of service had been.]

11. During the past year what changes have taken place in the key decision-making positions within your staff?

12. We understand that Jane Doe is our account manager and Bill Smith is her backup. For how many accounts and how much money is each responsible? What additional responsibilities, if any, does each have?

13. How much more in assets will each accept?

14. Attached as Enclosure A is a brief summary of your investment approach as we understand it. Do you believe this summary accurately reflects your approach? What changes would you suggest to make it more accurate?

    [*With each manager, it is helpful if we write our own summary of his investment approach in 100 to 200 words, using our own words. When we write it, we remove all the motherhood and apple pie from the manager's published description and focus on what distinguishes this manager from other investment managers. Also, the exercise forces us to articulate our understanding of that manager's unique approach. A manager's responding to this question by simply sending us a copy of the firm's published statement is an unsatisfactory response.*]

15. Have you used (or might you use) any derivatives in managing our account? If so, what kind, and to what extent?

16. Have you implemented any new policies or procedures this past year to further reduce the risk of unauthorized trading by members of your staff?

17. To what extent do you rely upon derivative valuations that are provided by your counterparties?

18. For transactions this past year involving non-exchange traded derivatives (including foreign exchange forwards), please list our account's counterparties, their credit rating, the type of contract employed (forward, swap, etc.), the year end notional value of the contracts, and the outstanding net asset value of each contract not marked to market daily.

19. Do any of our guidelines with respect to derivatives restrict you from doing any of the things you feel you should be doing?

20. Did you vote all proxies for stocks in our portfolio last year? Did you vote all of them solely in the interests of our plan participants?

21. If we should ask about an individual proxy vote, could you show us records of how you voted, and would you be prepared to tell us why you believed that vote was in the best interest of our plan participants?

22. What was the turnover on our account last year as a percent of the account's average assets, and what was the total amount paid for brokerage commissions?

23. What is the range and average of commissions paid for trades on our account last year?

24. Do you meet both the requirements and recommendations of AIMR Soft Dollar Standards? If not, how do you vary from those standards?
25. What amount of commissions, by broker, did you do with brokers that rebate a portion of the commission to our trust fund?
26. For all other soft-dollar brokerage you did for our account last year, please list the number of soft-dollar transactions (and % of total transactions), the number of shares traded in these transactions (and % of total shares traded), and the total dollar value of commissions involved (and % of total commissions).
27. Please list all the services you received through soft dollars last year, a description of the service, the name of the broker, the cost in soft dollars, and the conversion ratio (or alternative cost in hard dollars).
28. What are your internal policies with respect to employees trading for their own accounts?
29. What provisions have you made for disaster preparedness in the case of fire, earthquake, or whatever?
30. Is any client (including public funds and eleemosynary clients) paying a lower fee structure than we, net of any discounts in the form of contributions to eleemosynary clients, for essentially a similar investment management approach?
31. Do you have any investment services that are not the same as ours but are still somewhat similar, which operate with a lower fee schedule (net of any rebates) than ours?
32. If any client has a performance fee arrangement, please describe the arrangement.
33. Who is the owner of your firm? Who owns the parent company? Have there been any changes in ownership this past year?
34. What is the net worth of your firm?
35. Would you please comment on the profitability of your firm last year?
36. May we please have a certification from your insurance company that your firm is bonded as required under ERISA?
37. Aside from this bonding, does your firm carry any fiduciary liability insurance?
38. Are any litigation or enforcement actions (including enforcement actions initiated by the DOL or SEC) outstanding against your firm, any of its affiliates, or any of its investment professionals? If so, would you please comment on these actions?
39. Do you know of any conflicts of interest—actual or potential—that could conceivably affect our account?

Enclosure A:
Investment Approach
of [Name of Manager]

Bottom-up stock selection based on:

- Classic value: low P/E, low price/cash flow, low multiple/ growth rate, strong balance sheets.
- Special long-term value: unrecognized assets or earnings, recovery prospects, price anomalies, or some other unrecognized value attribute.
- Mainly market caps of $1B to $10B.
- Good price-appreciation potential with low downside risk on an absolute basis.
- Quality companies that are cheap, but undeservedly so.

Sell when (a) price seems to have little upside potential, based on historical ratios, or (b) if the reasons for purchase are no longer valid.

Stay fully invested until buying opportunities no longer exist.

The overall portfolio is a composite of four equal subportfolios— three of them formed independently by [name], [name], and [name], and the fourth coordinated by [name] mainly from stocks that are included in the first three subportfolios.

Appendix B

Dollar-Cost Averaging

Suppose we are about to invest $10 million in a common stock program (an index fund or mutual fund) that is currently selling for $100/share. We currently hold the money in cash equivalents. Assuming we have no ability to predict the price movement of the fund, which of the following three approaches would have the highest probability of bringing us the most shares?

1. Invest the full $10 million now.
2. Invest $2 million now and every 7 days thereafter until the full amount is invested (dollar cost averaging).
3. Buy 20,000 shares now and every 7 days thereafter until the full amount is invested.

Approach B is likely to prove better than C, as we will buy more shares when the price is lower and fewer shares when the price is higher and thus wind up with more shares in total.

(Conversely, if we are *selling* shares instead of buying them, then C is clearly better than B, because under B we would sell more shares when the price is low and fewer shares when the price is higher.)

But between approaches A and B—plunk all of our money down now, or dollar-cost average—which offers us better probabilities? Off hand, it would seem as if B, dollar-cost averaging, is better. For example:

Approach A (Buy Now)				Approach B (Dollar-Cost Average)			
Day	*Invest*	*Price*	*Shares*	*Day*	*Invest*	*Price*	*Shares*
1	$10,000,000	100	100,000	1	$2,000,000	100	20,000.00
				8	2,000,000	101	19,801.98
				15	2,000,000	99	20,202.02
				22	2,000,000	98	20,408.16
				29	2,000,000	102	19,607.84
			100,000				100,020.00

Remember, however, if we don't invest the full amount now, we can earn short-term interest on the balance. But also, there is a long-term underlying trend for the value of a common stock fund to rise. If that trend should exactly match the interest rate on short-term money, the two would cancel each other out, and approach B would be more advantageous than A.

On the other hand, if the long-term underlying trend for common stocks is 5 percentage points *higher* than for cash equivalents (it's actually been 7 points higher over the last 72 years), and if our best guess is that this trend will continue in a straight-line basis, then in most cases we will be further ahead with A, investing the full amount now. For example:

Approach A (Buy Now)				Approach B (Dollar-Cost Average)			
Day (a)	Invest (b)	Price (c)	Shares (d)	Day (e)	Invest (f)	Price (g)	Shares (h)
1	$10,000,000	100	100,000	1	$2,000,000	100.0000	20,000.00
				8	2,000,000	101.0946	19,783.46
				15	2,000,000	99.1854	20,164.25
				22	2,000,000	98.2755	20,350.96
				29	2,000,000	102.3825	19,534.59
			100,000				99,833.26

Where g = The price in the prior table times an annual increase of 5%, or $(1.05)^{days/365}$

h = f/g

The investor receives more shares under approach A than B ($100,000 - 99,833 = 167$, or 0.17%, more shares. Only if the price is very volatile, perhaps with a standard deviation of more than 30% per year, would it pay to dollar cost average into the position—and then only over a period of 4 weeks, not 4 months.

The main advantage of dollar cost averaging, if there is one, seems to be psychological. Investors do not have to make a decision of as great a magnitude now, and subsequently, they may be less subject to criticism and Monday-morning quarterbacking by their boss or clients.

All of this may hold true only *on average*—in the long run if the decision is the kind we are making periodically, multiple times over the years. But what if it's a once-in-a-lifetime decision? The law of large numbers doesn't help us with a one-time decision.

An approach to a one-time decision is to *minimize the maximum regret*. If we bought all on Day 1 and then the price went down, we'd be kicking ourselves. Would we have as deep a regret if, following our decision to dollar-cost average, the price went up by a similar magnitude and we had to buy more shares at a higher price? If our answer is no, then our maximum regret would be if the price went down, in which case dollar-cost averaging would minimize our maximum regret.

Chapter 7

Investing in Real Estate

W hen we talk about pension or endowment investments, we all too quickly think in terms of stocks and bonds. We fail to think about many other kinds of viable—and valuable—asset classes. We shall discuss many of them in Chapter 8. This chapter is devoted to the largest alternative asset class—private real estate. But first an introduction to private investments.

Private Investments

We use the term private investments to denote illiquid assets—ones that may be difficult to sell within a year, or perhaps impossible to get out of for the next 5, 10, or 15 years. Are such illiquid investments prudent? As long as we have enough marketable securities that we can convert to cash in time to meet any potential payout requirements, illiquid investments can be as prudent as marketable securities.

Most pension and endowment funds hold far more liquid assets than they need, and by doing so, they may be incurring a material opportunity cost. As a general rule, the more marketable an asset, the higher its price is bid up, and therefore the lower the return we can expect from it. That's why prices of the largest, most active stocks generally carry a "liquidity premium" over prices of less actively traded stocks. We pay a price for liquidity.

Conversely, prices of illiquid investments *should* be lower. There *should* be an "illiquidity premium" to the *net return* on private, illiquid investments. The word *should* is italicized because *caveat emptor* applies especially to private, illiquid investments, which come with fees far higher than typical fees on normal common stock accounts. But if we can invest intelligently in a diversified group of private, illiquid investments, we should expect a somewhat higher return per unit of risk than on marketable securities.

There is one drawback that applies to all private, illiquid investments. That has to do with the quality and timeliness of valuations. At the end of any quarter, for example, we know the quarter-ending value of a marketable security by the end of the last day of the quarter. It can take two to four months after the end of a quarter before the manager of a private, illiquid fund gives us his quarter-ending valuation. And then, the valuation is one that could be materially different from the prices at which the fund's investments could have been sold at that quarter-ending date.

Securities in private corporations are held at book value until there is either (1) a transaction, such as a private sale of additional shares, at which point the price per share will be changed to that transaction price, even if that transaction occurred two years ago; or (2) in the view of the fund manager, the value of the investment has become sufficiently impaired that he judgmentally lowers the carrying value of the investment.

Real estate valuations are a little better, in that properties are periodically appraised by registered appraisal firms. But these appraisals are informed judgments that can be materially different from the price at which a property could actually be transacted at any given time. There is no substitute for placing a property on the auction block to find out what it really is worth.

For these reasons, private illiquid investments are inappropriate to include in a unitized fund (like a 401(k) or other commingled fund), where money is going into or out of the fund on the basis of the fund's unit value on the transaction date.

Of all private, illiquid investments, real estate funds are the asset class most widely used. Real estate is truly a major asset class, as perhaps half of the world's wealth lies in real estate. For this reason, and because there are multiple ways to approach investments in real estate, we shall devote a separate chapter to real estate.

One caveat: Just as with stocks, there are major overall cycles in commercial real estate. The cycles are worst when overbuilding combines with a poor economy, as in 1989–1992, and best when vacancy rates are low during a booming economy. It is worth trying to avoid the down cycles and take advantage of the up cycles, although few of us are able to do that very well.

Core Real Estate

We use Core Real Estate to mean long-term investments in high-quality commercial properties in the United States. The effort is to buy such properties well, manage them well, and hold them for the long haul. The expectation is to earn meaningful net income year after year plus long-term increases in both that income and the value of the property. The expected appreciation stems from the fact that over long intervals the underlying land will become more valuable and, because of inflation in construction costs, the replacement value of the property will increase, and its rents will increase.

For this reason, real estate is often viewed as an inflation hedge, and I believe real estate, while far from a perfect inflation hedge, is a better long-term inflation hedge than most other asset classes. Few asset classes have investment returns more highly correlated with inflation.

The offset that needs to be fed into this equation is the long-term *depreciation* of real estate. (Although land doesn't depreciate, it can rise or fall in value as real estate locations become more or less desirable over time.)

By depreciation, I am not referring to accounting depreciation such as is used in financial reports or for tax purposes. I mean, in part, the fact that property tends to get run down if not refurbished from time to time. That can be corrected through periodic capital expenditures, which must be built into the manager's cash flow expectations. Harder to deal with, and perhaps harder to predict, is the tendency toward obsolescence. For example, a well-located warehouse no longer can command top rental dollars if newer warehousing technology calls for warehouses whose ceilings are six feet higher.

Core real estate is generally unleveraged or only moderately leveraged,[1] with a mortgage usually equal to no more than 20% of the property's value. More about leverage later.

A good core real estate portfolio will be well diversified in three dimensions:

1. *By type.* Mainly office (downtown and suburban), retail (major malls and strip centers), industrial parks (warehouses and light industrial), apartments, and perhaps single family residential, hotels, and raw land.

---

[1] Leveraged means paid for partly with borrowed money.

2. *Geographically.*   The various parts of the country, such as North-east, Southeast, Midwest, Southwest, Mountain States, and Pacific. (For this purpose, the United States is often carefully divided into economic zones that have less correlation with one another.)
3. *Size of property.*   Such as those valued at less than $15 million, those between $15 and $75 million, and those valued at more than $75 million.

Diversification is advantageous because it lowers the volatility of our real estate portfolio. Pricing of real estate moves in cycles by type, geography, and size. For example, offices in one area may get overbuilt at one time, with values thereby declining, while apartment vacancies may fall unusually low in another area, resulting in premium rents and prices for apartments. These individual cycles are additional, of course, to the overall real estate cycles. Real estate managers try to forecast these trends and take advantage of them, but such forecasting is an inexact science to say the least.

What rates of return can one expect from core real estate? Because real estate is a private market, there are no reliable investment return figures going back 70 years or more as there are for stocks or bonds. The Frank Russell Company began in the late 1970s to construct an index of unleveraged institutional real estate returns by compiling the results of a large number of institutional investors. This index is known today by its sponsor's name, the National Council of Real Estate Investment Fiduciaries (NCREIF). The index catalogs returns by various types and locations of real estate and is the best index of real estate returns available. It shows that over the last 20 years aggregate net total returns (if we assume about 1% per year in management fees) have been about 8% per year (about 3½% *real* returns, net of inflation), with a standard deviation of 3.6% per year and a correlation with the S&P 500 of −.02. Given these figures, what should we expect of real estate?

The above return figures include the years of 1989–1993 when commercial real estate went through its worst depression since the 1930s. I expect that *real* returns in a more normal interval would be higher than the 3½%. For 20 years (1979–1998), real estate returns were nearly 10% per year lower than those of the S&P 500. While that difference is unsustainably wide, I still don't believe long-term we can expect quite as high returns from core real estate as from common stocks.

Why is this? Shouldn't we earn an illiquidity premium? I think there are two reasons for lower expected returns. One reason is that some equity real estate acts partly like fixed income. The classic example would be a sale-leaseback arrangement, which operates for the investor something like a bond. In any case, a dependable, substantial flow of rental income is a key part of expected return from real estate.

The other reason is that the expected volatility from real estate is lower—even though I don't believe the 3.6% standard deviation figure from NCREIF. Why don't I believe it? The index is based on appraised values at the end of each quarter, and appraised values don't begin to show the volatility that is truly inherent if a property were actually to be put up for sale. Appraisals have lagged materially when property prices were declining and have lagged equally when prices were rising. There is no concrete way to know what is the underlying volatility of real estate. While I believe volatility is materially higher than that shown by the NCREIF index, I still believe it is lower than for common stocks.

The one figure I largely believe is the correlation with the S&P 500 of essentially zero. While real estate and common stocks are both impacted by economic factors, they are impacted by different factors and at different times. While the stock market was enjoying an historic boom for the last 15 years, real estate net of fees returned less than 6% per year. A key advantage of real estate is that it is a good portfolio diversifier.

Venture Real Estate

An approach to real estate investing that I like better is what I call "venture real estate." Simplistically, it amounts to buying a property to which a manager can add material value (such as through construction, rehabilitation, or restructuring the leases[2]), then adding that value in a timely manner, and as soon as that value has been added, selling it to someone who wants to buy some good core real estate.

What do we mean by adding material value? The epitome of value adding would be development, converting raw land into a well-leased building of some sort, or even buying raw, unimproved land and investing in the sewers, roads, and other infrastructure that will allow it to be sold at a much

---

[2] *Restructuring leases* includes modifying the list of tenants (such as to increase their creditworthiness or the volume of their businesses), adjusting their locations in the building, and modifying the term of key leases.

higher price to a developer. Such development can earn the highest returns, or if the development is not successful in a timely manner, it can be a source of large losses. Much value can be added in a far less risky way than that kind of development. Examples would include:

- Buying a well-located Class C office building, rehabilitating it, and re-leasing it as a Class B office building.
- Buying a hotel that has not been managed well and installing new, more aggressive management. (Hotels are classed as real estate, but they are in some sense more operating businesses than passive real estate.)
- Buying an office building with a poor leasing structure, perhaps leased in such a way as to leave pockets that were unattractive to rent; then re-leasing the building so as to earn a higher aggregate rent.
- Buying a tired looking shopping center, refurbishing it, and— through the new owner's national affiliations—giving it more nationwide leasing clout.
- Buying an industrial park of warehouses and repositioning them so they can be leased for a higher and better use, such as light industrial, inexpensive back-office, or special retail uses.
- Simply buying a property that has been a loser for its owner, who has become a motivated seller in a market where values are about to appreciate.

Ways to add value are limited only by the creativity of the human minds of entrepreneurial real estate managers. The approach is far more management-intensive than core real estate and requires greater expertise. That's why I refer to it as *venture* real estate.

If we pursue this approach, we should be sure we have especially competent management, and we should target net investment returns that are higher than those on common stocks—at least 8% *real*. Individually, venture real estate projects may be more volatile than core real estate, but it is possible, through commingled funds, to obtain a highly diversified portfolio of venture real estate. I am not convinced that such a diversified venture portfolio is materially more volatile than core real estate. Nor do I think the correlation with common stock returns is any higher. I believe there is a higher degree of "diversifiable risk" in venture real estate (as opposed to "systematic risk," which cannot be diversified away).

Leverage

One way that venture real estate managers often try to add return is through leverage—borrowing up to 60% of the value of a property. Leverage can add a very attractive increment to the returns on a real estate program. But leverage is a two-edged sword. If the program is not successful, losses can be dramatic. Occasionally, the deed to a property must be turned over to the lender. Hence, leverage is usually more appropriate in lower risk situations.

Leverage may make eminent sense for some real estate programs, but the plan sponsor should evaluate the appropriateness of his real estate manager borrowing at prime[3] *plus* X% while his fixed income manager is lending at prime *minus* X%. My preferred approach for dealing with this dilemma is to try to avoid lending at prime minus X% (by minimizing traditional fixed income investments).

Another key consideration relative to leverage is unrelated business income tax (UBIT). To keep taxfree investors from enjoying an unfair advantage over taxable investors, tax authorities have established UBIT. The tax has applied, for example, to earnings resulting from acquisition indebtedness (leverage at the time of purchase). UBIT rules are quite complex, and I will not try to spell them out; we will want to hire a competent tax adviser. The rules do, however, allow for the taxfree use of leverage if done in certain ways. And sometimes, the case for leverage is so compelling that it is worth incurring UBIT on the resulting earnings. Suffice it to say that because of UBIT, leverage can be a very complicated matter.

Ways to Invest in Real Estate

There are basically three ways we can invest in real estate properties:

1. We can invest in real estate directly (by buying properties specifically for our own fund).
2. We can participate in a commingled fund, often a limited partnership, that will invest in a portfolio of properties.

---

[3] The prime interest rate is generally the lowest rate at which banks will lend money to businesses.

3. We can invest in a form of marketable common stock called real estate investment trusts (REITs).

Investing in Real Estate Directly

By investing in our own portfolio of properties, we retain the maximum control. We ourselves decide which properties to buy, how to manage them, whether to leverage them, and when to sell. We may hesitate to label directly owned real estate as illiquid, because we can usually sell any given property within a year. Also, we may avoid the substantial fees that tend to be built into commingled funds and REITs.

Drawbacks are that it takes a lot of real estate expertise to manage such a portfolio, and we will probably want to hire an investment manager to do that. Even so, overseeing such a portfolio will still take up a lot of our time and effort.

Another drawback is that we will find it difficult to get as broad diversification in our real estate portfolio. We may own 5, 10, or 20 properties, depending on the size of our fund. With that number of properties it is hard to get wide diversification across the many kinds, locations, and sizes of real estate.

Commingled Funds

Many limited partnerships and other kinds of commingled funds are available for institutional investors to participate in. The challenge is to find the best-managed commingled funds and then to negotiate a partnership agreement that aligns the financial motivations of the manager and the investors. These are major, time-consuming challenges.

Much of the work with such commingled funds is up front, because once we have executed an agreement, we are a limited partner (or the equivalent), with the emphasis on *limited*. Rights of investors are necessarily limited in a partnership if the investors are to have the benefit of limited liability. If investors participate meaningfully in decisions, they can be classed as "general partners," which means that they suddenly incur *unlimited* liability.

Frankly, I am not bothered by limitations on the role of investors. Few institutional investors have the in-house expertise in real estate to add value to a real estate investment program. When we invest in such a fund, we consider we are hiring the expertise of our real estate manager, not the real estate expertise of our co-investors. *If* we have done a good job in selecting the manager, we want him to have maximum authority to negotiate real estate transactions. (That, of course, is an important *if.*)

Sometimes a fund's properties are specified up front, but more often the manager decides—all in accord with the stated objectives and constraints of the fund—on the properties to buy, the degree to leverage them (if at all), how to manage them, and when to sell them.

I actually prefer commingled funds where the properties are *not* specified and the manager has total discretion to select them, because I think the manager can be more opportunistic. When he finds an attractive property, he can offer the owner a price and say, "Here, this pot of cash is yours if you say yes. I do not need to consult with anyone." That can be tempting.

Going about the selection of a real estate manager is not totally different from selecting any other kind of investment manager. We study the manager's track record and assess the predictive value of that track record based on the depth and continuity of the manager's organization. The difficulties are greater, however, because the manager may only have managed a couple of funds, perhaps not yet to the ultimate sale of the properties. That means the manager's track record is based partly on appraised values, which can be quite different from prices for which the manager could actually sell the properties. And benchmarks are far more fuzzy—especially for venture real estate.

Once we invest in a commingled fund, our staff's time commitment is usually minimal, as there should be very few decisions to make. We can't normally make any of the decisions we can make with a manager of marketable securities. It is necessary to monitor the progress of the fund, of course, but this can usually be done through quarterly reports from the manager, occasional visits by the manager, and meetings that the manager holds for investors, often annually, and sometimes at the site of one of the properties he purchased for the fund.

Some funds have advisory committees of investors, usually consisting of three or four of the larger investors. The manager discusses strategy with these committees, but committees of limited partners cannot have any real authority, or the committee members would jeopardize their limited liability status. In fact, *all* investors can get a hearing for their concerns and opinions about the fund, whether or not they are members of the advisory committee.

The two concrete functions that an advisory committee can serve are (1) to decide on issues where the manager might have a conflict of interest, such as the purchase of a property in which the manager already had a financial interest, and (2) issues that may arise with respect to the reported valuations of the fund.

Once in a great while, issues do arise on which all investors must vote, and an investor is much better prepared to vote intelligently if he has been monitoring the fund actively. Such issues might include:

- Appointment of the manager of the fund also as property manager (a separate function, which carries a separate fee), if the partnership agreement had not already provided for that possibility.
- Whether to extend the date for the final closing of a new partnership if the manager proposes to keep it open for an extra month or two to let one or a few additional investors come into the fund.
- Whether to extend the investment period if the manager did not invest all of the money committed to the fund within the investment period—the years specified in the partnership agreement.
- Whether to permit the manager to reinvest proceeds from the sale of a property if the agreement did not permit such reinvestment.
- Whether to permit leverage to a greater extent than specified in the partnership agreement, or whether to permit the manager to negotiate a bank letter of credit that would obligate all limited partners to the extent of their commitments to the fund.
- Whether to permit the manager to develop a new building on a piece of land owned next to a successful property in the fund (assuming the fund document didn't provide the manager with that authority).
- Whether to discontinue authority for further investments by the fund, or to appoint a new manager of the fund, if key people leave the manager's organization (assuming the partnership agreement gives investors that right if certain key people should leave).
- Whether to extend the term of the fund so the manager is not forced to sell into what he believes is a bad market for selling.
- Whether to permit the partnership to be converted into a real estate investment trust (REIT), which would then become a marketable security.
- Whether to buy an additional partnership interest from a partner who has offered to sell his partnership interest for a given price.

- Whether to sell our partnership interest to someone (usually a vulture) who has offered to buy our partnership interest for a given price.

The nature of these issues may suggest to you that more such issues are likely to arise during the latter stages of a fund, and that has indeed been our experience. Whenever these issues do arise, they can chew up a lot of time and effort on the part of the sponsor's staff, including that required to team up with other investors to influence the outcome of the issues.

We have spoken little thus far about the most important step once we have identified a commingled fund that we would like to consider. That is the negotiation of the terms of the partnership agreement. That's such a critically important function that we shall treat it separately in Chapter 9.

What benchmark should we use for a venture real estate manager? The benchmark I prefer to see built into the manager's performance fee is an absolute return—either a nominal or real IRR *net* to the investor. A secondary benchmark to use with hindsight when evaluating venture real estate managers is a comparison with other venture real estate funds that were closed in the same vintage year. That, however, is a much fuzzier benchmark.

Real Estate Investment Trusts (REITs)

Marketable REITs issue common stock but, unlike regular corporations, they pay no income tax. They pass their income tax liability on to their shareholders, which is just fine for a taxfree fund. To qualify for such tax treatment, an REIT must meet specific legal criteria, such as earning 75% of its gross income from rents or mortgage interest, and distributing 95% of each year's taxable income to shareholders.

REITs have been around for 25 years, but for a long time they were small in number, with a sizable proportion devoted to investing in high-risk construction lending. The number of REITs devoted to *owning* properties has mushroomed since the early 1990s, and their aggregate value has gone up 20 times. Yet today they may own less than 5% of total commercial real estate. Some industry observers expect that eventually REITs will own the majority of commercial properties in the United States. Some REITs are private, but an increasing percentage of them are publicly traded.

Should REITs become the primary vehicle through which pension and endowment funds invest in real estate?

I'm not sure I have a clear opinion on that as yet. Historical data on REITs probably carry little or no predictive value for years prior to 1992 or so, and the years since then are so short an interval that I am hesitant to draw firm conclusions from them. For example, what long-term rate of total return and volatility should we expect relative to common stocks— and relative to the underlying real estate?

Because REITs are common stocks, they will share to some extent in stock market cycles and have a somewhat higher correlation with stock market returns than real estate itself has with common stock. REITs will at times sell at a premium to the underlying real estate value, and at other times a discount. But because real estate is a relatively illiquid asset, it will be difficult to readily arbitrage these premiums and discounts. This is conjecture, however, not historical fact.

If REITs are priced at a premium to the real estate, the REITs can expand by buying more real estate and issuing more shares, or else by issuing more debt (within allowable limits). In this way, investors can at times earn higher returns through REITs than through real estate itself.

Many REITs invest mainly in core real estate, to the extent that they typically expect to hold a property for the long haul. Some REITs, however—despite the fact that they are allowed to derive no more than 30% of their gross income from the sale of property—are very aggressive and have strong venture components.

Should we rely on our regular common stock managers to invest in REITs, or should we hire a specialist in REITs? Because investing in marketable REITs requires a lot more real estate savvy than most investment managers have, and requires lots more research about the particular properties owned by each individual REIT, I favor at this time a REIT specialist manager.

International Real Estate

We have talked up to this point about U.S. real estate. What's wrong with considering international real estate? Nothing is wrong with investing in real estate in other countries. Conceptually, as long as we are not bothered by incurring foreign exchange risk on an illiquid investment, an international real estate portfolio should add diversification to our portfolio, and we might indeed find some opportunities abroad that are more attractive than those available in the United States.

The reason I have not been involved in investing in real estate abroad (except to the extent our common stock managers have invested in real estate stocks in the United Kingdom and Hong Kong, for example), is that I don't know how to do it in a knowledgeable way.

It is hard enough to judge which are the outstanding real estate managers in the United States. Our ability to do so abroad would be far more limited. Also, I am far from sanguine about the ability of outstanding U.S. real estate managers to invest effectively abroad. Real estate markets are predominantly local, and I expect that the good real estate firms abroad would be far more expert on real estate values in their markets.

Also, it is possible (though not easy) to negotiate terms with U.S. real estate managers so as to align fairly closely the financial interests of the manager and the investor. It would be much more difficult to negotiate such terms with firms abroad.

Suffice it to say that international real estate makes lots of sense in concept, but from a practical standpoint I think there are some serious impediments.

In Short

Real estate is one of the biggest asset classes in the world, and it's a fine diversifier for a portfolio of stocks and bonds.

We can invest in real estate by buying it directly, by participating in commingled funds such as limited partnerships, or by investing in publicly traded real estate investment trusts (REITs).

We can earn the highest returns through venture managers who buy a property, add value to it, and then sell it rather than retaining it as a core holding.

Chapter 8

Alternative Asset Classes

A pension fund's committee chairman once said: "If the stock market plummeted and our fund lost $1 billion, I could explain that to my board of directors, and they would understand, because every other pension fund would be losing money too. But if some unusual alternative investment program lost $10 million, I wouldn't know how to explain it to the board, and they wouldn't understand it. Therefore, I am greatly concerned about most alternative investments."

We can readily empathize with this committee chairman. His reaction probably is typical of most committee chairmen. I would contend, however, that this mentality has cost their funds valuable opportunities to increase return while moderating volatility.

An alternative asset class might be considered any asset class that our decision makers have not considered before. For some, any stocks but the largest, most prestigious U.S. stocks might be an alternative asset class. For purposes of this book, however, we shall define alternative asset classes as anything other than marketable stocks, marketable bonds, cash equivalents, and real estate.

Venture Capital Funds

One of the more common alternative asset classes is venture capital. There are broad and narrow definitions of venture capital, and here we'll use a narrow one: We shall define venture capital as investment in *private start-up companies,* more often than not high-tech companies. These companies may be as early-stage as an idea and a business plan, or as late stage as a private company that is already producing a product, needs expansion capital, and may be preparing to go public (make an initial public offering of its stock).

As thus defined, venture capital is probably the riskiest of investments. Most start-up companies fail to survive, and only a small percentage become highly successful. How can our fund invest prudently in such risky ventures?

Fortunately, there has developed in the United States the world's most effective environment for funding and nurturing start-up businesses. Its venture capital industry is one of the United States' real competitive advantages. A key to this nurturing process, and one that provides a sensible vehicle for funds like ours to invest prudently in start-up businesses, has been the development of sophisticated venture capital firms.

A venture capital firm consists of a small group of experienced people who have become expert at evaluating start-up enterprises, identifying the most promising, investing in the best of them, taking seats on their boards, putting them in touch with those who can provide expertise they happen to need, and advising them on business strategy and capital raising. These venture capital firms form limited partnerships and raise funds from wealthy persons or, today, more typically institutional investors like ourselves.

A fund like this may raise $100 million and invest it over a period of three to five years in some 25 different start-up companies, and it may take some 15 or even 20 years before the fund has been able to convert the last of its investments into cash through acquisition or an initial public offering (IPO)—or must write them off through bankruptcy.

Despite its manager's expert winnowing and nurturing process, a meaningful proportion of a partnership's investments are likely to be losers. Most of the rest may earn a modest rate of return. And a few may earn 10, 20, or more times the money invested in them. These few home runs will make the fund.

The process is very labor-intensive, and the fees charged by such venture capital firms are very high—typically 2½% per year of an investor's commitment to the fund, plus 20% of cumulative net profits.

Net internal rates of return (IRRs) to the investors over the life of venture capital partnerships range from −10% per year to +40%. That's a far narrower range than for individual start-up companies, but that's still an extraordinarily wide range of results from an investment with an average duration of seven or eight years.

The task for us as investors is to diversify among the best of the venture capital firms and to dollar-average into additional partnerships over time in order to reduce the range of our aggregate net IRR expectations. Time diversification is very important in venture capital as in other private investments, because there are common factors that impact returns to partnerships of each vintage year, and it is close to impossible to divine up front which vintage year's partnerships will be most successful.

Two variables appear to impact venture-capital results in a systematic way:

1. The amount of money invested at that time in venture capital—the greater the amount (as in the last couple of years) the lower the ensuing returns seem to have been.
2. The receptivity of the IPO (initial public offering) market at the time ventures have matured to the point of issuing public stock. There is no way to foretell the condition of the IPO market at any particular time in the future.

Properly diversified, a good venture capital investment program should achieve a net long-term IRR of at least 15% to 20%—well worth allocating several percent of our assets to. But we should recognize drawbacks.

Venture capital is *very* long-term investing. It may be 20 years into the future before we see what net IRR our overall venture capital program has finally returned to us. Our returns for early years are likely to be poor. This is because of the J-curve, reflecting the fact that reported results for the early years are negative—consisting mainly of fees and expenses. The managers' fees, of course, begin in full force on day one. Also, "the lemons ripen early, and the pearls take more time." We are likely to have some bankruptcies before we begin seeing some of our ventures benefit from IPOs or ventures being acquired.

In addition partnership valuations are sticky. A private venture is carried at book value until either (1) a transaction occurs at a different price, in which case shares will thereafter be carried at that price, or (2) the viability of an investment has been so impaired that the manager judgmentally chooses to write down its value. The current valuation of any given investment may be kept the same for years.

This valuation procedure makes a venture capital program appear to have relatively low volatility. But such low volatility is a sham. Few investments are as volatile in value as a start-up company, and while diversification reduces this volatility, the level of underlying volatility is still high. Hence, when assessing the volatility of our venture capital program, we must ask ourselves whether we are interested in (i) the volatility of our venture capital *carrying values* (as they impact the volatility of the reported value of our aggregate assets) or (ii) the volatility of our program's *underlying value* (which will be a great deal higher).

I would guess that the standard deviation in underlying values of a well-diversified venture capital program is in the range of 25% to 30%—but my guess cannot be verified and is subject to a wide margin of error.

Well, how do we go about knowing which are the premier venture capital firms? As with other management firms, there is a wide difference between the better and the poorer firms.

It ain't easy.

One way to avoid the challenge is to hire a manager of venture capital managers—one who forms a master fund that participates in a dozen or two dozen venture capital partnerships over a period of three years or so. Such managers-of-managers can sometimes gain participation in some of the most eminent partnerships, which are often greatly oversubscribed and difficult to get into.

Another advantage of managers of venture capital managers is that they should competently handle the "end game." When a holding of a venture capital partnership has an IPO, SEC rules require that the shares of the current owners may not be sold for a period of time, usually a year—a period called a *lockup*. At the end of that lockup, the partnership may sell the shares, but most often it distributes the shares in kind to the partners and lets them either sell or hold the shares.

Few plan sponsors are well-equipped to deal competently with this end game, so they sell the distributed shares immediately, often leading to (and selling into) a temporary decline in the market price of the stock. A manager of venture capital managers will shoulder this responsibility. And because the manager should have been following these companies starting well before their IPO, the manager should have an information advantage as to whether to sell the stock immediately or retain it and wait for a higher target price.

The disadvantage with any manager of managers is that it adds another layer of fees. A really competent, experienced manager of venture capital managers, however, can add material value to a long-term venture capital investment program.

In any investment area it is well to consider the possibility of diversifying abroad. In start-up venture capital, however, the United States is the place to focus. No country in the world has the infrastructure to nurture start-up companies—especially high-tech companies—like the United States.

Buy-In Funds

Buy-in funds (like venture capital funds) also invest in private companies, but ones that are more established, usually ones that are or have been profitable. Such companies need capital for expansion, for acquisitions, or perhaps even for turn-around. The fund buys privately issued common stock or convertible securities or a combination of bonds and warrants.[1]

Abroad, both buy-in and buy-out funds are usually referred to as venture capital funds, but they rarely invest in start-up companies.

The risk of investing in a going concern is clearly less than investing in a start-up company, but the opportunity to earn 10 or 20 times our investment is also much lower.

Why do going concerns raise money privately rather than through a public offering? After all, money raised privately is almost always more expensive money than money raised through a public offering. Advantages are the ability to raise money quickly and without a lot of publicity, and sometimes with lower investment banking fees. The best buy-in funds bring more than money—management expertise delivered by the principals of the buy-in firm who serve on the company's board of directors.

Investors pay fees to the manager of the buy-in fund which in total, including performance fees, are much higher than for a typical common stock program. Hence the investor should demand a premium return because of both illiquidity and increased risk. The investor should be highly convinced that, net of all costs, he can realistically expect to earn that premium return.

Part of this expectation should be an exit plan. Whenever the buy-in fund makes an investment, it should have a plan and time line for getting its money out—often through an assurance that a public stock offering can be held by a given date, or a promise that the company will be willing to buy back the securities at a certain price after a certain date (a put).

---

[1] Warrants are options to buy stock at a certain price up to a certain date.

Buy-Out Funds and LBOs

A buy-out fund purchases the whole company instead of simply providing a portion of the company's capital. In the process, it either gives strong support to the existing management team or installs new senior management. In either case, it usually ensures management's sharp focus by providing lucrative stock options to the senior executives.

Often, mainly in the United States, the company is acquired chiefly with debt—in what is known as a leveraged buyout (LBO). LBO funds typically finance some 70% to 90% of their purchase price with debt, including some secondary debt that is high yield, relatively high risk. The strategy takes advantage of the fact that interest on debt is tax deductible, which sharply reduces the income tax bill previously faced by the company. The strategy also leverages the investment for the relatively small number of outstanding common shares. Hence, if the company is moderately successful, the share owners can realize internal rates of return above 50% and possibly above 100%.

Such leverage also incurs high risk. A modest decline in the company's fortunes can leave it unable to meet its debt obligations and thereby lead it into bankruptcy. In that case, the common stock investors (and sometimes the high-yield bond investors as well) may lose their entire investment.

Hence, a very high premium is placed on the competency of the management of the buy-out fund in its selection of appropriate companies to buy and in its ability to install excellent managements in the companies once it buys them.

A typical buy-out strategy is to acquire a company in a stable industry with reliable cash flows, leverage it steeply, then use cash flow to pay off the debt. When successful, this approach leaves shareholders with common stock that has gone up sharply in price.

Another strategy is to sell off the company's divisions that are either less profitable or even losing money, or which are outside of the company's mainstream business—leaving a focused core business that has the potential for good growth. Management often uses the proceeds from selling these divisions to pay down the debt and reduce the leverage. But again, the entire investment is viewed as a 3-to-7-year investment, and the buy-out fund should have concrete plans to liquefy its ultimate investment through a sale to a larger firm or through an initial public offering (IPO).

The fortunes of both buy-in and buy-out funds are clearly affected by the general economy and the valuations of the public stock market. But the correlation of their returns with the stock market, while positive, is relatively moderate, for two reasons:

1. There is usually no good way to value private corporate investments. If the investment is private stock in a *public* company, the value of the private stock can be inferred from the price of the public stock—but with a discount, usually of 20% to 30%, to account for the fact that the private stock cannot currently be sold. But if no stock is publicly traded, convention calls for the investment to be held at book value either until additional shares of stock are sold or until it becomes clear that the value of the investment has become impaired. This stickiness in the valuation of such investments makes them appear far less volatile than they really are and makes their correlation with the stock market appear far lower than it really is.
2. Enough special factors impact funds like these that, on a cash-to-cash basis, I suspect buy-in and buy-out funds have a moderately lower correlation with the stock market than a similar portfolio of common stocks would have.

As with venture capital, the returns on buy-in and buy-out funds can be negatively impacted by the heavy flows of money going into such funds if the total supply of such money exceeds the available opportunities. Those flows have been very heavy in recent years.

Distressed Securities

Another category of private investors consists of the vultures of the world—the distressed security funds. And just as vultures contribute to the ecology by cleaning up the carrion, distressed security funds become buyers of loans or securities that other investors no longer want to own.

When a company heads into bankruptcy, many investors want out. One reason is that the holding is viewed as a blot on the investor's good name, which motivates the investor to move it out of his portfolio. The more rational reason is that helping a company avoid bankruptcy or nursing it through bankruptcy is a special skill that many investors do not have. The skill involves specialized legal expertise combined with negotiating strategies that are a far cry from those faced by most stock and bond investors.

As a result, motivated sellers have a tendency to over-discount distressed securities, and that spells opportunity for the more competent distressed security funds. The risk is still high, of course, as it is often hard to turn around the business of a company heading into bankruptcy, and the decisions of the bankruptcy courts are difficult to forecast. Critically important, it is hard to predict *how long* it will take for a bankruptcy to wend its way through the court process. There's a clock ticking on the rate of return, and the longer it takes, the lower the return.

There are basically two kinds of distressed investors: (1) One will try to become part of the bankruptcy proceedings and thereby influence the outcome. Such an investor may try to obtain as many of the outstanding shares or loans as possible so he can control the vote on any issues before the court. (2) Other distressed investors avoid becoming part of the bankruptcy proceedings, partly because of the process's heavy demands on their time and expense, but more often in order to retain flexibility. Such an investor can sell at any time, while one involved with the bankruptcy court becomes an insider and, in effect, has his investment locked up until the court's final resolution.

The more conservative investors buy distressed securities only when the wind-up value of the company—the value of its cash and salable assets—is greater than the price they pay for those securities. Returns on these investments may be attractive but rarely extremely high. Less predictable but potentially higher returns accrue to investors who expect the company to survive in some form and who value it on a going-concern basis.

The proliferation of LBOs and of high-yield bonds in recent years promises to provide a continuing supply of distressed securities, as a certain portion of these investments will predictably hit the skids. Because of the special factors surrounding distressed investments, I believe the underlying correlation of distressed investments with the stock market is a good bit lower than the correlation between buy-in or buy-out funds with the stock market.

Absolute Return Programs

Although these kinds of programs are impacted to some extent by the general direction of the stock market, they are typically evaluated by their *absolute* returns, not their *relative* returns. Absolute Return programs are overwhelmingly dependent on the skills of the investor.

Even closer to being market-neutral—with no direct impact from the stock and bond markets—are arbitrage programs. Arbitrage managers buy a portfolio of securities (they go long) and borrow a similar portfolio of securities that they sell (sell short).

As a simplistic example, we might invest $100,000 in General Motors stock and simultaneously borrow $100,000 worth of Ford stock and sell it (sell it short). We would be as long as we are short, and we wouldn't care if the market went up or down, or whether automobile stocks performed well or poorly relative to the market. We would care only about the performance of GM stock relative to the performance of Ford stock.

Mechanically, such accounts use a sophisticated broker through whom they buy their long portfolio and then borrow and sell their short portfolio. The broker retains proceeds from the sale of the shorts and invests them in high-quality short-term investments, such as T-bills.[2] The arbitrage account receives a portion of the interest on the T-bills—perhaps 80%—and the broker retains the balance to pay for his security-borrowing and other costs as well as profit.

Arbitrage accounts take many forms, and we will comment here only on some of the more common.

Long/Short Stock Accounts

Nobel laureate Bill Sharpe, a leading proponent of index funds, has said that a long/short strategy is his favorite active strategy.[3]

Conceptually, a long/short stock account is about the simplest arbitrage program—a long stock portfolio, and a short one. Making strong returns on such a portfolio is a tall order, as the investor has given up the wind behind his back provided by the long-term positive direction of the stock market. We have indicated that most investors cannot, net of fees, do as well as an index fund, which only *buys* stocks. A long/short manager has the challenge of adding value *both ways*—long and short. Moreover the fees for a long/short manager are very high—a fixed fee plus, typically, 15% to 20% of net profits above T-bill rates! Obviously one wants to consider only an exceptional manager for such a task.

---

[2] Short-term U.S. Treasury bills.

[3] Peter J. Tanous, *Investment Gurus*, New York Institute of Finance, 1997, p. 104.

We might think of long/short stock managers as being generally one of three kinds:

1. One kind will take no risk in industries nor perhaps in other common factors of the market as well (such as growth vs. value, or large vs. small). If the investor buys a large drug company, he will sell another large drug company—betting that the first is undervalued and the second overvalued, that is, betting on the *spread* between the two drug stocks. He will not place a bet on whether large drug companies as an industry are either overvalued or undervalued.

2. A second kind won't pair stocks quite so explicitly but will ensure that the aggregate composition of his long portfolio (as measured perhaps by BARRA factors) is the same as the composition of his short portfolio.

3. The third kind tracks how large stocks are priced relative to small stocks, or how "growth stocks" are priced relative to "value stocks," or how one industry is priced relative to another. This manager will buy a basketful of large growth stocks, for example, and sell short a similar-size basketful of small value stocks.

Why is the return of such funds measured against T-bill rates? Because the investor's most obvious market-neutral alternative is a cash-equivalent investment such as T-bills. Remember, the long/short fund earns most but not all of the T-bill return through the investment of the proceeds from the short sales. Hence, any long/short investor worth his salt should earn more than the T-bill rate.

What should we expect from a long/short stock account? We should certainly expect higher returns than T-bills, although this is by no means assured. With extremely good long/short stock funds we can earn 5 to 10 percentage points more than T-bill rates. Volatility, while dramatically lower than for a regular common stock account, is still materially higher than for a money-market fund. Correlation with the stock market is near zero, although much to my surprise, I have noticed that long/short managers often tend to perform better with their long portions than they do with their short. That is, they tend to exceed the relevant index more with their longs than they lag the index with their shorts.

Without the wind of the stock market behind his back, a manager who is as short as he is long should not be expected to achieve as high a long-term rate of return as an equally strong traditional stock manager. So why would an investor place money in a long/short stock account?

First, a long/short stock account *is* a great diversifier. A *good* long/short stock account should provide better returns than a bond account, with possibly an even lower correlation with the stock market than bonds have with the stock market. A long/short stock account is perhaps the best of all arbitrage programs for use as a *portable alpha*. We'll discuss portable alphas after we finish talking about arbitrage programs.

M&A Arbitrage

M&A arbitrage stands for merger and acquisition arbitrage. Company A bids to buy Company B for $60 a share, compared with Company B's current price of $40. The price of Company B rapidly zooms close to $60, but not all the way. After all, it is not known whether Company B shareholders will accept that price, and more important, whether the Federal Trade Commission will allow such an acquisition. Nor is it known how long it will take for the acquisition to be consummated, if indeed it succeeds in going through. And if the stock market should fall off a cliff, as it did in October 1987, the offer might be withdrawn.

This is where the M&A arbitrageur comes in. He assesses the probabilities that the acquisition will take place and how long it will take, and he offers to buy the stock of Company B for, say, $56 a share. Investors in Company B are pleased with the run-up in the price, and many don't want to be greedy and are happy to sell at $56.[4]

What's in it for the arbitrageur? He buys at $56 (and perhaps hedges the market by selling short an equivalent value of Company A). If and when the acquisition ultimately takes place he receives $60—a profit of $\frac{4}{56}$, or 7%. If the acquisition takes place four months from now, his annualized rate of return is 23%.[5] Sounds easy. But if litigation should drag out the acquisition for a full year, his annualized return is an unsatisfying 7%. And if the deal breaks, and Company A does not acquire Company B after all, then the price of Company B will probably plummet close to its original $40 per share, and our arbitrageur will have *lost* $\frac{16}{56}$, or 29%.

---

[4] If the purchase price won't be in cash but will instead be a certain number of Company B shares, then the arbitrageur sells short Company B. That way, the arbitrageur is insulated from market volatility. He is investing only in the *spread* between the prices of Companies A and B. In such cases, do M&A arbitrageurs *need* to sell short? They do unless they're willing to take the risks of the stock market.

[5] $1.0714^{12/4} - 1$.

A good arbitrageur is a true specialist. He must be able to assess the risks with a high percentage of accuracy, and this means engaging some high-priced legal talent capable of second-guessing the position that the Federal Trade Commission will take with respect to sensitive acquisitions. The arbitrageur thus performs a useful function that the average common stock manager is not equipped to perform well.

Some proposed acquisitions are no-brainers. Almost anyone can see that they will be consummated. If Company A's acquisition of Company B fits that category, the arbitrageur would probably not be able to buy Company B for less than $58—leaving him with an expected annualized rate of return of only a little over 10%. The good arbitrageur earns his best returns when acquisition offers are seen as having problems—when his insights can give him a lot more confidence about the acquisition than is discounted by the market price.

M&A arbitrageurs—like other arbitrageurs—charge high fees. Typical is a fixed fee plus perhaps 20% of all profits. Over long time frames, good M&A arbitrageurs may earn net unleveraged returns of 10% to 15% per year for their investors. Returns are influenced by the level of T-bill returns, because investment bankers often use the less risky M&A arbitrages as an alternative investment for their money-market accounts. When interest rates were double digit, arbitrageurs were able to earn as much as 30% or more in a year. But that is unusual. Net returns are in the low teens most of the time, and some arbitrageurs have had negative returns in years when an unusually large number of deals broke (fell apart). A reasonable expectation for volatility (annual standard deviation) of a good unleveraged M&A arbitrage program might be roughly 6%.

The correlation of most M&A arbitrage programs with the stock market is definitely higher than zero, perhaps as high as 0.3. This may be because more deals break when the stock market drops sharply, and there seems to be more M&A activity when the market is strong than when it is weak. After all, the larger the supply of M&A deals, and the more complicated they are, the more opportunity for arbitrageurs.

Returns on M&A arbitrage can be increased through leverage—by borrowing, say, half of the account value and investing that also in additional M&A arbitrages. That might still not raise the volatility of the account to that of a typical common stock account. But a tax-exempt fund would earn unrelated business taxable income—which is taxable (as UBIT) at corporate tax rates. It is difficult to leverage a tax-exempt account in such a way as to avoid UBIT, so M&A arbitrage accounts for tax-free investors are typically not leveraged.

Convertible Arbitrage

Good money can also be made in convertible arbitrage—buying a convertible security, whose interest coupon gives it a high yield, and simultaneously selling short the common stock into which the security can be converted. The dividend rate on the common stock would normally provide a much lower yield.

The arbitrageur thus invests in the *spread* between the interest rate on the convertible and the dividend yield on the stock. But it is more complicated than that. The arbitrageur may earn additional money if the price on the stock declines, because the price of the convertible security will be underpinned by its bond value. Conversely, if a convertible security is priced at a premium above its conversion value (the value of the stock into which it is convertible), and if the issuer of the convertible security should call that security—that is, force its conversion into common stock—the arbitrageur would lose money.

Unfortunately, rates of return on convertible arbitrage are low, perhaps only a few percent higher than T-bill rates, *unless the program is leveraged.* And for tax-exempt funds, leverage generally results in UBIT. Convertible arbitrage therefore doesn't tend to find its way into many tax-exempt portfolios.

A good, modestly leveraged convertible arbitrage account still has rather low volatility—less than 10% per year—and a low correlation with the stock and bond markets.

Leveraged arbitrage is actually a very complex mathematical process. A simplified example is shown in Appendix A.

Interest Rate Arbitrage

The *spreads* between two different interest rates vary over time. I'm referring to interest rate spreads such as those between long bonds and Treasury bills, between BBB-rated bonds and Treasury bonds of a similar duration, or between mortgage-backed securities (like GNMAs) and Treasury bonds. A manager may feel he has very little ability to predict the direction of interest rates (few managers have), but he may have good expertise at predicting the direction of certain interest rate *spreads*.

If so, he can capitalize on that expertise through a long/short portfolio, which is indifferent to the direction of interest rates in general. He can go long Treasuries and short mortgage-backed securities (for example) when he believes the interest rate spread is too narrow and is likely to widen, and vice versa when the spread seems too wide.

The manager doesn't make much money when he is right, however, nor lose much money when he is wrong. The only way to make the effort worthwhile is to use leverage. In some cases, he can invest 10 times the net value of the account in a long portfolio and an equal amount in a short portfolio and still have only a relatively modest standard deviation of returns.

Leverage 10 times?! That sounds like rolling the dice—high returns or disaster, and monumental volatility! Unfortunately, the word *leverage* is one of those emotion-laden words that get in the way of real understanding. Unleveraged investments—as in a start-up company—can be extremely risky, whereas a highly leveraged interest-rate arbitrage account *may* be less risky than a standard unleveraged bond account. The point is: leverage is not necessarily either good or bad. It all depends on how much leverage is used, how it is used, and what is the underlying volatility of the leveraged investment.

As we mentioned before, there's one thing bad about leverage. In many cases, it leads to UBIT. For a taxfree fund, that usually takes the fun out of a leveraged investment.

Can we get around UBIT? Yes, it is possible, but we better have a good tax lawyer working with us. One of the more common methods is to invest in an off-shore fund, such as one registered in Bermuda or the Cayman Islands. But even there we will want a solid Opinion of Counsel that is satisfactory to our tax lawyer.

If we can get over that hurdle, we should have an account that has essentially no correlation with the ups and downs of either the stock or bond markets. Will it make money for us? Only if we have a talented manager.

Caveat

But wait a minute! What happened in 1998 to Long-Term Capital Management, L.P., with its Nobel prize-winning strategists? It nearly went bankrupt and probably would have if the Federal Reserve had not taken some action to generate a rescue. Long-Term Capital was perhaps the ultimate arbitrageur. Doesn't that mean that arbitrage is, in fact, an area where mortals should fear to tread?

Long-Term Capital certainly gave arbitrage a bad name. But our constructive reaction should not be to shy away from sensible arbitrage strategies but to learn from Long-Term Capital's mistakes.

Long-Term Capital adopted a strategy I have urged throughout this book to reduce risk—diversification. It scattered investments among a great many kinds of arbitrages worldwide that have low correlations with one another—low correlations *over time*, that is. It failed to remember that on rare occasions, panics occur in markets worldwide, no one wants to buy anything that has even a semblance of perceived risk, and prices plummet. Correlations among arbitrage strategies that are normally very low suddenly zoom toward 1.0—as in a chain reaction.

Because natural market forces tend eventually to drive the spreads being arbitraged back to some semblance of normalcy, Long-Term Capital's strategy probably would not have been flawed if it had staying power—to survive the liquidity crisis. But it didn't.

Long-Term Capital had leveraged its *entire* $5 billion portfolio—not just well-chosen parts of it—*twenty-five times!* As prices fell, Long-Term Capital received margin calls—demands from its brokers to increase its security deposits. Long-Term Capital had based its strategy on the expectation that it could readily sell its holdings whenever it wished at reasonable prices. But when it went to sell, it found markets had dried up for all but the highest quality and most liquid investments. It was a time when virtually all arbitrageurs lost money—at least on paper—but they survived. Long-Term Capital, however, *was forced* to sell. Without an infusion of cash, Long-Term Capital would have to realize such large losses that its total liabilities threatened to exceed its total assets. That's a definition of the brink of bankruptcy.

So what's the moral to the story? We must analyze our investment programs and our overall portfolio by a realistic assessment of the worst that can happen and make sure that we have the staying power to outlast episodes of the worst. In concept, this is no different from the casino owner who has all the odds running in his favor. But he will be out of business if he doesn't have deep enough pockets to outlast a few high rollers who are lucky at the same time.

Portable Alpha

Over longer intervals arbitrage programs offer the attraction of a very low correlation with other investments, but only the more exceptional ones can be expected to provide the same high long-term returns as a common stock account. It is nice to diversify, but I always hate to give up expected return for the privilege of diversifying.

Well, here is a place where it is possible to have one's cake and eat it too—by combining an arbitrage program with an index fund (or a tactical asset allocation account) that is invested entirely through the use of index futures. We can invest in an S&P 500 index fund, for example, without buying a single stock. We can match the index fund with great precision by buying index futures and keeping our cash in a money-market fund.

We can turn the index fund into an actively managed account, however, by *not* investing our cash in a money market fund but instead investing it in *any* arbitrage program that has low volatility and a low correlation with the stock market. Why might we want to do that?

An exceptional common stock manager, net of fees, might over the long term be able to outperform the S&P 500 by 2 percentage points a year, and a good bond manager might outperform a bond index by 1 percentage point. But *if* we have a low-volatility arbitrage manager who can be expected to outperform T-bills by 3 or 4 percentage points per year (after fees), we can pair him with a manager of index futures (without either manager having to know he is so paired) and expect *the index return plus 3 or 4 percentage points*. What a great expected return!

Doesn't the combined account have a higher volatility than the index fund? Yes, but not much higher if the arbitrage account is really market neutral (zero correlated). If the expected volatility of the uncorrelated arbitrage account is 5 percentage points, it might add some 2+ percentage points (the square root of the 5) to the volatility of the index fund. That's a fair tradeoff!

Incidentally, why call it Portable Alpha? Because if we let alpha stand for "excess return above our benchmark," we can synthesize a high-alpha bond or stock portfolio by investing in an arbitrage program (the source of the alpha) and overlaying it with index futures (the benchmark). We *transport* the arbitrageur's alpha to a stock or bond account. We can mix and match as we please with Portable Alphas.

Portable Alphas are not yet widely used by taxfree funds—perhaps because they are complex, off-beat, and difficult for committee members to grasp. That leaves all the more opportunity to those taxfree funds that are enterprising and willing to open their minds.

Commodity Funds

To many investors, commodity futures[6] seem like spinning a roulette wheel. And clearly, that can be a good analogy. But it doesn't have to be.

We all too quickly associate commodity futures with pork bellies, one of the least traded commodities. There are about 28 exchange-traded commodities, including metals, agricultural products, petroleum products, foreign currencies, and interest rate futures.

Most of those who trade commodity futures are hedgers, businesspeople who are buying *insurance*. The farmer sells corn futures because he can't afford the risk of fluctuating corn prices at harvest time. The importer buys futures on the Japanese yen because he can't afford unpredictable fluctuations in his cost of goods sold. Hedgers are not always in equilibrium. At times, more need to buy than sell, or vice versa.

Liquidity to commodity markets is provided by *speculators*. That's another emotion-laden word that gets in the way of real understanding. Speculators serve a valuable economic function, and the better of them are among the more quantitative academics in the investment world. They absorb the volatility in most commodity markets. They minimize *their* leveraged volatility by investing in a wide range of commodities with little or no correlation with one another and rationally expect to make a long-term profit from their investment.

The BARRA MLM commodity index provides good evidence that a simple disciplined commodity trading strategy can indeed provide a long-term profit. Moreover, commodity accounts can have a modest negative correlation with stock and bond movements—meaning that commodities should be a good diversifier.

Is this a place for taxfree funds?

Goldman Sachs runs a form of a commodity index fund (unrelated to the BARRA MLM index), which has had moderate returns. For the most part, however, commodities are an area where caveat emptor applies. The costs of operating a commodity account are extremely high, and the past performance of a commodity trader can have a surprisingly low correlation with his future performance.

---

[6] An example of commodity futures would be a contract to buy an amount of corn by a specific date for $X/ton. We can buy that future for $Y today and are betting that we will be able to sell that future later for a higher price (and not have to take the actual delivery of the corn).

A commodity account can be a challenging area for a taxfree plan to invest in, but I believe the right kind of program can be a good thing with a small percentage of a plan's assets. Such an account should be extremely well diversified—not only by commodities, but by *traders*. The account should use multiple traders with different styles of trading, selected by someone who is a real student of the field. Even then, typical commodity programs are highly volatile.

In short, commodities can be a good thing for taxfree funds, but not one of the first asset classes a taxfree fund should tackle.

Hedge Funds

Hedge funds are one of the more difficult asset classes to define, because they cover such a wide range of funds. Virtually all hedge funds go short as well as long, but that may be where commonality ends. Some are fully hedged, market neutral, and quite conservative. Others are highly leveraged to the markets. Most invest mainly in stocks, others invest only in fixed income securities, and others invest in the gamut of assets, including many derivatives.

Most share one thing in common—high fees, often a fixed fee equal to 1% of asset values each year plus 20% of all net profits. We should not be surprised that many of the very best investment managers become hedge fund managers, because their compensation can be astronomical. And *if* the manager is good enough, the high fees can be worth our paying. After all, the only thing that counts for the investor is long-term returns *net* of fees, and hedge funds have provided some of the best returns available.

The problem is that the high fees of a hedge fund don't necessarily mean high returns. There have been well-publicized instances of investors' value in a hedge fund being completely wiped out by the manager's speculation, perhaps partly driven by the incentivized fee structure. We therefore must have extraordinary confidence in a hedge fund manager in order to agree to his extremely high fees.

The fact remains, however, that some of the best investment managers of our time are hedge fund managers, and they have made their investors rich. Do we think we're up to identifying who they are?

Oil and Gas Properties

Oil and gas properties are a volatile but diversifying investment for a taxfree fund. They offer better inflation protection than most asset classes, and their returns have had a meaningfully *negative* correlation with returns on stocks and bonds. They also provide strong cash flow.

Returns on oil and gas properties are highly dependent on energy prices, which have deep cycles that can last for decades. They are also impacted, but to a lesser extent, by the accuracy of estimates of a well's reserves.

Because of the uncertainty and volatility of energy prices, oil and gas properties are usually priced to provide double digit real returns, assuming the *real* (inflation-adjusted) price of oil and gas doesn't change. During the 1980s and the first half of the 1990s double digit real returns (or even nominal returns) were a mirage, as a result of weak energy prices. During the 1970s, however, oil and gas properties were *the* place to be.

Basically, there are three kinds of oil and gas exploration and production programs—producing wells, development drilling, and exploratory drilling.

1. Producing wells are the safest investment and are priced to provide the lowest returns.
2. Development drilling includes in-fill drilling, drilling between producing wells, and step-out drilling, which is drilling nearby but outside of existing wells. The probabilities of success can be very high with development drilling but, of course, not like a producing well. As the predictability of returns declines, the discount rate reflected in the price of drilling rights goes up. Many programs that invest in producing wells also earmark a portion of the investment for development drilling.
3. Exploratory drilling—where there are no existing wells—naturally has the highest expected returns, and the widest range of expected outcomes.

Other oil and gas investments encompass the gamut of oil service companies—from drilling supplies to pipe lines to gas storage salt mines—and these can be very effective and diversifying investments in a private energy portfolio.

The costs of investing in oil and gas, including hidden costs, can be very high. And we must invest in such a way as not to be an oil and gas *operator*, or else our taxfree fund will be subject to UBIT. Every time I venture into the oil patch, I feel a bit like the city slicker waiting to be fleeced. In short, I want an extremely competent manager who really knows his way around the oil patch. If we have such a manager, however, we should find it worthwhile long-term to invest several percent of our total assets in oil and gas properties.

Timberland

For the patient investor, timber offers outstanding diversification benefits and the prospect of high returns. Like oil and gas returns, timber returns are perhaps negatively correlated with those of stocks and bonds. Timber is one of the better inflation hedges. And forecasts of long-term *real* rates of return range from 6% to double-digit levels.

Patience is necessary because of the cyclicality of timber values and because active management of timberland takes years to pay off. But it can pay off handsomely. The case for timber is fairly persuasive.

- Since the turn of the century, the real price of timber (net of inflation) has fluctuated a good deal, but overall it has risen by about 2% per year. Many authorities see no reason why this should change in the years ahead.
- Increasingly, timber will have to come from timber farms, because natural forests have been cut so heavily and remaining natural forests are gaining more and more environmental protection.
- We're not likely to be surprised by a sudden increase in the supply of timber, as the supply for the next 15 to 20 years is pretty well known. It is already in the ground and growing.
- Despite the use of wood substitutes and the impact of electronic communications on the printed page, the demand for timber should continue to increase in the years ahead, especially as living standards rise in the developing countries of the world.
- Timber is a commodity that does not have to be harvested at any one time. Each year, a tree continues to grow, and it becomes more valuable per cubic foot until it reaches some 30 years of age (this varies with the kind of tree). Such in-growth amounts to 6% to 8% per year.
- The percentage of the world's timber that today is provided from timber farms is very small. As demand continues to rise, supply is likely to be constrained. Creating a new timber farm that is ready to harvest takes at least 20 years.
- Some of the best places for growing timber are in the southern hemisphere, such as New Zealand, Australia, Chile, Brazil, and South Africa. Many trees will grow twice as fast there as in the United States, where in turn, trees grow faster than in Canada or northern Europe.

Investments in timberland programs are long-term investments, but unless liquidity is particularly important to our fund (it normally shouldn't be), a few percent of our portfolio in timberland seems to make a lot of sense.

Farmland

Farmland is one of the world's largest asset classes, yet little used in institutional investing. Why? Other than its being illiquid, like many other asset classes, there is nothing innately wrong with farmland. It comes down to the bottom line: What kind of rate of return can realistically be expected?

The world has continuously more mouths to feed, and a growing percentage of people can afford to feed themselves properly. So with a limited amount of farmland in the world, we might think it would become increasingly precious. Yet progress in agricultural science has been so rapid that, at least in the United States, we need less, not more, agricultural land.

Perhaps this is part of the reason why I have never found passive farmland investment opportunities from which we could expect exciting returns. Farming is a high-tech business today, and land is only one small part of the necessary resources.

There are times when farmland values have jumped dramatically, and other times when they have languished. A successful market timer could do well in farmland. But as in other asset classes, market timing is a dangerous game.

Perhaps someday institutional investors will find a way to take good advantage of this large asset class. To date, however, I have not.

In Short

We have the opportunity to consider a wide range of alternative asset classes, many of which march to quite different drummers than our stock and bond portfolios. High returns on many of these asset classes are especially dependent on the skill of the investment manager.

Much extra work is required if we are to understand these asset classes and find premier managers in them. We can, however, find a rewarding pot of gold at the end of the rainbow if we put enough time and effort into it.

Appendix A

How Does Leveraged Convertible Arbitrage Work?

A typical arbitrage of a convertible bond (or convertible preferred stock) against its underlying common stock would be as follows:

- Invest $100,000 in a convertible bond.
- Sell short $70,000 of the underlying stock. (We sell short only 70% as much in stock because the stock price moves up and down faster than the convertible.)
- Leverage 5:1 (without leverage, it's hardly worth the effort).

There is a wind behind our back in terms of income:

- Interest on the convertible.
- Plus T-bill interest on the proceeds from selling the stock short.
- Less dividends we must pay the owner of the borrowed stock.

Because of its greater income and relative safety of principal, the convertible is generally priced at a premium over its conversion value. The premium on a convertible bond or preferred stock is the difference between (a) the current price of the convertible security and (b) its conversion value—the value of the common stock into which it can be converted.

In an attractive arbitrage opportunity, assuming the convertible's premium remains normal:

- If the stock price is unchanged, we'll earn a little money (the difference between interest on the convertible and dividends on the stock).
- If the stock price rises sharply, we'll earn more money, because as the bond price exceeds conversion value, its percentage increase should

largely keep pace with that of the stock, and remember, we are long more of the bond than we are short the stock.

- If the stock price drops sharply, we'll also earn more money, because the price of the convertible bond won't suffer as large a percentage decline as the stock, because the convertible's bond value will begin to support the price of the bond.

For this reason convertible arbitrageurs like volatility. Of course, we can also lose money. In late summer and fall of 1998, for example, prices of convertibles fell and their premiums over conversion value actually declined. For several months convertible arbitrageurs had negative returns. But if the arbitrageurs didn't sell their positions, they tended to earn back their losses as bond premiums returned toward normal over time.

Chapter 9

Negotiating Agreements for Private Investments

One of the most sensitive aspects of entering a private investment fund, such as real estate or venture capital, is assessing: Does the structure of this fund do the best possible job of aligning the financial motivations of the investment manager with the goals of the investors—and more to the point, with *our* particular goals? This is such a critical and complex matter that I am devoting a separate chapter to it.

Aligning the motivations of the investment manager and the investors is not an easy thing to do. Typical agreements that have come down through the years set a poor precedent, although there has been some marked improvement in recent years. Investors must be much more pro-active than they have been in the past, and if they cannot achieve satisfactory alignment of interests, then they should probably decline the opportunity.

Many (but not all) of the points of concern revolve around the fee structure. Fee considerations for a private investment are very different from those for a liquid investment. A liquid investment has two key differences: (1) if the investment manager sells an asset, he reinvests the money, and the basis for his fee stays the same, and (2) if the sponsor becomes disenchanted with the manager, it withdraws its money and fires the manager.

By contrast, if the manager of a private investment sells an asset, he must usually return the money to the investors, and the basis for his management fee may go down. And if the sponsor becomes disenchanted with

187

the manager of an illiquid fund, it cannot usually terminate the manager. The terms of the agreement must take these differences into account.

The fee of a manager of liquid investments is normally based simply on the value of assets under management. This traditional kind of fee is *not* appropriate for a private investment, as it gives the manager no motivation to sell the investment at an optimal time. A performance fee combined with a fixed fee is needed for private investments. Most partnership fees, in fact, are structured this way.

An ERISA Problem

There is, however, a problem, at least for ERISA[1] funds. Representatives of the Department of Labor (DOL) have indicated that a performance fee may well be a per se prohibited transaction unless specifically exempted by DOL action. The DOL's position is based on the fact that the investment manager can enrich himself (through the performance fee) by his investment decisions—even though he may be enriching investors proportionately. The one fee schedule that is always acceptable to the DOL is one calculated as a percentage of the market value of assets.

In a sense, for private investments, such market-value-based fees *are* incentive fees, and they give the manager the *wrong* incentive. Such fees incentivize managers to retain an asset as long as they can, or else their fees will cease. Furthermore, managers profit whether or not they achieve their clients' objectives.

How does an ERISA fund get around the DOL's rules? Short of getting a DOL Advisory Opinion, the ERISA fund must get an Opinion of Counsel that is satisfactory to its own counsel and affirms either of two things:

1. The investment fee structure for an ERISA Fiduciary is similar enough to one of three fee structures the DOL approved back in the 1980s through its Advisory Opinions. (Advisory Opinions are supposed to apply only to the particular applicants for those Opinions, but those three Opinions are about the only position statements the DOL has issued on the subject, so ERISA funds have had to lean on them heavily.)

---

[1] The U.S. Employee Retirement Income Security Act of 1974.

2. The investment meets certain specific requirements whereby it will be categorized as *not* a Plan Asset under ERISA. This means that the manager will *not* be a Fiduciary under ERISA. Why the DOL wants to motivate ERISA funds to exclude their managers from being Fiduciaries under ERISA is something I've never quite figured out. (In any case, all such managers *are* fiduciaries in my book, and we fully expect them to act accordingly.)

Through these two means, ERISA funds have through the years entered into a great many investment programs with performance fees. The best discussion of desirable terms and conditions for investors in private investments is the following, a 1998 paper prepared by a task force (in which I participated) of the Committee for the Investment of Employee Benefit Assets (CIEBA), an arm of the Financial Executives Institute (FEI). The footnotes are my comments on this paper.

Terms and Conditions for Consideration by Plan Sponsors When Investing in Private Investment Funds

CIEBA's Working Group on Private Equity Terms and Conditions is pleased to submit its *suggestions* of desirable terms for a private fund. These suggestions are intended to better align the financial interests of fund sponsors with the interests of fund investors and, as such, do not purport to establish standards to be uniformly applied to each private equity fund. Rather, the Working Group acknowledges that the terms and conditions of any private fund need to be considered as a whole; they depend upon the particular circumstances and are a matter of negotiation. There is not a single set of terms that is universally appropriate, and the following suggestions need to be carefully considered in light of, among other facts, the nature of the fund and market conditions. Following these recommendations does not ensure that any particular fund merits investment therein.

The terms and conditions of a private investment fund are a matter of negotiation between the fund sponsor and the fund's participants. The appropriateness of some of these terms, such as the magnitude of fees, varies with the nature of the fund.

With respect to all such funds, however, fund participants should negotiate vigorously to gain terms that do the best possible job of *aligning the financial motivations of the investment manager with those of the investors.* This is not easy to do, but the following principles are recommended:

1. In principle, all profits and high compensation to the manager (and affiliates) should come through performance fees. The fund should include some form of target rate or *hurdle rate* (internal rate of return) that must be exceeded before the general partner or fund manager receives a meaningful performance fee.

    (a)   The manager of a private investment program needs fixed fees to defray his costs of operations while managing the program. But the fixed fees should cover *only* such costs, excluding high base salaries. Fixed fees should be phased in and phased out to recognize the fact that the general partner or manager would otherwise receive overlapping fees in managing two or more funds.

    (b)   During the fund's investment period, management fees are sometimes calculated as a percent of the investor's commitment. If so, once the fund is fully invested or the investment period has expired, management fees should then be based on the investors' remaining invested capital.[2] Management fees should not be based on market value.

    (c)   A performance fee should be based on the fund's *cash flow (internal) rate of return to investors, net of all costs and fees.* (Time-weighted rates of return are inappropriate here.) The cash flow rate of return should reflect the amount and date of every contribution from and distribution to the investors, and it should treat every distribution the same, whether it results from income, a gain, or a return of capital. "Net of all costs and fees" means just that—including net of any Unrelated Business Income Tax or any other taxes.[3]

    (d)   For real estate funds, a performance fee might be based on the fund's *real* cash flow rate of return (its IRR net of

---

[2] Where a performance fee structure does not include a hurdle rate, failure to include this provision may leave the general partner or fund manager with a disincentive to sell and make distributions. If there is no hurdle rate, fixed fees might be stepped down progressively—for example, 1% of commitments for years 1–5, 0.8% for year 6, 0.6% for year 7, etc.

[3] Some tax-free investors also prefer a provision that the general partner must use its best efforts to avoid any UBIT at all.

inflation).[4] Because of the correlation between inflation and a property's replacement cost, well-managed equity real estate can be oriented toward real returns better than almost any other kind of investment, and managers should not be compensated for inflation.

(e) The performance fee should be based on the *total fund*, that is, on *all* assets combined, not on an asset-by-asset basis. The investor is interested in performance of the overall portfolio. So, equally, should the manager. The manager should be as interested in improving the returns of his losers as his winners, whereas an asset-by-asset performance fee focuses his attention only on his winners.

(f) If a performance fee has a "catch-up" provision[5] once a hurdle rate of return is reached, the general partner or fund manager should receive no more than 50% of the net profits during catch-up. There may be some trade-off between the catch-up rate and a higher hurdle rate.

(g) The performance fee should be a back-end fee, calculated on the *actual* return, cash to cash. Payment of a performance fee should begin only after the program has returned to the

---

[4] *Real* returns should be calculated correctly. For example:

Under 5% inflation, 13% nominal return does *not* translate into 8% real return.

$$(1.13/1.05 = 1.076, \text{ or } 7.6\% \text{ real return})$$

It would take 13.4% nominal return to provide 8% more buying power—that is, 8% real return.

$$(1.134/1.05 = 1.08, \text{ or } 8\% \text{ real return})$$

This may seem trivial until we consider Brazilian-type inflation of years past—say, 500% per year. A real return of 8% would require a nominal return of 548%, not 508%.

(6.00 (the wealth value under 500% inflation)*1.08 = 6.48, or 548% nominal return)

A 508% nominal return would result in 6.08/6.00 = 1.013, or 1.3% real return.

[5] An example of a hurdle rate and catch-up provision would be:Investors are to receive 100% of all profits until they have received a net internal rate of return of 8%. Next, profits are to be divided 50:50 between investors and the general partner until the general partner has received 20% of cumulative profits. Thereafter, investors are to receive 80% of all profits and the general partner 20%.

investors all their contributions. The ultimate value added by the manager (and therefore the ultimate performance fee) cannot be known until the last asset is converted to cash. If, instead, managers receive performance fees as each property is sold, they are likely to receive more than they should—especially since the longest-held assets are often below-average performers.[6]

(h)   If a back-ended performance fee cannot be negotiated, then investors should require an annual clawback provision[7] that makes the manager's firm and its individual members responsible for repayment of the clawback in the event that, as of the end of each year, the manager has received an overpayment.

- The clawback should be for 100% of the overpaid performance fee, not net of any taxes or other expenses that the manager's firm or its individual members have incurred.
- The repayment amount should include a meaningful interest rate (well above money-market rates) to compensate the investors for the time value of their overpayment.
- An escrow account for accrued performance fees adds further security.
- A new provision in some agreements calls for the performance fee to be paid every three years, with 25% of each payment held back and paid in subsequent years if still earned.

Comments

A well-constructed performance fee should motivate the manager to sell each asset when it is optimum for the investors—specifically, when the manager expects that asset's future incremental IRR (assuming the asset

---

[6] Many agreements provide that the partnership may make distributions to the general partner to enable it to pay taxes on income that it has not yet received. This is a reasonable provision. But such "tax distributions" should be deducted from subsequent distributions payable to the general partner and should be subject to clawback provisions discussed in paragraph 1(h).

[7] A clawback is a repayment by the manager or general partner to the investors.

were purchased today at whatever it could be sold for today) will fall below the target return. Conversely, the performance fee should motivate the manager to retain each asset as long as the manager expects that asset's future incremental IRR will equal or exceed the target.

Ideally, a performance fee might be constructed with multiple hurdle rates so as to provide the manager at least some performance fee even if the program falls short of its target. If unforeseen problems limit the results to a low return, managers should still have an incentive to boost that IRR—for example, from 1% to 3%. Otherwise, the manager will have no interest in improving the fund's return other than for the protection of his firm's reputation (although reputation is not normally an inconsequential motivation).[8]

2. (a) The manager should at least finance his own minimum partnership interest (usually 1% of commitments), and depending on the manager's financial capabilities, he should commit materially more. Some funds in the past have financed the manager's 1% interest in the partnership. This is inappropriate, as the manager should have some of his own money riding on the success of the program.

    (b) The credibility of a manager and the key individuals composing that manager can often be equated with the degree to which they commit a major portion of their own money to the program. The general partner or fund manager should invest a significant portion of its net worth in the partnership. For example, a minimum of 5% of total partnership commitments is desirable, or some multiple of the annual

---

[8] Devising a fee structure that satisfies all of the above criteria is a very challenging assignment, but highly worth pursuing. Some years ago when a colleague and I were discussing a prospective fund with a real estate manager whom we regarded highly, we told the manager we thought his proposed fee schedule misaligned our respective interests. "Well," he had the temerity to counter, "What would you propose?" We were put to the test.

Our best effort for a real estate fee schedule is shown in Appendix A at the end of this chapter. Calculation of the incentive fee admittedly violates the KISS principle (keep it simple, stupid), but it's not any more complex than a sophisticated manager or plan sponsor should be able to deal with. This fee schedule—or some variant of it—has since been adopted by a variety of real estate funds. But the fee structure is far from perfect. We would challenge others to devise fee schedules that fit the above criteria even better. The important thing is that we should be committed to these *criteria*.

fixed fee such as 3 or 4 times, if financially feasible for the general partner.

3. Co-investment by the general partner or fund manager in any particular deal should be on the same terms as the partnership, and the general partner should co-invest in *every* deal or not at all. Co-investment should be offered to other limited partners only when the fund has fully subscribed to its desired allocation of an investment opportunity.

4. The fund's up front organizational expense is best paid by the manager, as he then has an economic motivation to limit his promotional expense. If, however, organizational expense is to be paid for by the fund (as often is the case), a reasonable cap should be set.[9]

5. Ongoing expense that is to be payable by the fund should be defined explicitly. It should be restricted to third-party reimbursements and should exclude discretionary items such as travel.

6. For full alignment of financial interests, the manager's sole source of income should be the investors' fees. If the manager should earn additional fee income—such as investment banking fees, break-up fees, or fees for serving as directors on the boards of investee companies—all of these fees should redound to the benefit of the investors (the manager will earn his share of them through his performance fees). It may be unwise, however, to arrange for such fee income to be treated simply as additional fund income, because most of these fees might be treated as Unrelated Business Taxable Income. Funds typically deal with this problem by providing that such fee income shall first offset fees—current, previous, and future fees—otherwise payable by the fund to the manager. And if fee income should exceed fees payable, then the balance of fee income should go to the fund.

This treatment of other fee income minimizes potential conflicts of interest. A manager, in negotiating a private investment in a company, can structure the deal in multiple ways—such as higher fee income and a lower price. By treating all such fee

---

[9] Organization expense is usually paid by the partnership, as this expense would not be tax-deductible if paid by the general partner. The agreement might well provide, however, that any organization expense paid by the partnership is to be deducted from subsequent management fees.

income as recommended, the tradeoff becomes irrelevant to the manager, and he focuses only on what is the best overall deal.

7. In real estate funds, fees paid to the general partner, fund manager, or affiliate for additional services—such as property management, financing, construction development, and transaction or lease brokerage—can potentially dwarf the importance of performance fees and water down their motivational value to the manager. The manager's only motivation to provide the above services should be to make the fund more profitable, not to provide another source of manager income. The simplest way to avoid such conflicts of interest is to require all such services to be provided by third, unrelated parties. That, however, is not always in the investors' best interests. If such services may be provided by the manager or affiliates, then (a) such services should be defined up front, (b) fees for such services should cover costs only and therefore should not only meet most favored nation[10] provisions but also should be lower than competitive rates, and (c) the manager should be required to report all such fees quarterly so investors know fully what the manager and its affiliates are earning from the program.

8. Some investors have special concerns that the general partner sometimes chooses to address in side letters outside of the partnership agreement. The partnership agreement should provide that all side letters, and the terms of those side letters, be made available to all investors.

9. Preferably, there should be no multiple closings[11] of the fund. All partners should make their first contribution at once, and no partner at his closing should have the advantage of knowing more about partnership investments than any other partner at his closing. In many instances, however, multiple closings are often desirable from a practical standpoint. This creates a problem, because there is usually relatively little return to the fund between

---

[10] *Most favored nation* provisions assure investors that the manager won't charge the fund fees for any particular service that are any higher than the lowest fees it charges any other customer for the same or a similar service.

[11] A fund closing occurs when the general partner legally accepts the commitments of investors and begins operating the fund. Some funds have second or third closings at later dates when additional investors are admitted to the fund.

closings 1 and 2—a rate of return much lower than any investor expected from the life of the fund. To mitigate this disadvantage, a late investor should not only pay fees from the beginning of the fund but, in addition, should pay interest to the initial investors from the date of the first cash call to the date of his contribution, and at a rate of return closer to the fund's target rate of return, such as LIBOR[12] plus 6% (although there are varied opinions among plan sponsors as to what the rate should be).

10. A commingled fund should have first shot at *all* of the manager's investment opportunities that meet the parameters of the fund—especially ahead of any subsequent fund or subsequent separate account.

In addition, the general partner or fund manager should be precluded from starting to market a new fund until the current fund is at least 75% committed to particular investments.

11. The partnership should draw down contributions from investors only on an as-needed basis—just in time. This enables the investor to keep its money invested in other long-term investments longer, awaiting cash calls.

If it is inconvenient for the investor to meet cash calls on short notice, the investor can always place its committed money in a money-market fund and meet its cash calls out of that money-market fund.

12. The penalties for an investor who fails to meet a cash call should be catastrophic. The manager, to accomplish the ends of all investors, must be able to count on cash arriving when called. If an investor misses a cash call, the result could be very costly to all investors.

13. The general partner should pay out cash raised through proceeds from income, loans, or asset sales whenever a modest amount of cash has accumulated. The general partner should not automatically wait until the end of a quarter or retain any more cash than it really needs.

14. The role of any advisory board composed of investors should be limited to partnership governance issues and the resolution of conflict-of-interest issues between the manager and the fund. An

---

[12] The prevailing interest rate applicable to interbank borrowing, specifically, the London Interbank Offered Rate.

advisory board should not have a voice in investment decisions, except in recommending to the limited partners an amendment to the investment guidelines governing the fund.[13] Examples of useful functions of an advisory board include approval of valuations,[14] review (but not approval) of operating budgets, review of fund audits, and approval of any situation where the manager may have a conflict of interest such as the use of related parties for various paid functions.

Immediately after each advisory board meeting the general partner should send all investors a report containing (a) minutes of the meeting, and (b) total costs incurred by the partnership in connection with the meeting.

15. Any amendments to the partnership agreements that materially affect the rights, investment criteria, or governance of the fund should require the vote of at least two-thirds of the limited partners' interests.

16. The fund should provide for a no-fault divorce (termination of the manager or general partner) upon two-thirds vote of investment interests who are unrelated to the general partner or fund manager. This provides for unexpected events. If the manager won't agree, he lacks confidence in his ability to satisfy the investors. Consideration should additionally be given to automatic termination of the fund (unless investors vote otherwise) in the event that key person(s) leave the management firm.

   In voting for a no-fault divorce, the investors should be able to vote for any of the following outcomes:
   - To end the commitment period but otherwise for the fund to carry on.
   - To replace the general partner (or fund manager).
   - To dissolve the fund.

17. The general partner (or an affiliate) should be permitted to purchase limited partnership interests, including buying such interests from other limited partners. But if it does, (a) neither the

---

[13] Limited partner members of an advisory board may not serve as agents for other investors, or else their liability would extend beyond the amount of their investment. Hence, they should not be compensated by the partnership for their membership on the board.

[14] Additionally, *any* limited partner should have a right to challenge a valuation, and if agreement can't be reached, to have the matter settled by arbitration.

general partner nor any affiliate may vote those interests, and (b) the denominator for determining the percentage of positive or negative votes should be those limited partnership interests owned by parties unrelated to the general partner.

In addition, to avoid the possibility of any single limited partner gaining control of a limited partnership, the definition of majority vote in a fund should be a vote of at least two limited partners, each of whom is unaffiliated with the general partner and with each other, who together own more than 50% of the units owned by partners who are unaffiliated with the general partner.

18. The fund should have a limited life, extendible beyond that date only by a two-thirds vote of partnership interests.

19. There should be no provision allowing one investor to cash out of the fund before every other investor is cashed out, even if the fund has sufficient cash to accommodate. Such a cashout cannot be done fairly, as it would have to be done at current unit value (or some multiple thereof), and there is no way of knowing in a private investment how unit value relates to true market value. Investors should understand that they will be invested in the fund to the very end—unless someone buys out their interest on an arm's length basis.

20. The liquidation of partnership assets should be at arm's length to third parties unaffiliated with either the general partner or limited partners unless the limited partners approve such a liquidation by a two-thirds vote.

Occasionally the general partner of a fund that is to be invested in hard assets—such as real estate or timberland—tries to insert in the partnership agreement a provision giving the general partner or an affiliate the right-of-first-refusal when the property is eventually to be sold, or the right to buy the property at appraised value. Such a provision is inappropriate.

When a property is to be sold, it should be sold to the highest bidder. Bidding is a process of discovering the market price of the property. Anything that interferes with this discovery process hurts investors. Bidders will only go to the trouble of submitting their most aggressive bid if they are confident that, if their bid indeed is best, they will win the deal.

21. Many partnership agreements provide some possibility for making distributions in kind (distributing actual shares of stock, for

example) in lieu of a cash distribution. In such cases, agreements should include the following provisions to protect investor interests:

(a) Any in-kind distribution should be restricted to freely tradable securities.

(b) Each investor should have the right to choose between receiving cash[15] or the freely tradable securities, except the general partner should receive his share of such distribution in kind.

(c) For purposes of calculating performance fees, the per-share valuation of an in-kind distribution should be the alternative cash distribution or the immediately realizable value of the securities, net of any transaction and market impact costs.

22. Within 90 days[16] after the end of each financial year, the general partner or fund manager should send investors a report containing at least the following:

(a) Year-end financial statements.

(b) Statement showing each investor's capital account and contributions and distributions during the year.

(c) Valuations of portfolio investments, which should be estimated as close to current market-based values as possible. The methodology used to value the portfolio investments should also be described.

(d) Overview of all investment activities, plus a summary of companies in which investments were committed during the year, including a description of each investment and its terms, and a description of any material events that impacted the partnership or fund during the year.

(e) A list of all investors in the fund with their current ownership share.

If the financial statement is not yet audited, a letter sent with the subsequent audited statement should highlight any material changes from the earlier statement. Quarterly reports should

---

[15] In practice, the offer of cash is an offer by the general partner to sell the limited partner's shares and distribute the net proceeds. The net proceeds per-share of such sales should establish the valuation of the entire distribution for purposes of calculating the performance fee.

[16] Many investors believe the general partner or fund manager should accomplish this within 75 days after the end of each financial year.

also be provided. They should cover, among other things, item (d) above.

23.   The general partner should be required to disclose to the limited partners throughout the life of the partnership the general partner's time commitment to other business activities (especially the time commitment of key individuals), any real or potential conflicts of interest, any regulatory violations, any litigation that it or partners or affiliates have been or are likely to be involved in, and of course all financial statements for the partnership entity, including partnership operating budgets.

24.   Under most partnership agreements, the fund indemnifies the manager for costs incurred in managing the fund, except in instances where the manager has been negligent. Some agreements try to provide indemnification except in instances where the manager has been guilty of gross negligence, and this should be universally *un*acceptable.[17]

   In addition to negligence, reasons for voiding indemnification should include bad faith, willful misconduct, fraud, illegal acts, breach of partnership agreement, and breach of fiduciary duty. The indemnified parties should cross-indemnify the partnership or fund for such acts. Moreover, the partnership should not indemnify the general partners for legal disputes among themselves.

25.   Depending on the nature of the fund, consideration should be given to (a) limitations on the fund's concentration in any one investment or investment category and (b) limitations on the fund's borrowing authority, especially if the purpose of the fund is corporate buy-ins.

Some Other Terms and Conditions to Consider (Besides Those Discussed in the CIEBA Paper)

To avoid conflict-of-interest concerns under ERISA, the general partner should be required to distribute to limited partners an Opinion of Counsel

---

[17] ERISA plans are required to meet a "prudent expert" standard and, as such, may not indemnify an ERISA Fiduciary for negligence. Many lawyers contend it is also imprudent under ERISA for an ERISA plan to indemnify for negligence a manager even if he happens *not* to be a Fiduciary under ERISA.

after its first investment and periodically thereafter that the partnership is being operated as a "venture capital operating company (VCOC)" under ERISA. Failing that, limited partners should have a right to withdraw from the partnership.

A manager's second fund may co-invest with his first fund in any new opportunity, but the second fund should not be able to invest in any follow-on opportunity in which the first fund invested unless (1) the limited partners specifically vote to permit that investment or (2) the follow-on investment is also being shared in a substantial manner by an unrelated institutional investor. This provision is intended to prevent an investment in Fund 2 that might serve to bail out a problem investment made by Fund 1.

Many partnership agreements prohibit the reinvestment of proceeds from any investment that is sold. I prefer *to permit* reinvestment for X years. In that way, we are getting more money invested for our fixed fees and organizational expense. Also, we are encouraging the manager to sell an investment where he has been fortunate enough to achieve a quick gain but where incremental gains on that investment might prospectively not be as good as on an entirely new investment.

Some general partners today are establishing the general partner as a limited liability company (an LLC) instead of a partnership of the particular individuals who have formed the general partner. A limited liability general partner can be detrimental to the limited partners unless the principals of the LLC are held jointly and severally liable for any obligations to the limited partners (as through negligence or clawbacks).

Other Due Diligence Procedures

It is hard for any single investor to negotiate these terms unless the investor is willing to commit a large sum and become *the* lead investor. But there is strength in numbers. I strongly urge opening a dialogue during due diligence with other key prospective limited partners. This can greatly improve our bargaining position. We have found other prospective investors eager to work together in negotiating partnership terms. There's a world of difference between hanging together and hanging separately.

Also, in evaluating a new fund, it can be insightful to ask the manager to calculate past performance records on a pre-fee *and* after-fee basis, with the after-fee performance calculated net of the proposed performance-fee structure.

Unfortunately, the terms of many venture capital partnerships today still often fail to satisfy the above criteria. Traditional fee structures die hard, and investors have too rarely gotten together and demanded that these criteria be met. Some venture capital managers have such remarkable track records that investors are lined up to get into their new funds, almost regardless of terms. The plan sponsor must then decide whether it is worth giving in on principles of structuring fees in order to get in with the best investors. There are few managers, however, who have earned the right to be so arrogant, and it is extremely worthwhile for investors to negotiate hard on partnership terms and to enlist potential co-investors to do likewise.

Legal Documentation

Nothing appears more daunting than a 96-page draft of a partnership agreement. Once we receive such a draft, there is a natural impulse to shoot it off to our lawyer as fast as possible. That's a good instinct, as it is critical to have a good lawyer working with us.

But while a lawyer can help us with legal considerations, we are the ones responsible for the business considerations. Hence, we should not give it to our lawyer until we have reviewed the whole thing and noted all provisions with which we are not entirely satisfied, or which we don't understand. That's taking on a terribly tedious assignment, but it's a mighty important one. Only then should we pass it along to our lawyer.

In Short

Negotiating the terms and conditions of private investment agreements is critically important. Besides making sure that fees are reasonable, we should work hard to structure agreements so that the financial motivations of the general partner and manager are as congruent as possible with *our* goals and objectives.

A final thought: We must not fall in love with any particular investment fund or manager. Diversifying over time and over different investment strategies proves beneficial in achieving good long-term investment returns.

Appendix A

A Real Estate Performance Fee Schedule

(Where the Target IRR Happens To Be 8% Real)

Acquisition Fee: 1% of net purchase cost.

Annual Asset Management Fee: 0.50% of net invested cost (perhaps adjusted for inflation)

Alternatively: No acquisition fee.
Annual fee of 0.75% of commitment for first 3 years.
0.75% of net invested cost thereafter.

Note: The above rates should probably decline, based on the size of each investor's commitment to the program.

Performance Fee: None until distributions give investors their money back in real terms. Then, progressively:

	1% of distributions until investors' real IRR equals 1% net of all fees and expenses.
then 2% "	" " " " " " " 2% " " " " " "
then 3% "	" " " " " " " 3% " " " " " "
then 4% "	" " " " " " " 4% " " " " " "
then 5% "	" " " " " " " 5% " " " " " "
then 7% "	" " " " " " " 6% " " " " " "
then 9% "	" " " " " " " 7% " " " " " "
then 12% "	" " " " " " " 8% " " " " " "
then 15% of all subsequent distributions.	

Effect: If investors receive exactly 8% real IRR, manager will receive about 6.8% of profits.
Manager will receive 15% of all additional profits.

- Investors' IRR is based solely upon their contributions and distributions, from their First Contribution Date to the date for which the IRR is calculated.
- In the calculation, the amount of every contribution and distribution is divided by one plus the Change in CPI from the First Contribution Date. The IRR is the discount rate at which the present value of all contributions and distributions equal zero as of the First Contribution Date.
- The Change in CPI as of any date is a fraction. The numerator is the CPI applicable to that date less the CPI applicable to the First Contribution Date, and the denominator is the CPI applicable to the First Contribution Date. The CPI applicable to any date is the CPI reported for the nearest prior month ending at least 43 days prior to that date (for the convenience of making calculations promptly). The CPI is the U.S. Consumer Price Index-U, all items.

Note: The figures used in the Acquisition Fee, Management Fees, and Performance Fee are examples only and should be tailored to the economics of the specific fund.

Example of Calculation of Performance Fee

		Dates of Cash Flows						
		1/88	1/89	1/90	1/91	1/92	1/93	1/94
a)	Investments by Plan	1000	—	—	—	—	—	—
b)	Cash available for distribution	—	80	80	80	80	1350	400
c)	Inflation multiplier since prior date	—	1.05	1.05	1.05	1.05	1.05	1.05

Cash distributions needed by plan to restore purchasing power of investment (0% real IRR)

d)	Balance needed before distribution ($c \times$ prior f)	1000	1050	1019	985	951	914	
e)	Cash distributed to Plan	—	80	80	80	80	914	
f)	Balance needed after distribution ($d - e$)	1000	970	939	905	871	0	
g)	Remaining cash available for distribution ($b - e$)	—	—	—	—	—	436	

Performance fee calculation

h_1)	Additional cash distribution needed by Plan to achieve *1% real IRR*	56*
i_1)	Cash distributed to Plan	56
j_1)	Performance fee paid to manager $1\% \times i_1 \; / \; .99)$	1
k_1)	Balance of cash still available for distribution ($g - i_1 - j_1$)	379
h_2)	Additional cash distribution needed by Plan to achieve *2% real IRR*	58
i_2)	Cash distributed to Plan	58
j_2)	Performance fee paid to manager ($2\% \times i_2 \; / \; .98$)	1
k_2)	Balance of cash still available for distribution ($k_1 - i_2 - j_2$)	320
h_3)	Additional cash distribution needed by Plan to achieve *3% real IRR*	61
i_3)	Cash distributed to Plan	62
j_3)	Performance fee paid to manager ($3\% \times i_3 \; / \; .97$)	2
k_3)	Balance of cash still available for distribution ($k_2 - i_3 - j_3$)	257
h_4)	Additional cash distribution needed by Plan to achieve *4% real IRR*	63
i_4)	Cash distributed to Plan	63
j_4)	Performance fee paid to manager ($4\% \times i_4 \; / \; .96$)	3
k_4)	Balance of cash still available for distribution ($k_3 - i_4 - j_4$)	192

(continued)

* Calculated in same manner as lines d through g, except $c = 1.05 \times 1.01 = 1.0605$.

Example of Calculation of Performance Fee *(Continued)*

		Dates of Cash Flows					
	1/88	1/89	1/90	1/91	1/92	1/93	1/94
h_5) Additional cash distribution needed by Plan to achieve 5% *real IRR*						66	
i_5) Cash distributed to Plan						66	
j_5) Performance fee paid to manager $(5\% \times i_5 \,/\, .95)$						4	
k_5) Balance of cash still available for distribution $(k_4 - i_5 - j_5)$						122	
h_6) Additional cash distribution needed by Plan to achieve 6% *real IRR*						69	
i_6) Cash distributed to Plan						69	
j_6) Performance fee paid to manager $(7\% \times i_6 \,/\, .93)$						5	
k_6) Balance of cash still available for distribution $(k_5 - i_6 - j_6)$						48	
h_7) Additional cash distribution needed by Plan to achieve 7% *real IRR*						71	32
i_7) Cash distributed to Plan						44	32
j_7) Performance fee paid to manager $(9\% \times i_7 \,/\, .91)$						4	3
k_7) Balance of cash still available for distribution $(k_6 - i_7 - j_7)$ or $(b - i_7 - j_7)$						0	365
h_8) Additional cash distribution needed by Plan to achieve 8% *real IRR*							83
i_8) Cash distributed to Plan							83
j_8) Performance fee paid to manager $(12\% \times i_8 \,/\, .88)$							11
k_8) Balance of cash still available for distribution $(k_7 - i_8 - j_8)$							271
i_9) Cash distributed to Plan $(85\% \times k_8)$							230
j_9) Performance fee paid to manager $(15\% \times k_8)$							41
k_9) Balance of cash still available for distribution $(k_8 - i_9 - j_9)$							0
Summary							
m) Cumulative cash return to Plan (in excess of original investment)							995
n) Cumulative performance fees paid to manager							75

Chapter 10

The Master Trustee

If we have multiple managers in multiple asset classes, all making continuing transactions, who keeps the books? Who pulls everything together with unfailing accuracy so nothing falls through the cracks and so we can analyze both the individual trees *and* the forest?

A must for an institutional fund of any size is a master trustee (or master custodian). I use the term *master trustee* here to include any trustee of a single plan that has multiple investment accounts managed by different investment firms.[1]

The master trustee is a bank that takes custody of all assets and holds them in trust. At one time that meant keeping zillions of share or bond certificates stored in its vault. Today, the vault's contents are limited mainly to certificates of private investments. Virtually all publicly traded stock and bond investments are kept in central depositories. The trustee has a computer record from the depository showing how many shares it holds of each security.

None of our assets belongs to the trustee. It holds them in trust for us. If the trustee ever went bankrupt, its creditors could not get their hands on any of our assets. This is not true of a broker who holds client assets in a custody account, because the assets in that custody account are in *the broker's* name. If the broker ever went bankrupt, our assets would be in jeopardy.

---

[1] See Appendix A for a discussion of the development of the terms *master trustee* and *master custodian* and of the differences between the two.

Trustees of pension plans are usually *directed* trustees. That means the trustee has no investment discretion. Everything the trustee does is specifically at the instruction of the client or an investment manager—unless the client additionally gives the trustee investment management responsibility over a portion of the assets.

If all the master trustee does is to take custody, why is a master trustee a must?

First of all, it separates the function of custody from that of investment management. The investment manager doesn't get its hands on any assets. Nobody at the manager's firm can abscond with any assets as long as custody is with a different party. Nor can it lie to us about the assets it is managing for us. For most kinds of skullduggery, the trustee and investment manager (or their staff people) would have to collude—a less likely occurrence. Some notorious cases of fraud could hardly have happened if the client had used a master trustee.

But that's not all a master trustee does. In some respects, custody is a relatively minor function. The master trustee performs two essential functions:

1.   Keeps the official books on all assets and all transactions.
2.   Serves as a primary source of management information.

Let's look at these two key functions.

Keeping the Books

The master trustee executes every trade made by an investment manager. The manager arranges the trade with a broker and notifies the trustee. The trustee then settles with the broker—exchanges cash for the securities that it takes into custody. This exchange is almost always done electronically these days.

Meanwhile, today's trustee keeps every dollar of cash fully invested. After settling all trades, the trustee "sweeps" all accounts each day for cash. That means the trustee invests every dollar of cash from every account in the trustee's Short-Term Investment Fund (STIF), which operates something like a money-market mutual fund). The STIF provides competitive overnight investment rates, and all of the account's assets are available for use the next day if needed. No money lies around uninvested.

At the end of each month, the master trustee provides the client the following statements for each account *and* for the overall trust:

- An asset statement showing the month-end book value and market value, usually categorized into convenient asset groupings.
- A list of all transactions, including those that were accrued but not settled at the end of the month. Accrued transactions are noted on the asset statement as "Accounts Payable" and "Accounts Receivable."
- A daily log of all purchases and sales of securities during the month, as well as all contributions and all withdrawals or expenses paid at the direction of the client.
- A list of all income (interest and dividend payments) received.
- A list of all cash flows into (contributions) and out of (disbursements) the trust.
- Foreign investments are shown in terms of both local and U.S. currency.
- Specially requested reports, such as aggregate brokerage commission reports, or a listing of the largest 10 transactions during the past month.

The stack of these statements for a single month to a plan sponsor with multiple investment accounts can be many inches high (unless we choose to receive it electronically).

In years past, a plan sponsor with multiple managers and multiple custodians received separate statements on each manager from that manager's particular trustee or custodian—each statement prepared under a different format—and the sponsor had to aggregate all of these statements itself to figure out its total position. How medieval that now seems! Today's plan sponsors can't fully appreciate the magnitude of this single contribution of their master trustee.

Well, if the master trustee is keeping the investment manager honest, who is keeping the master trustee honest?

Each trustee is required by law to have annual external audits, including audits of its systems. Some clients also send auditors periodically to examine their trustees. The most effective auditor, however, is the investment manager itself.

We require that the trustee send a copy of each account's monthly statement to the manager of that account, and that the manager, within two weeks of receipt, review that statement and write a letter to the trustee (with a copy to us) saying either (1) it agrees entirely with the trustee's statement, or (2) it agrees except for the following items (and then lists each variance). The trustee and manager must then get together and resolve each variance, again with a copy to the client explaining the resolution. This procedure serves to improve the accuracy of both the trustee's and manager's records. The client's task is that of monitoring the mail—to make sure each manager responds to the trustee each month, and that each item of variance is resolved.

Why do I like this process? No one knows more than the manager about his particular assets and transactions. He is aware of more nuances than any outside auditor. Also, he has a vested interest in keeping the trustee's records accurate, because he knows we are relying on the trustee's statements, not his (the manager's). Moreover, any errors in the trustee's records can affect the calculation of investment performance, perhaps the most important management information of all.

The trustee also prepares and files tax returns and government reports as necessary.

Trusteeship today is a highly capital-intensive industry—with the capital all going into systems and software to carry out its monumental information-processing function. The needed capital can run into hundreds of millions of dollars. This has narrowed the field of really first-class master trustees to perhaps not more than half a dozen worldwide.

Much of this capital investment is for the provision of management information, which we will discuss next.

Management Information

Given all the raw data that a master trustee has about every investment account, who but the master trustee is better situated to provide us with performance and portfolio composition analytics? The range of analytics desired by clients is as broad as one's imagination, and each client seems to want to look at some different kind of analytic.

What kinds of analytics are we talking about?

Performance Measurement

I always liked to do performance measurement ourselves, in-house. That provides the greatest flexibility in preparing reports, in putting together a presentation, and in doing ad hoc analyses. Moreover, when we do it ourselves, we can maintain quality control and are likely to gain a better understanding as to what all the numbers mean.

On the other hand, master trustees have all of the raw data in their computers, and they have over the years developed increasingly better and more flexible performance measurement systems—systems that a plan sponsor can hardly keep up with. Most fund sponsors expect their master trustees to provide performance measurement services, and the relative advantage of doing it in-house is waning rapidly.

Routine reports should provide the performance of each account, of client-selected groupings of accounts, and of the entire plan, and all this for the last month, 3 months, year-to-date, 1 year, any number of multiple years, and since inception—all compared with one or more benchmarks. A good trustee keeps track of some 2,000 different indexes and combinations of indexes for use as benchmarks, as requested by its various clients.

The trustee, usually working with other trustees who share information (such as, in the United States, the Trust Universe Comparison Service or TUCS), has access to industrywide statistics so the trustee can also show us how our performance has compared with other pension funds over any interval, and what our percentile ranking was.

The trustee can provide similar kinds of data on each account's alpha and beta relative to its benchmark index, as well as its volatility, and its Sharpe ratio.[2] And it is equipped to do performance attribution analyses—breaking down the performance of a portfolio to show how different segments performed, by geography, industry, or stock characteristics.

The trustee can then present this information in any number of graphic forms. Some trustees can provide performance triangles such as those we introduced in Chapter 1.

Portfolio Composition

Today's trustee can slice and dice the composition of any particular portfolio by virtually any measure one can imagine—by industry, by country, by price/earnings ratio, by market capitalization, and by innumerable other measures. And it can display these in a wide range of graphic forms.

The trustee can also provide the same analytical information about the latest month's transactions so we can see at a glance if a manager is moving into smaller stocks, or stocks with a higher P/E, or is loading up on a particular industry.

---

[2] The ratio of (a) an account's performance in excess of the T-bill rate to (b) its volatility.

This information is extremely valuable to us, the client, as we try to understand—what each of our managers is doing . . . how well diversified are they . . . what are the heaviest bets they are making (both individually and as a group) . . . and how close is our overall portfolio to its target asset allocation? In short, the master trustee can provide more information than any of us can digest.

As a client, we must then decide what information will be most meaningful for us to follow, which information will materially help us in the decisions we must make, and what information is worth the trustee's extra fees . . . and is worth our time to analyze.

Also, we can get this information electronically as well as in paper. Through the Internet or a telephone hookup, we can access essentially real-time information and analyze it any way we want with the master trustee's powerful analytic programs.

Exception Reports

The master trustee can also arrange for exception reports—such as a listing of all derivatives, or of all holdings of a certain kind that together account for more than a given percent of our plan's overall portfolio. We have even had our master trustee watch each day the use of derivatives by each of our managers and let us know if any manager ever exceeds our agreed-upon guidelines. We never expect any instances of such excesses, nor have we had any, but the monitoring has contributed to our sound sleep at night.

In the future, some master trustees will be equipped to provide even more sophisticated analyses of portfolio-wide risks.

Flexibility

The convenience afforded by having all of our plan's assets under one roof gives us, the plan sponsor, remarkable flexibility. We can do things easily that would be difficult or impossible to do without a master trustee. For example:

- If we terminate a manager, we simply have to instruct our master trustee not to accept any more transactions from the terminated manager, and then to place the account under the direction of a new manager.

- If we have a manager of foreign exchange (FX) who is authorized to hedge all foreign currency exposure that is not otherwise hedged, our trustee can provide our FX manager a daily list of the total unhedged dollar exposure of our composite account to each foreign currency.
- We can have all of our assets made available to a single securities-lending agent—the most convenient agent often being the master trustee itself.
- We can arrange for the central, aggressive management of all cash across all of our accounts in a way such as that described in Chapter 11 under the section titled "The Bank."

Many pension plans also use their master trustee for a separate, major function—keeping the records of all plan participants and serving as paying agent to all retirees. Some master trustees additionally are acquiring actuarial firms so they can service pension clients soup to nuts.

An Extension of the Plan Sponsor's Staff

It is helpful for us as a plan sponsor to think of the particular people serving our account at our master trustee as an extension of our own staff. The care, accuracy, and timeliness with which they administer our account is critical to the smooth functioning of our fund.

Great dividends accrue if we get to know these people and help them understand not only what we are doing but *why* we are doing it. Everyone can do a job better if he knows why he is doing it, and he can enjoy it more at the same time.

We have found it helpful if, when we make a change of investment manager, we send our master trustee not only a statement of the action taken but a copy of the rationale that we presented to our committee. On periodic visits to our master trustee, we have found great responsiveness of its staff if we give them a presentation explaining our overall investment strategy and how we analyze our various accounts.

In fact, many companies as they re-engineer their processes in their quest for quality, define their pension administrative processes as if their staff and master trustee were a single organization. This has led to shortening cycle times, eliminating redundant operations, improving reliability, and reducing costs.

Criteria for Selecting a Master Trustee

To do a first-class job of providing the kinds of services we have described in this chapter requires a monstrous investment in computer systems. Only an organization that can amortize this investment over an extremely large client base can afford that amount of capital investment. Hence, there may be, at most, half a dozen world-class master trustees. How should we choose among them? Unlike investment managers, master trustees have no numerical track records to help us reach our judgment.

If I were looking for a master trustee, I would put on paper our detailed requirements (a major task) and ask each of the world-class master trustees why they think they would meet those requirements best, and what they would charge for it. I would ask how much money each was reinvesting in its systems and in its professional resources, and where those investments are being made. I'd want a feel for how the master trustee might be able to add value *tomorrow*.

I would also spend much time talking with present clients of our finalists, asking them not just about their overall satisfaction with the master trustee but also their experience with the particular requirements that are important to us.

The selection of a master trustee is an arduous task, burdened with great detail. But it's a crucial decision, as our master trustee is critically important to us—every day.

In Short

A master trustee (or master custodian) not only provides a convenient and secure repository for all of our plan's asset, it also is an extremely powerful source of management information that can help us understand what our managers are doing and how well they've been doing it.

To gain the most from our master trustee, we should regard the people who manage our account at the master trustee as among the most valuable members of our immediate staff. They are!

Appendix A

The Master Trustee/ The Master Custodian

by Robert E. Mainer
Senior Vice President, The Boston Company

Functionally, it's hard to see the difference between a bank's role as a trustee or custodian. In both capacities, the bank is responsible for safeguarding the assets, processing trades, collecting income, and so on.

A trustee is the owner of the assets held in trust. Once a donor places assets into an irrevocable trust for a designated purpose (and a pension trust is a specific type of irrevocable trust), it is almost impossible for the donor to retrieve the contributed assets or to change their purpose. The named fiduciary [usually the pension committee] for a pension trust can change the trustee but not the purpose of the trust.

As custodian, a bank does not have title to the assets in its care but performs its functions as *agent* for the owner. For example, a college's board of trustees has the ultimate fiduciary responsibility for the school's endowment, but usually the trustees will hire a bank to serve as their agent in providing custody for the endowment assets. A custodian, unless specifically instructed otherwise, ordinarily has no investment authority over the assets in its care, is not authorized to vote proxies, and must look to the fiduciary owner of the assets for instructions with respect to any discretionary matter affecting the assets in its care.

Prior to the 1960s, a trustee bank usually had full discretionary responsibility for investing the plan assets held in a pension trust. In the 1960s and 1970s, plan sponsors began appointing independent investment managers, and the bank's status changed in many cases to that of *directed trustee*. A directed trustee is a trustee in all respects except that the named fiduciary has delegated investment authority to a third-party investment manager(s), and the trustee is instructed to accept directions from the investment manager(s) with respect to all investment matters.

At about the same time, because of acquisitions and start-ups, many companies found themselves with multiple pension plans for different subsidiaries, each with different benefit schedules and different trustees. Multiple trustees are both costly and inconvenient. This led to the development of the master trust.

In establishing a master trust, each of a company's several pension plans contributes its assets to a single master trust and, in exchange, receives unit interests analogous to shares in a mutual fund.[3] A master trust also can be compartmentalized, with separate commingled funds for stocks, bonds, and cash equivalents, for example. Each individual pension plan can then have its own asset allocation—its own unique mix of interests in these various asset classes as suits its particular situation.

Over time, the term *master trust* has acquired a broader definition. Today, any large pension trust with complex asset structures is apt to be called a master trust, regardless of its actual legal configuration, and the bank is referred to as master trustee. Similarly, a bank acting as custodian for a large, complex fund managed by multiple investment managers is likely to be called a *master custodian*. In this usage, the adjective master recognizes that a bank's transaction processing generates a large amount of data about a plan's assets and the events affecting them. Thus a bank can logically serve as the master source of data used by a wide variety of accounting, control, analytical, performance measurement, and other management information systems.

---

[3] In some cases, as an alternative, the participating plans are given a percentage interest in the master trust, proportional to the assets each has contributed.

Chapter 11

Bells and Whistles

Once we have established a master trustee/custodian and a well-diversified investment program, it is time to see if we can add a little value here and a little value there through special programs that may not make us rich, but which add up meaningfully over time. In this chapter we shall talk about four such ways: the bank, security lending, hedging foreign exchange, and soft dollars.

The Bank

As we have mentioned earlier, cash provides the lowest expected long-term rate of return of any asset class, and therefore we should try to minimize the amount of cash we hold at all times.

This is not easy. For example, if we have multiple investment managers, each retains a certain amount of cash in the account he manages for us—typically from 1% to 10% in our account. He is usually not trying to time the market (an effort not likely to add value), but the cash is simply "noise," his "working capital" as he buys and sells securities for us. Over the years we have found that multiple managers, as a group over time, tend to average roughly 5% cash in our accounts.

We could instruct our managers never to hold more than 1% of our portfolio in cash, but I believe this would be dysfunctional. Many managers would find such a limit difficult to live with. It would get in the way of their preferred approach to managing investments.

Furthermore, if we have a futures account, one that's kept in cash overlayed by index futures (such as a synthetic index fund or a Tactical

Asset Allocation account, see Chapter 4, page 85), that is additional cash. And in any case we have our own Checking Account,[1] our pension plan's working capital account, from which we pay benefits and we fund new investments.

Our trustee/custodian is happy to sweep cash from all of these accounts every day into its Short-Term Investment Fund (STIF), which earns short-term money market rates, but why not do something more constructive with this money? Why not start our own "Bank"?

A bank takes in money from multiple depositors, pays them a set rate of interest, and invests the money at a higher rate so it can show a profit and pay dividends to its shareholders. Our Bank can do the same:

- Take deposits from the account of every manager's account (excluding commingled funds, of course, where we don't have access to the cash). We tell our managers (the Bank's "Depositing Managers") they may not manage the cash in their account, even though we pay them for managing those assets. Our trustee/custodian sweeps all cash in their account every day into deposits in our Bank.
- Promise all of our Depositors daily interest at our trustee/custodian's STIF rate[2] (to be accrued daily and paid by our Bank at the beginning of each month).
- Make the money deposited by each account available each day for use by the manager of that account if he needs it.
- Invest the Bank's money more efficaciously.

But how should we invest the Bank's money? We can initially divide our deposits into two categories:

1. Cash that is pretty much embedded and is never expected to leave the Bank (the Bank's Embedded Asset Account), and
2. Cash that is truly working capital, cash that we may not have for long (the Bank's Working Capital Account).

---

[1] Unlike many personal checking accounts, the balances in this Checking Account are always kept invested at money market interest rates.
[2] The rate of interest that our trustee/custodian's Short-Term Investment Fund is paying depositors.

Embedded Assets Account

This includes whatever percentage of our Depositing Managers' assets we believe is truly embedded in cash (typically an average of 5% of their aggregate assets). This is cash we are likely to hold permanently and which we should therefore invest in a long-term program, perhaps a common stock account.

Another possibility is to overlay the cash in the Bank's Embedded Assets Account with index futures (as with a synthetic index fund or a Tactical Asset Allocation account), where the cash will be available for some unpredictable rainy day. In more than 15 years of running such a Bank, we have never experienced a day rainy enough that we had to call on any of this rainy-day cash, but it does give us a warm fuzzy feeling of comfort.

Funny thing about an account like this. We are talking about the possibility of the Bank's Embedded Assets Account being invested in cash overlaid by futures, so that account's cash would be deposited right back into the Bank. This time, however, it ought to go into the Bank's Working Capital Account, and we should be careful not to double-count those assets.

Working Capital Account

This encompasses all other cash in the Bank. But there is no need to put it all in very short-term securities like our trustee-custodian's STIF. Why not hire a capable but aggressive cash manager, who is authorized to buy liquid fixed income instruments with maturities up to 2½ years provided his *average* maturity is not longer than one year?

It is extremely unlikely that all of the Bank's cash will be withdrawn at once. By allowing our cash manager to invest up to 2½ years maturity, he can earn money (in a positive yield-curve environment) by "riding down the yield curve" (see Chapter 4, pages 78–79). Typically, two-year paper (fixed-income securities with a maturity of two years) has a materially higher interest rate than 90-day paper, an initial advantage for our Bank. Because by definition such paper has a declining maturity over time, its interest-rate normally declines with its maturity, which means our manager can sell it at some later date and realize a capital gain.

Our cash manager can be more aggressive if we communicate regularly with him about large withdrawals we know are coming up in the next 10 days or the coming month. Even so, once in a great while we will have some surprisingly large withdrawals, and it may be necessary for the manager to sell a Certificate of Deposit at a disadvantageous price. Tough! The extra transaction cost will be offset many times over by the additional money he can earn by being aggressive as we have suggested.

Figure 11.1 is intended to show how the Bank works.

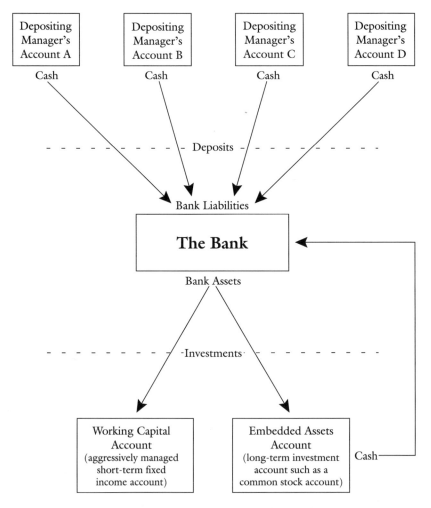

Figure 11.1   How the Bank Works.

Owner's Equity

Like any bank, our Bank has assets (its investments), liabilities (its deposits), and the difference, which is known as *owner's equity*. Every bank is in business to earn a profit for its owners, and so is our Bank. Every month our Bank will earn more money (or less) from its investments than it must pay out in interest to its depositors, with the difference reflected on the Bank's balance sheet as owner's equity.

It is possible, in fact, that our Bank might lose money in its first year and end up with a negative owner's equity. That is likely to happen in a year where we invest the Embedded Assets Account in common stocks, and the stock market heads sharply downhill. But again, it's a long-term game. We can run for a while with a negative owner's equity, always with the possibility, if necessary, that we could prop it up by transferring some assets into the Bank from one of our long-term investment accounts—a capital infusion. I doubt if this would be necessary, but at least it's possible.

Over time we are likely to build up retained earnings in our owner's equity, and we should periodically declare a dividend. The dividend is paid from the Bank's owner's equity to our Checking Account, which is one of the Depositors in the Bank. Hence the cash doesn't leave the Bank. But our Checking Account will now need less money from our other accounts in order to pay benefits or to fund new investments.

Besides managing dividends, we must also manage the amount of money in the Bank's Embedded Assets Account. We should periodically review the total assets of managers' accounts that are depositors in our Bank, and compare 5% of those assets (if that's the percentage we decide on) with the current market value of the Bank's Embedded Assets Account. Some significant differences may occur over time, either because the Embedded Assets Account is earning a higher or lower rate of return than the average rate of return that must be paid to Depositing Managers' accounts, or because we added to or withdrew money from the Depositing Managers' accounts. In any case, if the difference is material, we should rebalance by transferring assets between the Bank's Working Capital Account and its Embedded Assets Account.

Isn't it possible that at some point the aggregate amount of cash in the Depositing Managers' accounts may drop below our assumed 5%—say, to 3%? That means that the Depositing Managers' accounts would, in effect, be leveraged by 2%. Horrors! It is probably an ephemeral occurrence, in which case I would ignore it. On the other hand, if that now seems to be the norm for our Depositing Managers' accounts, we should change our algorithm to 3% (instead of 5%).

The Bottom Line

So what do we get out of all this complexity? Well, let's assume over the long term with 5% of our depositing accounts we can earn 5%/year more on our Embedded Assets Account than on STIF. That would add 0.25% (5% times 5%) to our annual compounded return on those depositing accounts. If the Depositing Managers should earn 10%/year on their accounts, then the difference of that 0.25% over 10 years *for each $1 million in the Depositing Managers' accounts* would be $60,000.[3] That's worth having.

And if, with our Working Capital Account, our aggressive cash manager can average 0.50% more per year than STIF (say, 6% vs. 5.50%), the difference over 10 years *for each $1 million in our Working Capital Account,* would be $83,000.[4] Again, we'll take it.

Securities Lending

The stocks and bonds held by our trustee/custodian have a value in addition to their market value. There are people who will pay us a rental fee for lending them some of those securities. The rental fee isn't much, but if we can do it with essentially no risk, why not do it? Those extra dollars add up over time.

Who would pay us to borrow our stocks and bonds? Dealers who make a market in stocks and happen to have sold more than they have bought at some point. Also, other investors who want to sell a stock short. For example, if someone wants to invest in an arbitrage by buying Stock A and selling Stock B, he can only do that by first borrowing Stock B. When he borrows Stock B from us, he must pay us the dividend as soon as he gets it, but he does get the privilege of voting the proxy.

---

[3] $(1.1025^{10} - 1.10^{10}) \times \$1,000,000 = \$59,555.$

[4] $(1.06^{10} - 1.055^{10}) \times \$1,000,000 = \$82,703.$

What's the Risk?

Isn't it risky to lend Stock B? Not really, because at the same time we lend Stock B to the borrower, he must give us collateral consisting either of cash or of high-quality short-term paper like T-bills that have a value of 102% of the current market value of Stock B (105% if we're lending a non-U.S. stock). And every day the collateral gets "marked to market." If the stock rises in price, the borrower must give us more collateral. If the stock declines in price, he may ask for some of his collateral back.

We can recall Stock B at any time on three days' notice, and if the borrower doesn't return it we have the right to buy him in—to buy Stock B on the market and return any excess collateral to the borrower. If the price of Stock B had just gone up and the collateral isn't sufficient for us to buy the stock, the borrower owes us the difference. Our risk is if (1) the stock price suddenly rises *and* (2) the borrower goes bankrupt. Since the borrower is usually a large brokerage house with a satisfactory credit rating, this confluence of events is extremely unlikely.

What Do We Earn?

How do we get paid? We invest the cash, or we receive the interest on the T-bill we were given as collateral. Of course, the borrower has negotiated a rebate whereby we must pay most of the interest back to him. The net interest we earn on the loan may be less than an annual rate of 0.25%. Sounds like a lot of work for little return, doesn't it?

The better trustee/custodians offer a security lending service where they do all the work for a portion of our net interest (in fact, I understand it's one of their higher profit-margin services). The entire program is pretty much invisible to us, even though 10% to 20% of our assets may be out on loan at any one time. Net net, in the course of a year we may earn some 0.02% on the aggregate value of our loanable assets. You're right—it's not much. But why not take it?

More Risk for More Return

By taking a little more risk, it is possible to squeeze out a little more profit. We can hire a lending agent who will make all loans in exchange for cash collateral, and then we take responsibility for investing the cash collateral.

We hire an aggressive cash manager to invest our cash collateral, perhaps the same one who manages our Bank's Working Capital Account, although he might manage our collateral account slightly more conservatively. After a time we may find that 5% to 10% of our portfolio is always loaned out, and the collateral for that portion is essentially embedded. If our collateral manager understands this, he can take longer maturities on this money and earn higher interest rates than the rates (usually based on overnight interest rates) assumed by our lending agent when he negotiates rebates with the borrower.

With any sizable portfolio, I find it hard to justify *not* hiring a lending agent, and the most convenient (although not always the most remunerative) is usually our own trustee/custodian.

Hedging Foreign Exchange

Hedging forward exchange means buying forward contracts on a foreign currency, such as promising to buy a million Japanese yen three months from now with a fixed number of dollars, so we can insulate our Japanese securities investments from the ups and downs of the dollar value of the yen. Hedging can also be accomplished with futures or options, but most often it is executed with forwards.

Assuming we invest part of our portfolio abroad, *should we hedge all of our foreign exchange risk?* After all, our obligations are in U.S. dollars. Moreover, overseas stock markets tend to be more volatile than the U.S. stock market, even in the developed countries. There is a cost to hedging, of course—think of it as an insurance premium. But for currencies of the developed countries of the world, the average cost of hedging is very small, some say perhaps 15 basis points (or 0.15%) per year.

An obvious answer is: Let's hedge if we think the dollar is going to strengthen relative to other currencies, and go unhedged if we think the dollar will weaken. I don't believe investment committees or investment staffs (or most investment managers) are any better at predicting the direction of the dollar than they are at predicting the direction of the stock market or interest rates.

If we're not going to try timing the market, the key question is: Does hedging reduce the volatility of our overall portfolio? The answer, as with so many things: it depends.

First off, on an annual basis, foreign exchange fluctuations have roughly a zero correlation with the stock and bond markets. But there is evidence that over longer time frames—two to five years—the correlation may actually turn negative. So the first step in answering our question is whether we are concerned about volatility over one year or over longer time frames. A negative correlation over longer time frames indicates that going unhedged should actually reduce volatility.

Well, let's say we are concerned about *annual* volatility. The addition of an asset class with zero correlation tends to reduce overall portfolio volatility. But with foreign exchange, it is not an *additional* asset class. We are not putting additional assets into that asset class. Foreign exchange fluctuations are an attribute of an *existing* asset class, and any hedging we do is an overlay on that asset class.

Therefore, in theory, any exposure to foreign exchange fluctuations tends to *increase* the annual volatility of our aggregate portfolio. But, depending on the nature of our portfolio, the impact on annual portfolio volatility is negligible—certainly not worth the insurance premiums—if our exposure to foreign exchange is less than 20% to 30% of our portfolio. For exposures beyond that, the impact on portfolio volatility is said to rise by increasing magnitudes. Therefore, if 20% to 30% of our portfolio is invested outside the United States, we might think about hedging 50% or more of our exposure.

Hedging is viable with respect to currencies of the developed countries and is becoming increasingly viable (although still very expensive) relative to currencies of some of the emerging markets.

Active Hedging

Managing foreign exchange actively is a different kind of activity from managing a stock portfolio. There is more serial correlation in foreign exchange prices than in stock prices. That means, if the price of a currency goes up on day 1, there is a slightly higher than 50/50 probability that it will go up also on day 2—not as close an approximation to random walk[5] as with stock prices. As a result, many of the most successful foreign exchange managers believe that technical information (price movement) is

---

[5] *Random walk* means there is no information in the movement of prices today, this week, or this year that will help us predict the movement of prices tomorrow, next week, or next year.

more important than fundamental information (relative inflation rates, or purchasing price parity[6]).

In short, managing foreign exchange is a different art. Many common stock managers don't believe they are good at it and sensibly don't try to make money on foreign exchange, although they might hedge from time to time as insurance.

It is possible, although not easy, to find managers that specialize in foreign exchange *and* are good at it. By good, I mean they can make money in foreign exchange more often than they lose, and make money over the long term.

Provided we can gain confidence that we have found a good foreign exchange (FX) manager, I prefer an active hedging program. Our FX manager can do it in a way that is invisible to our stock and bond managers. We can let all of our stock and bond managers hedge as they think best (I hate to put constraints on good managers), but inevitably there will be a vast majority of our FX exposure that is not hedged.

A good trustee/custodian can (1) aggregate and summarize our unhedged exposure every day electronically and make it available to our FX manager, and (2) alert us if ever our FX manager should exceed his limit, which is to hedge currencies *up to but not beyond* our actual unhedged exposure to each currency.

With respect to any particular currency, our FX manager can then choose to hedge or not, depending on whether he thinks the currency will rise or fall in price. He can hedge any portion of our unhedged exposure to each currency—none of it, part of it, or all of it. And, if we consider our natural position should be *un*hedged, we will judge our FX manager on whether or not he makes money for us.

Our FX manager will lose money for us if he buys a 90-day forward contract to buy yen with dollars at a certain price, and if at the end of those 90 days the price of the yen has declined. We must cough up the difference in price, which means we must advance money to our FX manager to cover his losses.

On the other hand, our FX manager will make money if the price of the yen has increased. We can pocket the difference in price.

Administratively, we can put a small, set amount of money into the account of our FX manager at the beginning of a month to cover possible losses. If he loses more than that during the month, we must stand ready

---

[6] *Purchasing power parity* refers to the relative price that consumers have to pay for the same package of goods and services in two different countries.

to replenish his account immediately out of our Checking Account. At the end of the month, if there is less money in the account than at the beginning, we will replenish it up to the set amount. If there is more money than at the beginning, we will transfer the excess to our Checking Account.

Some months our FX manager will lose money, and in other months he will earn money. There will even be years when our FX manager will lose money. But if he is good, he should make money most years. If our FX manager is good, active hedging should both add to the total return of our aggregate portfolio and reduce annual volatility.

The fee schedule for an active FX manager may appropriately consist of a small fixed fee and a percentage of his net profits over time—provided the performance fee includes a high-water mark (see page 115).

This would apply if we consider our base position *unhedged*. But the same approach can be adapted if we consider our base position either 100% hedged or 50% hedged. It would simply be a matter of redefining the term "net profits" for purposes of calculating the FX manager's performance fee.[7]

FX as a Separate Asset Class

If our FX manager is good and we limit him to hedging our unhedged FX exposure, we are missing a good opportunity by not making the most of his talents.

For example, our manager may believe the dollar price of the Japanese yen will increase (meaning the yen will weaken). But we don't have any unhedged Japanese assets, so our manager is not permitted to buy a forward contract on the yen. And he may never *sell* forward contracts when he believes the dollar price of the yen is going to decline. Another possibility: he may believe the yen is going to weaken relative to the euro, but he is unsure whether either is going to change value relative to the U.S. dollar. It would be outside of our hedging guideline for him to cross hedge—to buy a forward contract on yen denominated in euros. In such instances, we are unable to take advantage of his insights.

---

[7] If we considered our base position to be 50% hedged, then we would expect our FX manager to hedge exactly 50% of our unhedged FX exposure and to deviate from that in one direction or the other only when he saw an opportunity to make money (or avoid losing money). The definition of his net profits would then become the difference between (a) the money he made or lost through his FX transactions and (b) the money he would have made or lost if he had always been 50% hedged.

As with any manager, if we are confident he is good, why shackle him with unnecessary constraints? Instead of limiting him to our unhedged exposure, why not tell him that—without any knowledge of our unhedged exposure—he may go long or short any currency but may not incur greater gross exposure (the sum of all long and short contracts) than $X million, nor any greater net exposure (the difference between long and short contracts) than $Y million. If we are right about the FX manager being outstanding, such flexibility should increase both the consistency of his earning money for us and the amount that he earns for us long term.

Well, wouldn't such an overlay program add to the volatility of our aggregate portfolio? Our experience was that it did *not* add to our overall volatility. Our managed FX results therefore must have had a slightly negative correlation with the volatility of the rest of our portfolio.

Soft Dollars

Soft dollars refer to the fact that brokerage commissions are typically higher than necessary to cover transaction costs, so brokers offer free services or rebates as a come-on to use their brokerage services. I will handle this subject in two parts—philosophical considerations and pragmatic considerations.

Philosophical Considerations

Let me say up front, I don't like soft dollars, even though the Securities and Exchange Commission (the SEC) has generally said they are legal. The very name *soft dollars* suggests something is under the table, and I think there are aspects about soft dollars that sustain that impression. Brokers have long offered their customers free research and related services for doing business with them, the more business, the more services. Brokers even price many of their services in soft dollars—the dollar amount of commissions it will take to acquire a certain service.

I am for unbundling—charging hard dollars for transactions, for research, and for every other service individually. Why?

- Whenever we buy something, we should make a cost/benefit judgment. Is that service worth the price? When we get a freebie thrown in, we don't tend to make that judgment, certainly not in the hard-headed way we would if we were buying it for hard dollars. I suspect a lot of brokerage customers are getting things that aren't worth to them their hard-dollar value.

- When investment managers receive research or other services for soft dollars, those are *their clients'* soft dollars! Those are things the investment manager should be buying out of his own pocket as part of his cost of doing business. Granted, if the investment manager had to buy all those services with hard dollars, he might have to raise his management fees to clients—but perhaps by less than he would save in transaction costs, because he would buy only those services he deemed worth the hard dollars.
- There is an inherent conflict of interest in soft dollars.

At the very least, we should ask our investment manager each year what services he bought with soft dollars, and what dollar value and percentage of our transaction costs he used to pay for those services.[8] Such a sunlight approach may cause the manager to think before acquiring a service that wouldn't look good when included on such a list.

Large fund sponsors are aware of soft dollars and want a piece of them. They locate brokers who will provide special services (or simply rebates) *to the fund sponsors* for soft dollars. Consultants often garner clients with this approach, offering their consulting services in exchange for the fund sponsor directing its managers to do a certain volume of transactions through a particular broker who will pay the consultant for his services to the fund sponsor. This, too, is probably legal under ERISA, but it can raise issues of conflict of interest relative to the independence of the consultant. The Association for Investment Management and Research (AIMR), which has drafted new and fairly stringent standards for the use of soft dollars and reporting to clients, advises: "Plan sponsors should avoid soft dollar conflicts of interest by hiring only consultants with no financial arrangements with brokerage firms."

Typically, an investment manager will be willing to apply 20% to 30% of commission dollars for our account to one or more brokers who are providing services (or rebates) to us.

---

[8] See the generic annual questionnaire for all of a sponsor's investment managers, questions 23–27 in Appendix A at the end of Chapter 6 (pages 146–147).

All too often, we may smile about getting a service for free. I'm not sure it's really free. We may request the manager to direct brokerage dollars to one or more particular brokers on a best-execution basis, but the direction still serves to remove some of the responsibility from the manager. Directed brokers are not usually ones who can provide the best execution, and it is possible that we—thinking we are getting something for free— may actually be paying incrementally more total transaction costs than the value of the service we are getting. At the very least, soft dollars reduce the need for us to make a hard-headed cost/benefit evaluation of the service we are receiving.

Moreover, directed brokerage sometimes allows the client to buy services his committee's approved budget might not otherwise permit. The committee's lack of funding for the service may be short-sighted, but a soft-dollar subterfuge should not be the solution. And if the service were one that would otherwise be paid for *by the plan sponsor* instead of out of plan assets, then the possibility arises of a Prohibited Transaction under ERISA.

If a client is going to direct brokerage, I think he should always have the broker rebate cash directly to the trust fund instead of accepting a "free service." A rebate is clean, can't be diverted for inappropriate uses, and both the rebate and the hard-dollar expenditure for services show up on the financial statements sent to the auditors.

Better yet, I like to find a list of about a dozen brokers who are willing to provide discount brokerage, usually at 2¢ a share or less, for any transaction in which our fund is involved, no matter how small the participation of our fund in the overall transaction. We then send that list to our managers, encouraging (but not directing) them to use those brokers whenever the total transaction costs are not expected to be higher. A commission of 2¢ a share is generally lower than regular commissions net of the rebate we can receive through soft dollars. But I don't like to *direct* managers to use these brokers. That removes some of their fiduciary responsibility to do the best thing. Moreover, I don't like to interfere with what managers think are the best ways of doing things.

Philosophical Rebuttal

Many people in the investment community disagree with me, and they have a point. If all transactions were priced on the basis of transaction costs alone, and all services were priced only in hard dollars, far less investment research would get done. Large investment managers, who already do most of their research internally, would do more of it internally, and small managers would not be able to afford to buy brokerage research. Pressure would grow for small managers either to merge with large managers or to disappear. Less research would be done on small companies than is done today.

The argument goes on that better quality research makes for better decision making. A reduced amount of research and a smaller number of investment managers resulting from the elimination of soft dollars would lower the market's efficiency and increase its volatility.

Obviously, under the present system, large managers are subsidizing small managers, and many people think that's entirely OK. I'm one who distrusts interference with the laws of economics, and such subsidies do just that. I'm not sure what all the results would be if soft dollars were ended, but I believe in time the investment community would become more efficient for all.

Pragmatic Considerations

The fact of the matter is that most managers do not like to use discount brokers. They depend on their own use of soft dollars, and the use of discount brokers complicates their life.

One manager, for example, refuses to do any trades at 2¢/share or for anything more or less than that manager's standard commission rate. But the manager will accept directed commissions for up to 20% of an account's brokerage dollars. Should we say we don't like soft dollars and thumb our nose at potential "commission recapture" for our trust fund? Since there is no legal problem with using soft dollars in this way, there seems to me no sense in passing them up.

We can't deal with the system as we would like it to be but must deal with it as it is. For us, then, that means encouraging managers to use discount brokers at 2¢ a share or less wherever it makes sense for them to do so, and to encourage soft-dollar commission recapture where that makes most sense.

In 1997, an ERISA Advisory Committee went so far as to say, ". . . if a plan sponsor does not direct [brokerage commissions], then their plan may be subsidizing every other pension plan's research. . . . A properly structured commission recapture program can assist investment managers reduce plan costs, and help plan sponsors fulfill their fiduciary responsibilities."

The Committee's report went on to say that managers should be required to give each client full disclosure of all trades for that client involving soft dollars. In addition, investment managers should be required to provide a description of their policies involving soft dollars.

In the final analysis, net of everything, are our managers' *total transaction costs* as low as they should be? *Net total transaction costs* are what count, and of course, they include not only commissions but also market impact costs, which can be far larger.

Market impact costs are any extra price we must pay (or give up) in order to induce another party to buy from (or sell to) us. For example, a market maker in a stock will offer to buy that stock at a "bid" price or to sell it at an "offer" price. His two prices are often 12.5¢ apart. Sometimes, if we have a large block of stock that we are eager to sell, we may have to reduce our offer price by a full dollar to coax enough investors to buy it all. There is no agreement as to how to measure market impact costs. Simplistically, market impact costs might be thought of as the difference between our transaction price for a stock and the average price at which that stock traded throughout that same day.

Analyses done by Abel Noser, Elkins McSherry, and others can enable us to look at the total transaction costs of each manager and those of each broker he used, and then to ask our manager informed questions.

In Short

Once we have decided on our asset allocation and hired the managers for each asset class, we can—with a bit of creative effort—arrange a variety of programs that will add pennies to our bottom line. Since we can garner these pennies with low risk and fairly high consistency, we are missing a good thing if we don't go after them.

These pennies compound over time into money that's worth having.

Chapter 12

Information Retrieval
System (Files)

This short chapter covers the mundane but important subject of our filing system. Few functions involve more paper than pension investing, and it helps if we can find what we want when we want it. The files we should maintain include the following:

Committee Meeting Records

A file for each committee meeting (kept in chronological order) should begin with the meeting minutes. Since our committee is a legal body, minutes of committee actions should be maintained as if for a board of directors. Along with the minutes we should keep a copy of every presentation made at the meeting.

It is surprising how often we refer back to presentations made to the committee in earlier years. What specifically did we tell the committee about the parameters of this particular program? What was our rationale for that program?

To make this meeting file useful, we might keep two indexes. One is simply a chronological log of all meetings, with one line about each report made or action taken at each meeting. When did we deal with proxy voting policy? A quick scan of this log will give us the date and direct us to the file with our presentation in it.

The second index is an alphabetical list of each of our present and prior investment managers, together with the dates of meetings when action was taken involving that particular manager. When did we hire Manager X, and why? It's remarkable how often we use this index.

Contracts and Agreements

We should keep all the contracts and agreements we sign with managers or investment funds in a very accessible manner, in alphabetical order by manager. This is another file we often refer to. What are the agreed-upon terms relative to some situation? What terms for a new contract might we plagiarize from an old one?

In each manager's file it helps to keep *prior* contracts in case a question should arise about a situation that occurred before the date of the current agreement.

Besides being excellent reference material for ourselves and any new staff person or consultant who joins our team, these files of meeting records and contracts and agreements are critical when the plan sponsor is "lucky" enough to have a fiduciary review, such as the Department of Labor carries out from time to time.

Permanent Files on Each Manager

We should keep a permanent file on each manager. It should contain, if nothing else, the information we leaned on to support the hiring of that manager, together with another copy of the presentation material we also included in the committee meeting file.

This Hiring File, which we should establish as soon as we hire a manager, is our paper trail if anyone should ever challenge the prudence of our hiring a particular manager. Prudence is an a priori matter—what due-diligence did we do *before* we hired the manager, not what happened afterwards.

In one of the few legal suits on this subject, the 1991 Department of Labor suit against a pension plan *(Martin vs. Tower)* for negligence in the selection and monitoring of an investment manager, part of the settlement stated: "The process by which such candidates are identified shall be documented."

In this permanent "Hiring File" we also include the infrequent additional special documents that we might want to refer to some years from now.

Financial Reports

We actually need to keep *two* files of periodic financial reports on each manager—one for reports from the trustee/custodian, and one for reports from the manager. The trustee/custodian's reports, of course, are our official data that serve as the source for our performance measurement calculations.

Each month or quarter, every manager sends us a financial report, usually showing rate of return, the composition of the portfolio, transactions, and sometimes special analyses. This report usually duplicates what we receive from our trustee/custodian, but it is helpful to retain this report for the benefit of the manager's quarterly commentary, and also in case questions should arise. Manager reports also let us see if we and the manager are deriving the same performance numbers for his account.

Quarterly reports from the managers of our illiquid investments—such as real estate or venture capital—are even more important to retain. Our trustee/custodian's quarterly reports contain each venture's valuation as of the *prior* quarter end. The venture manager's valuation arrives one to three months after the end of the quarter it is reporting on, sometimes later still, and the trustee/custodian's prior quarter-end report needs to be revised to reflect the new valuation.

Copies of trust reports and reports from investment managers should be retained for the greater of seven years or until released by the plan's tax adviser subsequent to review by the Internal Revenue Service. A plan's tax adviser sometimes recommends retention even longer if there are any outstanding questions with the Department of Labor or the Pension Benefits Guarantee Corporation (PBGC).

Current Correspondence File

The current file of correspondence with our managers is one that should be kept current or it will get too fat and unwieldy. We should retain the current and prior year's correspondence and destroy correspondence from years before that.

Manager Notebook

For frequent, convenient reference, we find it helpful to keep a file—I prefer a notebook—containing all *current relevant* information about our managers (see Chapter 6). Specifically, for each manager:

- The manager's latest questionnaire response, with our marginal notations on it.
- Notes from meetings with the manager during the past year.
- A performance triangle of the manager's performance (two or more triangles if we like to compare the manager's results with two or more benchmarks).
- The manager's latest year-end portfolio composition analysis, together with a "motion picture" of his portfolio composition over time.
- Our latest written evaluation of that manager.

Money Manager Files

We meet a large number of managers over time whom we do not hire, but we should keep reference material on those meetings in what we call Money Manager Files. We might consider keeping five alphabetized files:

U.S. common stock managers

Non-U.S. common stock managers

Fixed income managers

Real estate managers

Alternative asset managers (everything else)

These files would be monstrous and not very user-friendly if we kept all of the presentation materials given to us. But if we remove the covers and keep only those pages with substance that we might want to refer to some day, we will keep the file manageable. These pages often contain marginal notes we made during the meeting, and on the first page we always mark the date of the meeting and the names of all who attended.

In Short

Over time we accumulate a wealth of information. We need some of it to meet fiduciary audits. We can make great use of much of it as a living library.

Only if we keep this information in a well-organized, readily retrievable way can we realize its true wealth.

Chapter 13

Keeping Score III: Liabilities

This chapter applies only to defined *benefit* pension plans. Because assets of a defined *contribution* pension plan (such as a 401(k) plan) belong beneficially to its respective plan participants, its assets and liabilities are by definition equal. An endowment fund has no obligations other than amounts the sponsor intends to withdraw; this subject is covered separately in Chapter 17 on endowment funds.

A defined benefit pension plan has very concrete liabilities—the promises the plan has made to its plan participants—*benefit obligations,* we call them. But how do we value those liabilities? If we promise to pay someone $1,000 ten years from now, what is our liability today? Certainly not $1,000. We could put a lesser amount in the bank today, and that would grow into the $1,000 we need ten years from now. That lesser amount, realistically, is our liability today. The trouble is, reasonable people can't agree on the dollar amount of that liability today.

Obviously, we want to have more assets than liabilities at any given time. But if someone tells us the ratio of the plan's assets to its liabilities, we can in good faith look him quizzically in the eye and say, "What do you mean by *liabilities?*"

Measuring a Pension Liability

The problem is tougher yet when the promise is for $X a month for the rest of your life. The *present value* of that pension obligation to you depends on how long you live. Actuaries are the mathematicians who deal with this problem, and the best they can do is to weight the $X for each future month by the probability that you will be alive to receive it. If you were the only participant in the plan, there would be great uncertainty about this. But if a pension plan has several thousand participants, an actuary can predict the probabilities within a pretty narrow margin of error, thanks to the law of large numbers.

The actuary must then bring these future probability-weighted payments back to a present value. That is, he must discount each future payment by an expected rate of return. If a reasonable rate of return were 7%, then how much money would the plan need to invest today at 7% interest to exactly equal all of its payments in the future? With modern computers, that's easy to figure.

What's not easy to figure is what discount rate[1] to use. Should we assume a discount rate equal to prevailing long-term interest rates on high-grade corporate bonds? Some would say that's unduly conservative if we are investing plan assets mainly in common stocks, because over the very long term, common stocks have always earned a higher return than bonds. And the higher the discount rate, the lower the present value of the liabilities.[2] (And vice versa.)

Others would argue that we should use whatever discount rates insurance companies are currently using to sell annuities—a "market" discount rate assuming we were to turn our pension liabilities over to an insurance company. This is an extremely low discount rate, as insurance companies invest conservatively, and they not only provide for their meaningful expenses, but they also assume that when their current bonds mature, the interest rates on the bond proceeds that they must reinvest will be much lower than at present. Their assumptions lead to a very high present value of liabilities.

What interest rate is right to assume? It depends. The Financial Accounting Standards Board (FASB), which specifies how our company must account for our pension plan in the footnotes of its annual report to shareholders, assumes our pension plan will be a going concern and mandates

---

[1] The interest rate that is assumed for purposes of calculating present value.

[2] The present value of liabilities declines as the discount rate is increased, because the higher the interest rate, the less money we need now to provide for a given payment any time in the future.

the use of a prevailing interest rate. The SEC says that means an interest rate no higher than that on high-grade corporate bonds.

The Pension Benefit Guaranty Corporation (PBGC), an arm of the U.S. government that insures corporate pension plans in case they terminate without enough assets to cover their liabilities, takes a much more conservative approach. The PBGC mandates the use of a discount rate that is much closer to that which insurance companies are currently using to price annuities. After all, the PBGC is an insurance company.

Either way, as interest rates change from year to year—as they inevitably do—the present value of our plan's liability for any single existing *retiree* can change quite substantially. And the percentage change in our plan's liabilities for *active* plan participants will probably be greater still.

Twenty-five years ago, before FASB had spoken on the subject, actuaries tended to adopt a given discount rate and assume that rate year after year so a plan didn't show great volatility in its liabilities from year to year. While reasonable people can argue about what an appropriate discount rate should be, I personally believe that the discount rate should be tied in some way to prevailing rates, because future investment expectations *do* fluctuate from year to year, and reality, to me, means we have to reflect this fact.

Our actuary can help us select our interest rate assumption for FAS purposes. He can tell us what other companies are doing and what makes sense to him. But ultimately, our company must decide for itself.

Pension Liabilities for Active Employees

Our discussion has been very simplistic so far, as we have talked mainly about liabilities for existing retirees. The matter gets much more complicated for active employees, especially for a plan that bases pension benefits on "final average salary"—such as one's average salary over the three years prior to retirement.

Think about a typical pension formula—say, 1.5% of final average salary for each year of service with the plan sponsor. Sounds simple. But the math gets very complex. Each year the pension benefit that I accrue goes up by 1.5% of "final average salary" *plus* the percentage increase in my "final average salary" over what my "final average salary" was a year ago. If my salary goes up by an average of 4% per year over my 35-year career, the pension benefit I will be due at age 65 goes up somewhat exponentially over my 35 years. That increase is greatly amplified by the present value calculation of

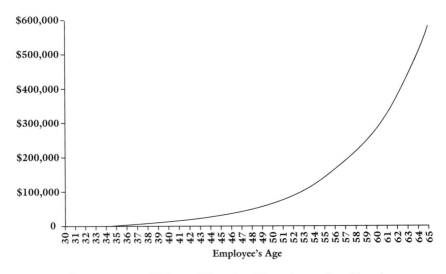

Figure 13.1   Present Value of Pension Promises of an Employee Earning $30,000 at Age 30.[3] (Courtesy of Towers Perrin.)

the pension benefit. Whatever pension benefit I accrue by age 35 has 30 more years to be discounted than the pension benefit I accrue by age 65.[4]

Assuming I join the plan sponsor at age 30 and retire at age 65, look at how *the present value* of my cumulative accrued pension grows over those 35 years:

Figure 13.1 shows that the present value of the pension I have accrued by age 45 amounts to only some $26,000. It grows to some $130,000 by age 55. Then it grows at an astonishing rate during my last few years, to some $568,000 by age 65! If I leave my employer at age 45, or if the employer should terminate the plan when I am 45, my pension will be worth very little.

This fact has major implications for the design of pension plans, which we shall deal with briefly in Chapter 16, but it creates a major challenge in valuing a plan's liabilities for an active employee.

Should we value the plan's liability for that active employee on the assumption that the employee will earn no future benefits? (As unlikely as it

---

[3] Assuming a 4% annual salary increase and 7% discount rate.

[4] "More years to be discounted" means the pension plan has 30 more years to earn investment returns on money it invests when I am age 35 than on money it invests when I am age 65.

may be, the company sponsoring the plan can always freeze the plan—discontinue crediting benefits for future service.) Or should we take a going-concern approach? That way, we would assume an average annual increase in the employee's salary, weight each future year's accrual by the probability that he will not have resigned by that year, calculate the resulting pension he will have accrued by retirement age, then calculate a percentage of that pension equal to his years of service to date divided by the years of service he will have by the time he reaches retirement age.

Sounds complicated? Well, that's a simplistic view of the calculation required by the FASB, although the explanation does spell out the principle.

Financial Accounting Standard 132 (FAS 132) requires a company to report its going-concern liability—which it calls projected benefit obligation (PBO). FAS 132 will not explicitly consider a plan underfunded, however, unless its assets fall below its *accumulated* benefit obligation (ABO)—which is something of a no-future-benefits liability.

Which of these two measures should we focus on? From a practical standpoint, assuming the pension plan could earn an investment return equal to its discount rate, a plan sponsor would, in theory, need essentially no more assets than its ABO at any time it happens to stop crediting benefits for future service. So if the discount rate is reasonably conservative, why should we want any more assets? (Of course, the PBGC wouldn't agree that the discount rate is reasonably conservative!) If we should discontinue future benefits while we have what seems like excess assets, we would not know whether we *really* had excess assets until either (1) the last plan participant had received his last pension payment, a couple of generations in the future, or (2) we bought an annuity from an insurance company (at very high cost) for all remaining pension promises (and then the obligation would be that of the insurance company).

Afterwards, if excess assets really remain, the plan sponsor can redeem them after paying a redemption tax *plus* corporate income tax—and even the plan sponsor's right to that net redemption is sometimes called into question by legislators. The legislators' question: Should excess assets belong to the plan sponsor or to the plan participants? The answer seems perfectly clear to me. Because the plan sponsor incurred the risk of having to contribute more to the pension plan if investment returns turned sour, any excess assets should belong to the plan sponsor. Somehow, not everyone sees the matter as I do.

Back to the question of whether we should focus on ABO or PBO, we must recognize that nearly all pension plans are going concerns. We must also recognize that PBO is (and must necessarily be) an arbitrary going-concern calculation—a measure that may be 50% or more higher than ABO for a plan sponsor with few retirees and a young work force, or perhaps only 10% higher for a plan sponsor with a lot more retirees than active employees.

In any case, a plan with assets equal to only 100% of ABO has no room for disappointing investment returns. The plan could become dramatically underfunded if a declining stock market occurred at the same time interest rates plummeted, causing the present value of plan liabilities to skyrocket.

That same scenario could well lead to underfunding even if plan assets started out equal to PBO. Hence, a plan sponsor must recognize that unless plan assets exceed PBO by a large magnitude, the plan is likely at some time to become underfunded—and plan sponsors hate to report to employees and investors that their plan is underfunded. But plan sponsors (and employees) should recognize that occasional underfunding is likely to occur at some point, and unless the underfunding is dramatic, it should not be a source of worry to the plan sponsor or the employees. Somewhat increased contributions by the plan sponsor, plus the natural tendency of markets to correct themselves, should bring the plan out of underfunding before very long.

Pension Expense and Pension Contributions

For any given year, pension *expense* and pension *contributions* can be two very different amounts.

The FASB has spelled out in FAS 87 and FAS 132 how plan sponsors should report pension expense each year for purposes of corporate profit and loss. On average over the long term, this calculation is targeted at maintaining pension assets at roughly the PBO level. This means that, generally, if pension assets materially exceed PBO, a plan sponsor must recognize "pension income" instead of "pension expense" for the year. Yet at no time can plan sponsors make a *negative contribution* (a withdrawal) from their pension plan even though their pension *expense* may be negative.

FAS 87 requires use of the "projected unit credit" actuarial method to calculate annual pension *expense*. Generically, the projected unit credit method is also most widely used to calculate annual pension *contributions*. But the particular way that FAS 87 requires the method to be applied is not acceptable under Department of Labor and IRS regulations, so pension plans are forced to contend with different calculations of pension expense and contributions.

Actually, plan sponsors can choose from a wide range of methods for calculating their annual contributions.

In theory, what kind of a method would make sense? The most simplistic target would be to maintain assets at ABO, so let's devise a method to accomplish that. Assuming that at some time in the next 1,000 years the plan will be terminated, any assets above ABO would be . . . excess. Therefore, let's make a contribution each year in whatever amount is necessary to bring plan assets up to ABO, and let's make no contribution whenever plan assets exceed ABO.

Theoretically, not a bad method—except for two major shortcomings. First, annual contributions as a percentage of payroll will tend to rise over the years if the average age and years of service of the work force should increase. At some point, however, the average age and years of service in any organization tend to stabilize.

Second—and far more serious—the plan sponsor would incur phenomenal volatility in its year-to-year contributions. That could be modified by introducing a smoothing technique—such as amortizing over- or underfunding over a 5- or 10-year interval, although this would still lead to more volatility in contributions than most normal actuarial methods.

One could also modify the method to target an average overfunding of 10% to 15%—just to be conservative.[5] In any case, there would still remain one very serious shortcoming: The method would not be legal in the United States and in a number of other countries. Other than that minor fact, I like the concept. It would minimize the present value of contributions, and it would avoid large overfunding.

What's wrong with large overfunding—aside from the question some day as to who owns excess assets? Overfunding brings a psychological risk that management of the plan sponsor will regard a dollar in the pension plan as worth less than a dollar in corporate cash and will find that the overfunding is burning a hole in its corporate pocket.[6] There have

---

[5] I prefer a funding target of ABO + X% rather than a target of PBO. As indicated earlier, depending on the percentage of retirees to a company's active workforce, the ratio of PBO to ABO can vary widely.

[6] Companies with labor unions sometimes find union leaders bargaining for increased pension benefits as soon as pension assets exceed liabilities to any degree.

been many instances of a plan sponsor sweetening plan benefits, with or without a concomitant employment downsizing, which the sponsor probably wouldn't have done if it had had to fork up the extra cash out of its corporate pocket. I would maintain that companies should regard a dollar in the pension plan, through the present value of its impact on future contributions, as just as valuable as a dollar in corporate cash—albeit that pension assets are obviously less accessible. Some would say pension assets are even more valuable because their investment returns, unlike returns on corporate assets, are tax free.

In fact, while defined-benefit pension assets are clearly fiduciary money and must properly be kept permanently separated from corporate assets, I believe it is appropriate in assessing the health of a company to look at the company's extended balance sheet—one that includes both pension assets and pension liabilities.

The most common method to calculate pension contributions 25 years ago was one that calculated the uniform average percent of pay a plan sponsor would theoretically have to contribute over the career of every employee, and then applied that percentage to the plan sponsor's total payroll. Actuaries called variations on this approach the "Aggregate Method" or the "Entry Age Normal Method," among others.

For any employee approaching retirement age, this method leads to a contribution much smaller than the incremental value of pension benefits that that employee accrues for that year. But for all other employees, it leads to a contribution much greater than the employee's incremental accrual. And since the average age of a plan sponsor's work force is typically between 35 and 45, it is obvious that overall, the method leads to a contribution well in excess of the work force's annual ABO accrual. The result is that plans which use such methods are targeting assets far in excess of PBO—an inappropriate target in my opinion.

The projected unit credit method, now most widely used, targets a funding level more or less equal to PBO—not far in excess of PBO.

We have intentionally treated alternative actuarial methods very simplistically—detailed only enough to convey the basic underlying principles and distinctions. Actuarial methods, in their full detail, are much more complex. They require additional assumptions such as those relating to retirement age, the integration of benefit levels with Social Security, and legislated maximum benefit levels. Also, they often incorporate the use of additional actuarial probabilities as well as various amortization devices to help smooth changes in year-to-year contributions.

If we are responsible for a plan sponsor's actuarial work, then it is important for us to understand the actuarial dynamics of our plan. Otherwise, I think it is enough if we simply understand the concepts discussed here.

Immunization

One approach some plan sponsors have pursued in order to minimize and hopefully eliminate volatility in contributions is to *immunize* plan assets. We could do this by forecasting the amount of benefits our plan must pay out each year, and then investing in whatever high-quality bonds will produce each year the same combination of interest payments and proceeds from maturities as our benefits that are payable that year. By definition, our fixed-income investments would have the same duration as the duration of our liabilities. If we can invest our assets precisely in this manner, the market value of our assets should rise or fall each year precisely in line with the present value of our benefit obligations.

The concept is superficially attractive because it should essentially eliminate risk. There are serious disadvantages, however.

First, we have no way to immunize payouts forecasted to occur beyond 30 years. We would have to invest for a maturity up to 30 years and then be dependent on our being able to reinvest maturing proceeds at interest rates at least equal to today's rates. We cannot eliminate this reinvestment risk.

Second, the approach doesn't work well for active plan participants. We simply cannot forecast the future payouts to them very accurately. Hence, the use of immunization is typically limited to a plan (or portion of a plan) where no active employees are continuing to accrue additional benefits. Immunization certainly doesn't allow for the possibility of any uplifts—inflation-related increases in pensions for existing retirees—in case the plan sponsor should ever choose to declare an uplift.

Third, and most significant in my view, is that the reduction of risk through immunization comes at a very high opportunity cost. Historically, annual investment returns on bonds over long intervals have averaged at least several percentage points a year less than returns on equity investments. A 1% per year reduction in a plan's investment return can increase the plan sponsor's *annual* contribution to the pension plan by 1% to 2% of payroll, or more, depending on the ratio of pension assets to payroll.

If a company's pension benefit obligations stem overwhelmingly from retired lives *and* if the company cannot afford the possibility of sometime having to make a surprisingly large contribution, then maybe immunization has a role. But with it goes a large opportunity cost.

Impact of Liabilities on Investment Strategy

How, then, should a plan's funding status—its ratio of assets to liabilities—affect its investment strategy?

Some say if a plan is underfunded or narrowly funded, its investment strategy should be more conservative, as a decline in the market value of assets would seriously hurt its funding status. Others say that if the plan is seriously underfunded, its investment strategy should go for broke. If investments are successful, the plan will become properly funded. If investments are not successful, the sponsor can terminate the plan and "put" the liabilities to the PBGC. Of course, the PBGC has become increasingly wise to that game.

My own view, perhaps a minority view, is that investment strategy should not usually be greatly influenced by funding level. If the sponsor views its plan as a going concern, then it should be willing to incur a reasonable volatility of assets and contributions in order to earn a high return and minimize contributions long-term.

Standard & Poor's has said: ". . . over the long-term, the credit quality of [defined benefit] pension plans approximates that of their corporate sponsors."[7] It follows that a company with a weak financial structure may not be able to afford an unexpectedly high increase in pension contributions.

Another exception to my above-stated view may be where (1) a plan is so overfunded that strong investment performance would increase overfunding to a point where the plan sponsor could never benefit from the overfunding, but where (2) large negative performance might return the plan sponsor to the point of having to resume making contributions.

One thing to keep in mind: Actuaries are not trained to be investment strategists. Actuarial disciplines are distinctly different from investment disciplines, although some consulting firms do offer both disciplines.

---

[7] Standard & Poor's *Creditwatch*, October 11, 1993.

Impact of Pension Expense on Corporate Budgets

The typical corporation adds its annual pension expense under FAS 132 to its other employee benefits and allocates total employee benefits across all company units as a percentage of payroll. I don't think this is the most helpful cost accounting. There should be no such thing as negative pension expense in cost accounting, as cost accounting should be unaffected by the pension plan's funding status.

A company's employees earn increases each year in the company's pension promises to them. These increases are the company's incremental costs for the year. For each employee, these increases, measured by PBO, are called "service cost"—and they are totally unaffected by whether the plan is overfunded or underfunded.

Therefore, I believe a company should include in the cost of employee benefits (which it allocates to every unit of the company) only its "service cost" for that year—no more, no less, even though total pension expense is likely to be materially higher or lower. The difference—plus or minus—should be an unallocated corporate expense (or credit), treated the same way as expense for the company's board of directors meetings. This additional amount is irrelevant in assessing what is the company's true cost for any particular unit of the company, and it can get in the way of good corporate decisions.

In Short

Valuing our liabilities—our pension benefit obligations—must necessarily be an arbitrary process. Their valuation relative to the market value of our assets should drive our *funding* strategy—when and how much we contribute to our pension plan. But under most circumstances, I don't think we should let funding ratios drive our *investment* strategy. While we want to invest in such a way as to limit volatility in our funding ration, overconcern about funding ratios can divert us from making the most of our investment opportunities.

Chapter 14

Governance

Who is responsible for what decisions? That's what governance means. Ultimately, the organization's board of directors is responsible for the management of a pension fund or endowment fund. But it's not practical for boards of directors to make investment decisions for those funds, so they almost always appoint a decision-making committee to take on this responsibility.

The board exercises its fiduciary responsibility in the care it takes in appointing this committee and in its oversight during the subsequent years to assure itself that its committee appointees remain appropriate. The board should exercise oversight by receiving a report on the policies and performance of the fund at least once a year.

U.S. corporate pension law, ERISA, requires that a "named fiduciary" be appointed for each pension plan. This named fiduciary is usually the committee appointed by the board of directors. The members of this named fiduciary committee are *individually* responsible for investment policy and all other decisions of that committee, which means they can be sued as individuals for any decisions that violate that fiduciary responsibility. I believe this named fiduciary concept is an appropriate way to view the responsibility of all such committees, whether for public pension funds, foreign pension funds, or endowment funds.

Standards to Meet

There are four other concepts established by ERISA that I believe should be universally applicable:

1. All decisions should be made "solely in the interest of participants and beneficiaries" and exclusively to provide benefits to them or pay reasonable administrative costs. This makes illegal any conflict of interest that should creep into an investment decision. The provision is actually a simplifying concept, because it frees committee members to focus entirely on the risk and return aspects of investment opportunities as appropriate for that pension fund and to ignore extraneous considerations.

2. The investment portfolio should be broadly diversified—"by diversifying the investments of the plan so as to minimize the risk of large losses, unless under the circumstances it is clearly prudent not to do so."

3. "The risk level of an investment does not alone make the investment *per se* prudent or *per se* imprudent. . . . An investment reasonably designed—as part of the portfolio—to further the purposes of the plan, and that is made upon appropriate consideration of the surrounding facts and circumstances, should not be deemed to be imprudent merely because the investment, standing alone, would have . . . a relatively high degree of risk."[1]

    Specifically, the prudence of any investment can only be determined by its place in the portfolio. *This was a revolutionary concept,* as the old common law held that each individual investment should be prudent of and by itself. There are a great many individual investments in pension funds and endowment funds today—such as start-up venture capital—which might not be prudent of and by themselves but which, in combination with other portfolio investments, contribute valuable strength to the overall investment program.

4. The standard of prudence is defined as "the care, skill, prudence, and diligence under the circumstances then prevailing that a prudent man acting in a like capacity *and familiar with such matters*

---

[1] Preamble to Final DOL Reg § 2550.404a-1, reprinted in *Preambles to Pension and Benefit Regulations,* 80,352 and 80,354 RIA (1992).

would use in the conduct of an enterprise of a like character and with like aims." [Italics added] This is often referred to as the "prudent expert" rule and strikes me as an appropriate standard. Everyone involved in decision making for the fund—committee members, staff members, investment managers, and consultants—should be held to this standard.

That said, I fear that the words "fiduciary" and "prudence" have all too often been *impediments* to investment performance because of the scary emotional overtones those terms arouse. Such emotions lead to a mentality such as: "It's OK to lose money on IBM stock but don't dare lose money on some little-known stock." Neither should be more or less OK than the other.

Prudence should be based on the soundness of the logic supporting the *purchase* and *retention* of that stock in the context of the whole portfolio, and on an a priori basis—not on the basis of Monday morning quarterbacking. IBM may be a wonderful company, but I would maintain that a portfolio composed entirely of the stocks of similarly wonderful companies might not be very prudent.

Another aspect of my concern is that the terms *prudence* and *fiduciary* all too often motivate decision makers to look at what other funds are doing instead of applying their own good sense of logic to their own research into portfolio management.

Fiduciary Committees

Composition

Well, who should be on this all-important fiduciary committee? A committee may consist of outside investment professionals, as is often the case with the endowment committees of large universities, or the committee may be composed of a group of senior corporate officers, as is often the case with corporate pension funds. It could even be a committee of the board of directors. I believe either an inside or outside committee, or any combination of the two, can be perfectly satisfactory. And both have the potential to be impediments to good investment results.

What does the fiduciary committee do and how should it function? The committee should set fund objectives and investment policies, establish asset allocation, and decide whom to hire and retain as investment managers.

That's a big responsibility! How can the committee do that effectively when it meets for only a relatively small number of total hours each year?

It simply can't—by itself. It must rely on a professional staff to do the research and make recommendations. (Or, in the case of a small endowment fund, the committee must rely similarly either on a subcommittee of one or two members who are experienced in portfolio management or else on an outside consultant.)

This reliance on staff is the first thing that committee members must recognize—they can't do it themselves. Their greatest responsibility is to choose the staff or consultant they will rely on. They must expect to approve most of the recommendations of staff or consultants. And if they have lost confidence in their staff or consultants, they must replace them and get ones in whom they can have confidence.

Does that mean that once the committee has a staff or consultant in whom it has confidence, it should essentially turn all decisions over to them? No, the decisions are still the committee's unless it has turned the entire responsibility over to an investment manager who is registered with the SEC as an investment adviser. And even then, the committee has responsibility for monitoring results.

Should the committee seriously consider delegating all decision making to an investment manager or consultant? This is done rarely, and "rarely" is a good thing. Why?

First, decisions on investment objectives are not readily delegated. They should be developed in the context of the needs and financial circumstances of that particular plan sponsor. How readily can the corporation meet unexpected contribution requirements? Must the fund rely only on the assets presently in the fund, or can additional contributions reasonably be raised? How much does a university rely on the annual income it receives from its endowment fund?

Second, few investment managers are well equipped to take overall responsibility for a pension fund or endowment fund. Many investment managers are highly experienced in investing in stocks and bonds, but not in the full spectrum of investment opportunities that the fund should be considering.

This is the potential danger of having investment professionals as committee members. In many cases they contribute valuable experience to the committees. But because their experience is focused on particular investment areas, they may be less comfortable considering recommendations concerning other investment areas. Do they understand their limitations? To be successful committee members, they must become generalists, not specialists. Unless they can make this transition, their investment experience can actually be a drawback.

How about an in-house committee—a pension committee composed of senior corporate executives? Don't they bring built-in conflicts of interest? That's a good question. How easy is it for the corporate executive to take off his corporate hat and put on his fiduciary hat? This depends heavily on the character and ethics of such committee members. Fortunately, I have seen this done very successfully over the years.

A key advantage is that a corporate executive's fiduciary responsibility to shareholders is not often in conflict with his fiduciary responsibility to plan participants. Both groups have an overwhelming interest in gaining the best possible investment return within a reasonable level of risk. To be successful they must be comfortable accepting a level of risk high enough to gain the investment-return advantage of a long time horizon.

Conflicts can arise if the plan sponsor or a committee member has a special relationship with an investment firm. Such a relationship has the potential for conflict of interest. Fortunately, I have more than once seen pension committees terminate an investment manager where one or more committee members sat on that manager's own board. I have on many occasions been asked to meet with certain investment managers with whom a committee member had a relationship or friendship, but never have I been pressured to alter the criteria for hiring a manager or in any other way to give preferential consideration.

Role of Committee Members

So . . . if committee members can't do it all themselves, what should they do? The committee members, acting in the best interests of plan participants, should ensure that the fund's objectives are consistent with the financial condition of the plan sponsor (is the sponsor likely to be able to make future contributions as needed?) and they should ensure that the fund's investment policies are consistent with the plan's objectives. Then they should review each recommendation from the following standpoints:

1. First and foremost, is the recommendation consistent with the fund's objectives and policies? If not, should the committee consider modifying its objectives and policies, or is the recommendation therefore inappropriate?

2.   Is the recommendation consistent with the committee's target asset allocation? If not, should the committee consider modifying its target asset allocation?
3.   Is the recommendation internally consistent?
4.   Has the staff (or consultant) researched all of the right questions relative to things such as:
     (a)   Character and integrity of the recommended manager.
     (b)   Nature of the asset class itself.
     (c)   Validity of the manager's reported past performance, and its predictive value.
     (d)   Credentials of the manager's key decisionmakers.
     (e)   Depth of the manager's staff.
     (f)   The manager's decision-making processes and internal controls.
5.   What alternatives did the staff (or consultant) consider?
6.   Have adequate constraints and controls been established, especially with respect to derivatives that a manager may be authorized to use?
7.   Does the fee structure seem appropriate?
8.   Is the recommendation consistent with the plan document and all applicable law?

Criteria for Committee Members

Does this sound like a heavy-duty demand on investment sophistication? While investment sophistication helps, I don't think it's a requirement for a committee member. Then what criteria should a prospective committee member meet? For example:

- High moral character, ready to avoid even the perception of conflicts of interest.
- Knowledge of how the fund relates to the financial situation of the plan sponsor.
- A healthy dose of common sense—the ability to reason in a logical manner, to apply abstract principles to specific situations, and to relate questions at hand to everything else he knows.
- A flexible mind, willing and able to consider, weigh, and apply new concepts and ideas, and to challenge previously held concepts, including one's own.

- A willingness to accept a level of risk high enough to gain the investment return advantage of a long time horizon.
- A willingness to learn—about the kinds of concepts discussed in this book and about individual investment opportunities.

"What is the difference between competent and incompetent boards?" write Ambachtsheer and Ezra.[2] "Competent boards have a preponderance of people of character who are comfortable doing their organizational thinking in multiyear time frames. These people understand ambiguity and uncertainty, and are still prepared to go ahead and make the required judgments and decisions. They know what they don't know. They are prepared to hire a competent CEO[3] and delegate management and operational authority, and are prepared to support a compensation philosophy that ties reward to results."

Committee procedures usually call for decisions to be decided by a majority vote. In practice, most decisions should be achieved by consensus—a unanimous vote, if you will. This is important because every member of the committee is a party to the decision, and if the decision were subsequently to be challenged on a fiduciary basis, each member would be individually answerable for the decision.

That doesn't mean that everyone agrees that a decision is always the best possible, but everyone should ultimately agree that it is at least a *good* decision. If a committee member clearly believes the decision is inappropriate and subject to subsequent legal action, that member may have to resign.

Number of Committee Members

How many members should compose the fiduciary committee? There is no set number. But I favor a smaller committee of members who will take their responsibility seriously and will attend meetings regularly. A committee of five might be optimal for purposes of generating good discussion, giving each member a feeling he is important to the committee, and—not inconsequentially—the ease of assembling the committee for a meeting.

---

[2] Keith P. Ambachtsheer and D. Don Ezra, *Pension Fund Excellence,* John Wiley & Sons, Inc., 1988, p. 90.
[3] The pension fund's chief executive officer. For example, the staff's director of pension investments.

It is for the last reason that I am wary of the inclusion of out-of-town members on a fiduciary committee. Out-of-town members can bring special qualifications, but there can be problems with their ability to get to meetings regularly, especially when a meeting needs to be called on relatively short notice to address a special investment opportunity or an unexpected problem. The committee can mitigate this difficulty, of course, by the use of conference calls in combination with the mailing of presentation materials well in advance. But still, to get a group of busy people together at the same time can often be a challenge.

This is why some corporations appoint a single person (rather than a committee) as their "named fiduciary" for investments. That places a lot of responsibility on that person, and he should be more knowledgeable about institutional investing than most committee members. But in cases of a one-person committee, I recommend the establishment of an advisory counsel that can review objectives, policies, asset allocation, and performance. Such an advisory council can serve as a sounding board for the fiduciary and can also evaluate for the plan sponsor whether the fiduciary is doing a good job.

The advantages of a small or one-person committee are: focused accountability and, of course, flexibility—the ability to act without getting tied up in bureaucratic procedures. Flexibility can also be a disadvantage to the extent it facilitates actions without sufficient thought or without inquiry from multiple points of view. An advisory council can help to offset this disadvantage, especially if the fiduciary is required to share promptly with the members of the council copies of all recommendations the fiduciary approves, including the full rationale supporting those recommendations. An advisory council should meet at regular intervals, plus whenever the fiduciary believes he could benefit from its advice and counsel, and also whenever any member of the advisory council requests a meeting.

Staff

Criteria for Staff

What should a committee expect of its staff (or whoever is making recommendations to the committee)? Senior staff members should generally meet the criteria we listed for committee members, but in addition, they should be full-time investment professionals—able to think through and articulate recommended objectives and policies and then apply them. They should be familiar with the full range of asset classes and kinds of investment opportunities that can be found in each asset class. Their job is to do the research, to recommend asset allocation, and then to dig out the particular investment managers and investment programs to recommend to the committee. Their job is also to monitor existing investment managers, to be sure each is worth retaining, and to assemble data on the fund's overall performance and present it to the committee in the most helpful way possible. This means they must have strong communications skills—both verbally and in writing.

In short, the senior staff professionals must be the experts and the ones who do the work. But they should always remember that the fiduciary committee is the one deciding on the objectives and policies, making the actual investment decisions, and shouldering the final responsibility. The staff cannot be moving in one direction and the committee in another.

Responsibility for Committee Education

This fact leads to what I believe is the number-one responsibility of the staff: to provide continuing education to the committee members. Few committee members start out with a broad grasp of the kinds of things that fill the pages of this book. It is up to the senior staff members to teach them. Such education—including the setting of realistic expectations for return and volatility—should be provided on a continuing basis. Each decision opportunity should be related to the fund's investment policies.

The most useful thing we have done (for staff as well as for the committee) is to get all committee and staff members off site for a 2-day retreat every few years, to meet with a group of outstanding investment professionals with highly diverse backgrounds to consider the committee's policies, investment allocation, and general investment strategy. Such conferences can't be pre-programmed except to the extent of the questions that will be asked of the group initially. Some committee members find it eye-opening to see the extent to which top investment professionals disagree with one another. Letting the chips fall where they may has always expanded the perspective of our committee members and helped them and the staff subsequently to develop a consensus about the investment directions in which they want to be heading.

Relatively few organizations may be able to arrange for such a conference. But all staffs can work on the task of continuing education.

There are senior staff people who at times have come upon a highly attractive but offbeat investment opportunity but would not consider recommending it to their committee for fear they would be laughed out of the room. To the extent this is true, it is a sorry reflection on the open-mindedness of the committee, a reflection on the staff's inadequate education of the committee, or both. Offbeat opportunities may require much greater due diligence and more careful explanation to committees than more traditional opportunities. But offbeat opportunities, if they pass this test, can add valuable diversification to a fund's overall portfolio.

Organization of Staff

How large should the staff be? That all depends on the size of the fund and the complexity of the investment program. Some funds are too small to justify even a single professional staff person. Endowment funds of such small size may be fortunate enough to have a committee member who is an investment professional staffing another institutional fund and can rely on that person for staff work. Most such funds, however, must find a competent consultant to serve in the capacity of its professional staff.

With a larger fund, consulting can also be very important but serve a different role. Because of the staff's continuing interaction with the committee and its undivided focus on its own fund, the staff of a larger fund can monitor its investment portfolio and develop recommendations more appropriately than its consultant. Consultants can serve as a valuable adjunct to staff, filling in expertise where the staff has less experience or providing analyses that the staff may not have the systems to do. But for a larger fund, the *staff* should make all recommendations, not the consultant. Moreover, the staff should not need the consultant's "Good House-keeping seal of approval" for each of its recommendations.

How should the staff of a large fund organize its senior professionals when it does no in-house investment management? There are two basic extremes:

1. Divide the staff by asset class—for example, someone responsible for U.S. equity investments, someone for foreign stocks, someone for fixed income, someone for real estate, and so on.

2. Have no specialists. Make every senior staff member responsible for everything. This approach is very demanding on staff members, making a shambles of anything close to a 40-hour work week.

I favor the second approach, especially if we can keep our staff small. This approach has worked well for me. It avoids any semblance of parochialism. One cannot consider an opportunity in asset class A without considering how it stacks up against opportunities in asset class B. Frequently we find that what we learn in one asset class has application in other asset classes as well. It forces each staff member always to consider the fund's portfolio as a whole.

From a practical standpoint, it makes sense to assign a "lead" staff member to each new investment opportunity. That person will carry on the correspondence and negotiations, and if it reaches that point, will make the recommendation to the committee. But due diligence on that opportunity is everyone's responsibility, and the decision to move ahead should be the result of informed consensus of the staff.

The staff of a large fund should also have a strong professional person responsible for support services. This critical function should include:

- The operation of the staff's management information system.
- Performance measurement.
- Portfolio composition analyses and diagnostics.
- Principal day-to-day contacts with the trustee/custodian.
- Audits and administration of all bills to be paid.
- Review of all routine manager controls (including follow-up to ensure that each manager reconciles with the custodian's statement each month).
- Physical preparation of graphics for presentations.
- Preparation of government reports (such as a pension fund's 5500 report) and all surveys.
- Establishment and maintenance of user-friendly filing systems that are kept up-to-date, and of all other secretarial and clerical requirements of the office.

What should be the size of the staff of a large fund (assuming the staff is not managing assets in-house)? No quantity of people can possibly be as effective as a few top-flight professionals. Hence I favor a small staff of dedicated senior professionals. A small staff of high competency allows manageable processes that bring informed and experienced judgments to bear on every opportunity. Much is expected from each such staff member, and assuming they deliver, they should be treated and compensated in a way that will encourage them to make a career with that fund—passing up highly compensated opportunities with other funds or with Wall Street.

The work of pension investments is based on a solid grounding in two academic disciplines: discounted cash flow and probability theory. But that's just the beginning. An in-depth knowledge of the pension investments field is a *long-term process*. Hence I believe it is counterproductive to rotate high-potential corporate executives through the pension investments position for stints of several years each. Many decision rules are different from those of the normal line operation of a business. For example, there are times when we may want to add responsibility (more money) to an underperformer and take responsibility away from an overperformer. That's not the normal approach for managing most corporate operations.

In short, pension investment positions should be viewed as career positions. The work is a lifelong learning experience.

Interaction of Committee and Staff

Committee Meetings

We might well set dates a year in advance for four to 10 committee meetings, whatever number may be expected to be necessary. That way committee members can plan their calendars around those dates. If the staff happens not to have sufficient business to justify a meeting, the staff should arrange to cancel the meeting. If a 2-hour meeting is scheduled and the staff needs only half an hour of business, it should notify committee members as far in advance as possible.

If an urgent matter comes up that can't wait for the next scheduled meeting, a special meeting should be called at whatever date most committee members may be available. If the matter is simple and routine enough, the staff can avoid a special meeting by circulating to committee members a "consent to action," which when signed by a majority of the committee is sufficient to authorize action.

Committee members should make every effort to attend meetings, if not in person, then by conference call—which I have found can work very well.

In any case, relative to recommendations, committee members will appreciate the staff sending them copies of its full presentation materials several days before each meeting. If committee members have been able to review and think about a recommendation in advance, they will be prepared to ask better questions during discussion at the meeting. The danger is that the committee member may decide how he will vote on the recommendation prior to the meeting. This he should avoid. Advance preparation should lead to questions, not pre-conceived minds.

At the meeting I have found it helpful to review each recommendation page by page. This does not mean reading out loud each page, which every committee member is quite capable of reading, but the staff person should discuss briefly the *meaning* of the page. This tends to elicit more and better discussion and gives greater assurance that no key considerations have been glossed over.

Ultimately, after the committee is convinced that the staff has truly done its homework, the committee should probably approve 90% to 98% of all recommendations. A lower approval rate suggests that the committee does not have sufficient confidence in staff. Remember, the committee *must* rely on staff. And if the committee can't build adequate confidence in its staff, it should get a new staff in which it *does* have confidence.

Reviewing Performance

One meeting each year should be designated for reviewing the previous year's performance. The staff should provide a detailed performance analysis of the overall fund and of each manager in the context of the various market averages and perhaps the results achieved by funds of peer pension funds or endowments.

Recent performance—whether of the whole fund, of a particular index, of a specific group of managers, or of an individual manager—is best given in the context of long-term perspective. The best format for doing that, I have found, is the performance triangle in Table 14.1 (similar to the triangle on page 18). The triangle won't let us look at recent performance without also seeing the long-term.

Another advantage of the triangle is that it serves well as the basic tool we as staff use in analyzing performance, so the committee is looking at performance exactly the same way we are.

Table 14.1 Manager XYZ vs. EAFE Non-U.S. Stock Index

To End of	87	88	89	90	91	92	93	94	95	96	97	98
						From Start of						
98	1	0	1	0	1	1	2	4	3	3	4	7
97	1	1	2	0	0	0	1	3	2	1	2	
96	2	2	3	1	0	1	1	4	2	0		
95	2	2	3	1	0	1	2	5	4			
94	3	3	4	2	1	3	0	6				
93	4	4	7	4	3	7	8					
92	3	3	6	3	2	7						
91	3	3	6	1	4							
90	4	5	11	4								
89	4	5	19					MV = $92M				
88	4	10										
87	3											
Actual	28	18	30	–19	8	–5	40	1	7	6	0	13
Cash Flows						$+96	–	–		$–27	$–36	$–18

Note: The numbers on the left and at the top reference the year.

—Number on a white background are percentage points per year by which the manager outperformed its benchmark. Numbers on a gray background are percentage points per year by which it underperformed its benchmark. (For presentation purposes, I prefer using blue numbers for outperforming and red for underperforming.)

—The line toward the bottom marked "Actual" shows the manager's actual performance for each year.

—The bottom line, labeled "Cash Flows," shows that we contributed $96 million to his account in 1992 and withdrew $27 million in 1996, $36 million in 1997, and $18 million in 1998.

—The vertical dotted line shows that the manager was hired in 1992.

—At right above we see that the market value of the account at year-end 1998 was $92 million.

Table 14.1 shows how we can add to the triangle further valuable information, such as the current market value and the history of all contributions and withdrawals since the year the manager was hired.

Staff's comments about a manager should summarize concisely its reasons for retaining the manager (unless it recommends termination). The focus should be on the same criteria we use for hiring managers, such as that in Chapter 5, pages 101–102.

How about monthly and quarterly performance reports? I believe strongly we should avoid monthly performance reports to the committee. They are entirely too myopic. I have been able to glean little that is useful for decision making from monthly performance reports myself, and I believe circulating such reports to the committee members only wastes time of both staff and committee members and invites counterproductive inquiries.

I feel much the same way about quarterly reports to the committee. Certainly, a full-blown performance presentation each quarter is a waste of time for both the committee members and the staff members, who could be devoting their time to activities that are more likely to benefit the bottom line. Circulation of a 1-page quarterly performance report to committee members may be appropriate, with more detail only on an exception basis.

At one extreme, even that 1-page performance report once elicited criticism from my committee's chairman. "Rusty," he said, "you spend all this time trying to teach the committee members not to be myopic, and then you give them a golden opportunity to be myopic by circulating your quarterly performance report!" We discontinued the report, of course.

Periodically, as during a market panic, it makes sense for staff to update the committee on interim performance. From a communications standpoint, one of my more satisfying moments occurred at the end of October, 1987. The market had dropped by more than 20% and our pension fund had lost over $1 billion in unrealized gains. So at a meeting that had been pre-planned for the end of that month we presented a 1-page report letting our losses all hang out.

At the conclusion of the 1-minute report the chairman turned to the committee members and asked, "Are there any questions about that report? . . . If not, we'll go on to our next item of business." And they did.

We had reviewed often with the committee the historical fluctuation of the markets, including the devastating crash that occurred in 1973–1974. What great evidence that our committee members had internalized those lessons!

Recommendations to the Committee

In making a recommendation to hire a manager, we should cover concisely the key questions the committee *ought to* ask about that manager. Generally, such a presentation should provide:

- The precise recommendation, including the full name of the manager, the amount of money to be assigned to its management, and the particular asset class it will manage.

- How does the manager fit into the portfolio's overall asset allocation and policies? This should include information about the asset class itself if the asset class is relatively new to the committee.
- Who is the manager?—corporate affiliations, date of founding, location of offices, size of staff, and so on.
- How does the manager invest? What distinguishes his approach from other managers in his asset class?
- The manager's past performance, and why we think it has predictive value. Why do we think he is the best we can get in that asset class?
- Who are the key people and why do we have confidence in them? How deep is the staff, how long have they been with the firm, and what turnover of people has the manager experienced?
- Who are the manager's other clients, especially for the same kind of program we are recommending? (This consideration is often overemphasized, as it is not the actions—or inactions—of other funds that should determine what we do.)
- What's the fee schedule, and why is it appropriate?

As staff, our presentations should cover only the salient points, not try to snow the committee with the whole story nor, in fact, provide any more than a committee member might be expected to absorb. Does the committee really need to know this? How can we say this in a way so the members will grasp our point more quickly? We shouldn't try to cover our tail by giving an information dump. Of course, we should have a rich depth of additional information and background so we can answer briefly but with authority any reasonable questions that might come up.

Candidness is perhaps our number one criterion. We must gain and retain the committee's complete trust. That means if there is negative news or negative aspects about a manager, we must be forthright about them— including our reason for not proposing action as a result (assuming we think no action is needed).

Preparation of the recommendation is, in my opinion, one of the staff's best steps in due diligence. We start by asking ourselves what questions the committee *should* ask, and then write down candidly our responses. As we look at what we have written, does it hold together? Is it convincing without our having to doctor it up? If our answer is not a strong yes, then the recommendation is probably not one we should make.

Upon coming upon an exciting new opportunity, I have multiple times roughed out a recommendation to the committee, backed off, then taken another look at it, and decided ultimately I could not marshal enough cold logic to bring it before the committee. Liking something intuitively is not enough.

Meeting with Managers

It is customary for many committees to meet the recommended manager and sometimes to meet the "finalist" managers one after the other in what I call a "beauty contest." I recommend *against* bringing the managers to meet the committee. The committee can, at best, determine how articulate a manager is. But articulateness has a low correlation with investment capability. In 20 to 30 minutes, a committee's interview can be little more than superficial. Committee members can not bring the perspective of meetings with hundreds of managers, as the staff does, nor can it do the kind of homework the staff should have done. Ultimately, the committee's decision comes down, after discussion with the staff, to whether the committee has confidence in the staff and believes the staff has done its homework adequately in this case.

I don't even recommend bringing managers to the committee for performance reports—for much the same reasons. I have sat through countless manager reports to committees. These reports generally cover the manager's outlook for the economy, his interpretation of the account's recent performance, and the particular transactions he has made recently. The reports are superficial, often myopic, leaving the committee members little better off other than the feeling that they have "done their fiduciary duty." A cogent, concise report by the staff can do a better job of surfacing issues and placing things in a helpful perspective for decision making.

Working with New Committee Members

Whenever a new person is appointed to the committee, we should devote much effort to bringing that person up to speed quickly with the rest of the committee. We should immediately give him key documents, such as the fund's objectives and policies, and its target allocation, together with their underlying rationale.

Understanding the why of everything is critically important, and the above documents may well need to be supplemented by one-on-one sessions with the staff's director. Also helpful may be a brief meeting with the fund's legal counsel to outline the committee member's legal responsibilities.

Advice of Counsel

The committee's legal counsel is an important member of the team, especially for a pension fund. Each plan needs numerous legal documents—a trust agreement, plus a management agreement with each of its investment managers, as well as consulting agreements. Private investments, such as limited partnerships, usually require far more complex legal work. In addition, our counsel should serve more day-to-day functions.

The staff should review every recommendation with counsel before presenting it to the committee. ERISA is a complex law, and so are the laws of the SEC and IRS, and we must be mindful of them all. Our attorney should be able to steer us away from recommendations, and from certain statements in our presentation materials, that might conflict with any of these laws. To do this well, our attorney needs to understand our investment program, to *be* a part of the team.

Committee meetings should be documented as formally as those of boards of directors, with agendas distributed to committee members well ahead of time, and minutes carefully recording each decision and who is instructed to implement that decision. Minutes should record that each decision was made "subject to the advice of counsel." Once a decision is made, implementing it can involve a lot of legal work. Legal roadblocks can sometimes arise that require the matter to go back to the committee for further decision or even causing a show-stopper, making it impossible to implement the decision.

To staff, legal counsel can be a pain in the neck and our best friend—both at the same time. It is mighty frustrating to be told that a sensible investment opportunity cannot be implemented for some arcane legal reason, but when a Department of Labor inspector moves into our office to examine our investment program, we are extremely thankful that our counsel has made us jump through all the legal hoops.

Of course, it is not the job of a good counsel to just say no. A good counsel tries to understand what we want to accomplish and more often than not can suggest an alternative way for us to achieve the same objective. Our counsel can do that best if he is treated as a true member of our team.

Proxies

Many people associate the word "governance" with the voting of proxies for the many common stocks in our fund. Those people are really concerned about the governance not of our fund but of the companies we invest in and our responsibilities as a share owner. Certainly, as a share owner, we should see that our proxies are voted, and responsibly. The Department of Labor has even issued a statement to that effect.

But who should vote our proxies? I feel strongly that the investment manager who holds a stock in his account should be the one to vote it. He is in the best position to know what vote would most likely promote the value of that stock. Of course, if we are managing the stock in-house, then we should vote it ourselves.

We as sponsor of our fund should make sure that our managers are exercising their responsibilities. We should require each year a statement from each manager that he has voted every proxy he has received (he would not receive the proxy for a stock that is out on loan), also that he has voted each proxy in the sole interest of our pension plan participants,[4] and that he could explain to us in each case why he thought his vote was in our participants' best interest (see page 146).

Incidentally, if two different managers of ours hold the same stock, we should not be upset if at times the two managers vote their proxies differently. Different opinions are what make markets.

In Short

All who are involved in decisions for a pension fund or endowment fund are fiduciaries and are held by law to a very high standard.

Final decisions are often made by a high-level committee that typically devotes a relatively few hours per year to the fund. The committee must have a competent staff (or consultant) to rely on. One of the staff's foremost responsibilities is seeing to the continuing education of committee members.

---

[4] Endowments and foundations may have additional considerations for proxy voting, as discussed in Chapter 17, page 290.

Chapter 15

Coordinating Pension Financing at a Company's Subsidiaries

Let's say we are responsible for pension investments at a global company with a dozen subsidiaries around the world, each with its own pension plan. Each is investing its pension money differently depending on local laws, conventional investment wisdom in that country, and whatever consulting firm it happened to start working with years ago. Moreover, each subsidiary is calculating its annual pension contributions differently. How do we get our arms around all this and ensure that pension financing is being done in an optimal way at each subsidiary?

That's a complex and frustrating assignment, partly because the laws and customs are so different from country to country. Most subsidiaries are small enough that the function of pension financing is a 15th added responsibility held by a human resources or treasury staff person, who prioritizes his time accordingly.

The assignment is also, however, a window of valuable perspective and insights. We get to test our policies and strategies in a very different context, and we are forced to assess which policies measure up as having some universal qualities and which may simply be the way we've been accustomed to doing things in the United States.

Each subsidiary may have somewhat different pension *benefits,* but in financing those benefits, each should be trying to do the same thing—to finance the benefits in a way that will provide security to employees but at the lowest long-term cost to the company, and in a way that will minimize the effort needed to administer the plan.

Global Policies

I believe it makes sense for a multinational company to have pension financing policies that it applies worldwide. That sentence is a mouthful, as circumstances vary so greatly from country to country. What kinds of policies might make sense globally? Let me suggest a few:

1. Each subsidiary will strictly obey the laws of its land. But it will disregard the pension funding or investment *customs* in its land.

2. The multinational company should adopt for use worldwide a single actuarial method to determine contributions.

   - A global actuarial method will implicitly define how well funded every pension plan is targeted to be. The method should provide for adequate funding but discourage large overfunding.

     Overfunding can rarely be reclaimed directly by the company, although it can be absorbed through "contribution holidays." But managements—when faced with the happy circumstance of large overfunding—sometimes treat it as free money and are more generous with it than they ought to be.[1]

   - No single actuarial method will be legal in every country. Where the company's global method is not legal, it should be used as a target method. The subsidiary, in applying the legally required method, should adjust actuarial assumptions to the extent the laws allow so as to bring contributions as close as possible to the level of contributions indicated by the global method.

---

[1] Subsidiaries of large global companies can prudently target a narrower margin of pension funding surplus than an indigenous company of modest size that has no parent to fall back on. If, for example, markets turn sour and a subsidiary's pension funding drops below liabilities, the plan participants should not have to worry. To preserve its reputation in all countries, a global company cannot afford to allow its pension promises in *any* country to go unfulfilled.

- The parent should appoint a worldwide actuary to calculate annual pension contributions and pension expense in every country. This will ensure that the company's global actuarial method is applied uniformly. Any subsidiary should be free to use another actuarial firm for consulting purposes, but its contributions should be calculated by the worldwide actuary.
- The parent's pension investments staff should review and approve all actuarial valuations, including the actuarial assumptions, and should approve any variance in contributions from those indicated by the global method.

3. A subsidiary should finance its pensions with book reserves wherever (a) book reserves are legally permissible *and* (b) the laws of the nation do not permit flexible tax-free investing of pension assets, meaning that the plan cannot expect to earn a net rate of investment return that is at least equal to the parent company's net average cost of capital.

4. Each subsidiary should have written pension investment policies that are approved by the parent's pension investments staff. These policies might include (to the extent allowed by law):
   - To base investment decisions solely on what will be best for the plan and its participants, with no other considerations but that of investment effectiveness, and avoiding any perception of conflict of interest.
   - To gain broad global diversification.
   - To achieve, within a given volatility limit, the best possible long-term rate of investment return (net of fees and any taxes).
   - To hire within each asset class the best investment manager (or managers) that the subsidiary can access—regardless of the location and nationality of the manager—starting with index funds if the subsidiary cannot access a manager with a high probability of net investment returns well in excess of the index.

5. Wherever feasible, every subsidiary should use the same trustee/custodian, usually the one also used by the plan of the parent company. At present this is possible in only a few countries, such as the United States, United Kingdom, and Canada, but this list of countries will grow in the years ahead. Use of the same trustee/custodian establishes appropriate standards, facilitates the

flow of information, and provides a common performance measurement service.

6. The parent's pension investments staff should advise all subsidiaries on investment policies, asset allocation, and the selection of investment managers, and the staff should approve each subsidiary's final asset allocation and choice of investment managers.

 To gain maximum benefit from the research and due diligence of the parent's pension investments staff, subsidiaries around the world should appoint common managers and invest in the same commingled funds wherever possible.

 A multinational company can afford one first-class pension investments staff, not multiple ones. That staff should have global responsibilities.

7. The company should appoint a common auditor for all its pension plans worldwide.

We might say, great! We'll establish some policies like these and then it will be just a job of administering them. Right? Not so! Applying such policies runs head-on into the following roadblocks:

- Local laws limit any set of global policies for pension financing.
- As described at the beginning of Chapter 4 (page 66), conventional investment wisdom differs dramatically from country to country. This can create strong local resistance to any common investment policies.
- Many a subsidiary has its own fiduciary committee that takes its responsibilities seriously (which it should) and in some cases feels independent (which it may be, legally). The attitude often, and understandably, is, "Mother, I'd rather do it myself!"

 Some committees are required to have up to 50% employee representatives. Company-appointed members must balance their fiduciary responsibility with recognition that they are company appointees to the committee.

- If global policies sharply alter a subsidiary's approach, such as forcing a change from insured annuities, the rigidities of the old way can create major problems (and expense) in getting from here to there.
- Few companies can afford an experienced pension investments person. As mentioned before, the pension investment function is often someone's nth additional responsibility. Hence, it is often—

understandably—difficult to gain enthusiastic attention to pension investments at the local level.

The challenge is clear. How to deal with that challenge in each individual case is not clear. But taking on the challenge is clearly worth doing. Even a small increase in the long-term rate of investment return will make it all worthwhile.

One precondition necessary for success: Such an effort must have the *total support of the company's senior management people* and their willingness to enforce these policies. Without that level of support, the effort is doomed to frustration.

Can One Size Fit All?

An advantage of wrestling with how to invest pension funds around the world is that it raises the question: Assuming there are no taxes and that laws permit complete investment latitude, is there a basic optimal asset allocation that would be as appropriate in Switzerland as in the United States as in Hong Kong? Why should optimal asset allocation differ from one country to another?

Here are four reasons (other than taxes and legal investment constraints) why asset allocation perhaps ought to differ a little:

1. Liabilities are in local currency. Hence, to avoid a mismatch of assets and liabilities, assets should also be predominately in the local currency.

    This would be especially true in a strong-currency country, and perhaps untrue in a weak-currency country. In any event, foreign exchange exposure can usually be hedged at low cost.

2. The nature of a plan's liabilities. If most of the liabilities are for active employees, equities may do a better job of hedging liabilities. If most of the liabilities are for retirees, a larger allocation to long-duration fixed income may be appropriate.

    To minimize contributions long-term, we will want an aggressive investment approach in either case. I suspect that differences due to the nature of liabilities will prove relatively small.

3. The plan's funding ratio. If our plan is way overfunded and we are making no contributions, then it is argued that we should invest more conservatively, as we won't be able to reap commensurate rewards from strong future returns, in that the company can seldom redeem grossly excess pension assets; yet an investment pothole could return us to a position of having to reinstate contributions.

Alternatively, if our plan is weakly funded and our company cannot afford to increase its contributions, then it is argued that we should invest more conservatively so as not to jeopardize the security of our employees' pensions.

I believe a common investment approach needs relatively little modification to meet the above two extreme situations. And under all other funding ratios, we should be able to justify the same aggressive investment approach. In any case, with optimal diversification, it is not necessary to have a highly volatile pension fund.

4. A small pension fund cannot access as broad a diversification as a large fund.

That is true, as a small pension plan must usually confine itself to marketable securities. But it can still achieve valuable diversification through global investing.

I do not view these four considerations as show-stoppers for a basic one-size-fits-all optimal asset allocation. What it does mean is that a universally optimal asset allocation needs to be tailored for each plan on the basis of taxes, legal constraints, and each of the above considerations. But I suspect that efficient-frontier studies will rarely show dramatic differences from a universally optimal asset allocation.

Figuring out a universally optimal asset allocation is another matter. This effort is highly dependent on the assumptions we enter into our computer for expected return, volatility, and correlation. But, adjusted for such things as taxes and currency, our assumptions should be consistent around the world. That is why, after we have made all adjustments, our optimal asset allocation in most countries worldwide should have a great deal of similarity.

Each of our global policies referred to earlier in this chapter—including asset allocation—should apply equally to our main parent-company plan. If the policy doesn't fit in the United States, for example, then maybe we should adjust either our global policy or our procedures with respect to the U.S. plan.

The advantage can be gleaned best if the parent's pension investments staff doesn't always take the attitude that "Mother knows best." Even part-time pension staffers abroad may come up with good ideas or insights. We must listen thoughtfully with care and work hard to remain objective.

In Short

A global company can reduce its global pension costs long term by seeing that the pension investment policies and programs that it has researched so well at home are also applied wherever possible at subsidiaries around the world. This task is one of the most challenging in the pension world. It requires strong top management support . . . and also an extraordinary dose of understanding, patience, and determination.

Chapter 16

Defined Benefit Plans vs.
Defined Contribution Plans

This book is focused entirely on defined-benefit (DB) pension plans and endowment funds, not on defined-contribution (DC) plans such as 401(k) plans. But for perspective, this book would be incomplete without briefly contrasting DB and DC plans. What are the key differences?

- A DB pension plan defines the benefit the participant will receive (such as 1½% of the participant's average salary over his last three years for every year of service), and the participant has no interest in how successfully the pension fund is invested as long as the plan pays him the benefit that it promised.
- A DC plan defines the amount of money the sponsor will contribute to the plan each year for each individual participant, and over the years the value of that participant's account will be fully impacted by how well or poorly that account is invested. Usually, the participant decides how his account will be invested, choosing among a range of funds offered by the plan.

A *Cash Balance Plan* has aspects of both a DB and a DC plan. It is DC in the sense that the plan defines the amount that will be added to a participant's account in any one year. But the participant is not impacted by investment results, because the plan defines the rate of interest that will be credited to his account each year. A Cash Balance Plan is really a DB plan,

274

because the sponsor decides how the money is actually invested and bears the risk, in just the same way it would with a more traditional DB plan.

In the past 10 years, there has been a tremendous expansion in both the number and size of *DC* plans while the number of *DB* plans has essentially not grown at all. The trend is also moving in that direction around the world. In the United States, the amount of money today in DC plans rivals the amount in DB plans, which heretofore have been the backbone of private pension plans. Why?

- With DC plans, an employer knows exactly what his pension costs will be as a percent of payroll. It believes it has no material additional liability (unless it considers fiduciary liability). A DB plan entails highly arcane valuations, and future costs are unpredictable.
- Because they can see hard dollars, employees think they understand DC plans better and therefore appreciate them more.
- DC plans appeal far more than DB plans to younger employees, most of whom today do not expect to spend a career with their employer. A *typical* DB plan provides little value unless the employee spends his career with his employer. A DC plan provides essentially the ultimate in portability. Of course, so does a Cash Balance Plan.
- Some employers fund their DC plans with employer stock, which some employers feel is a cheaper way to fund and also gives employees an ownership interest in the employer.
- Government regulations have made DB plans increasingly complex to administer. Governments have therefore, unwittingly, motivated employers to switch to DC plans.

While a DC plan makes a splendid adjunct to a DB plan, I believe there are serious problems with sole reliance on DC plans. These include:

- In the long run, DC plans cost more. Per dollar of employer contribution, a DC plan can provide materially *less* retirement benefits than a well-run DB plan. This is mainly because plan assets cannot be invested nearly as effectively under a DC plan as under a DB plan. Also, participant accounting tends to make administrative costs higher for DC plans.
  — A DB plan can prudently afford to invest plan assets far more aggressively than a DC plan. This is because of the law of large numbers and a longer time horizon. Within a fairly narrow

band, a DB plan knows about how much it must pay out in benefits in each of the next 10 years. An employee participating in a DC plan has no such advantage. He doesn't know whether he and his spouse will die next year or at the age of 102. Such uncertainty should cause the prudent employee to invest his DC money far more cautiously.

— Relatively few employees have enough investment knowledge to invest their DC money in an optimal manner. A few are too speculative; most are too risk averse. Even with the best education programs that a sponsor can provide, many employees will never be well equipped to invest their 401(k) money in an optimal way.

— Many employees will want to hire a financial counselor. This means they will have to pay a large annual fee, either directly or indirectly.

— DC plans cannot offer employees the diversity of investment options that a DB plan can take advantage of. For example, a DB plan can invest in a large number of private investment programs that could not readily be offered in a DC plan.

• With DC plans that offer a company match, the lowest paid employees often fail to take advantage of the company match because they feel they can't afford their portion of the contribution. Hence they don't build up an adequate nest egg for retirement.

• If employees have most of their retirement money in a 401(k) plan or an IRA, where will they be if eventually we get hit by another bear market like 1973–1974?

• DC plans that rely mainly on employer stock are asking for trouble. At very successful companies like Microsoft, employees have undoubtedly gotten rich. But there are too many factors outside of a company's control that impact its fortunes. Placing most of one's investment eggs in any one basket is patently imprudent.

Another drawback of a DC plan to the sponsor: The sponsor must make a relatively fixed contribution in cash each year, come hell or high water. With a DB plan, the present value of the sponsor's contributions are reduced by whatever increment the pension fund can earn over its interest-rate assumption. And when the sponsor does need to make contributions, it has considerable discretion, within limits, as to the amount and timing of its contributions.

If DC plans have such drawbacks relative to DB plans, then why are DB plans losing their following? Besides overregulation (which some government officials now *appear* to begin recognizing), DB plans typically have two major drawbacks: lack of portability, and low accretion of value for new and midcareer employees. Benefits for employees who leave before retirement are puny.[1] Consequently, employees who aren't sure they'll stay to retirement attach little or no value to a DB plan.

Is there a way to cure this lack of portability? Yes. Some DB plans in the United States have adopted benefit schedules that accrue more of an employee's pension benefits earlier in his career—such as a Cash Balance Plan. Remember, Cash Balance Plans add a specific dollar amount each year to every employee's lump-sum retirement accrual, and his cumulative dollar balance increases each year by a particular interest rate. That is the company's liability to the employee. The employee can take it with him any time he leaves. But the employer can continue to invest as aggressively as it now invests its DB plan, and it can have the same hope it has now of reducing future contributions through effective investing.

It can be very costly, however, to make a typical DB plan more portable while targeting equivalent retirement benefits for all employees. Transition provisions that are needed to keep existing employees whole are expensive. Older employees will continue getting their current high pension accruals each year while younger employees will get far higher pension accruals (although later in their career not as much as older employees now receive). The cost is somewhat like that of moving forward the date when we must pay our taxes. There may be no increase in the tax rate, but the overlapping payments during the transition amount to a large one-time increase.

Yet because of the importance of a good pension plan in the recruitment and retention of young employees, I believe many companies in the years ahead will find a way to transition their DB plans to something more portable, such as Cash Balance Plans.

Changes in the Public Sector

Countries around the world are finding they can ill afford to maintain their traditional social security benefits. Chile and Argentina have

---

[1] See Figure 13.1 on page 240 for a chart showing how the present value of pension benefits builds up over one's career.

changed their social security plans completely from DB to DC. That solves the government's funding problem but creates the kind of problems noted above that are common to DC plans. There has been discussion in Washington about inserting DC elements into the U.S. Social Security program, although it is unclear at this time where that idea is likely to go.

One thing is clear worldwide: Governments are increasingly looking to employers to provide a greater portion of retirement income. Whether this will be done more with DC plans, or with DB plans that have better portability features, only the future will tell.

A Word about Lump Sums

Increasingly, retirement benefits are being provided in the form of lump sums. Benefits of DC plans and Cash Balance Plans are *defined* in lump sums. Some regular DB plans offer retirees a lump sum alternative to the pension promise of $X/month for life, and most retirees currently choose the lump sum.

Plan participants *like* lump sums. Lump sums are concrete, participants feel in control, and the sheer size of lump sums is tantalizing. Moreover, anyone with a shorter than average life expectancy would naturally choose a lump sum over a pension.

I personally worry, however, that many retirees will regret opting for a lump sum. My reasons:

- We can never *spend* our lump sum. We must live pretty much off its income. If we live to be 95, we still can't spend the principal as we don't know whether we will live to 105. With a pension, we can spend our monthly check completely because we know there will be another next month.

    Of course, if our purpose is to leave behind the principal for our children's inheritance, the lump sum is attractive. Most retirees, however, are naturally more concerned with having enough money so they themselves can live comfortably.

- Most retirees are not well-equipped to deal with how to invest their lump sum effectively. Some retirees, of course, are indeed well-equipped—at the time they retire. But many of them, as they get into their 80s, will find their investment responsibility increasingly burdensome. And eventually, someone else is likely to take control of their investments.

- Many retirees are smart enough to know they need investment assistance. But whom should they lean on? Few are well-equipped to sort through the choice of personal investment counselors. And once they decide, the counselor's fee comes right off the top.
- A few retirees, unfortunately, are sitting ducks for fast talkers or are otherwise unfrugal enough to spend their lump sums long before their time. Then what? Are they to become wards of the state?

These are a few of the reasons why I believe retirees, and society as a whole, will suffer if traditional DB plans decline relative to DC any more than they have already.

One way to mitigate part of the drawbacks of lump sums would be for plan sponsors to offer a combination lump sum/annuity option—any combination of the two. For example, an employee at his retirement could choose an annuity starting only when he reaches his eightieth birthday, and he could take the balance in a lump sum. Such an annuity would cause only a modest reduction in his lump sum and he could afford to *spend* his entire lump sum by the time he reached 80.

In Short

Defined contribution plans make a wonderful adjunct to a defined benefit plan. But I think the headlong worldwide movement toward DC plans *instead* of DB is a mistake. DC plans are more costly to employers than a DB plan needs to be, and I think most retirees will end up worse off.

Chapter 17

Endowment Funds

What is the purpose of an endowment fund? Its purpose is to throw off a perpetual stream of income to support the operations of the sponsoring organization. All endowment policies should flow from that purpose.

Key criteria for endowments:

- For planning and budgeting purposes, the stream of income should be reasonably predictable.
- For the health of the organization, the magnitude of that steam of income should, over the long-term, maintain its buying power.

The traditional approach to income recognition by endowment funds is materially flawed. It defines *income* by the accounting definition of dividends, interest, rent, and sometimes net *realized* capital gains as well. If an investment approach is kept reasonably in tact, the year-to-year stream of dividends, interest, and rent is quite predictable. But the impact on income is a key consideration if anyone suggests a major change in the endowment's investment approach. Moreover, if realized capital gains are included in the definition of income, that creates a wild card.

The trouble with income defined as just dividends, interest, and rent is that it impacts investment policy both seriously and detrimentally. To provide a reasonable amount of income, the sponsor is motivated to invest a major proportion of the endowment in bonds and stocks with high dividend yields. And if income is running short of what is needed, the sponsor can adjust the investment portfolio to increase the dividends or interest.

Such an approach dooms the second criterion, of maintaining the endowment's buying power over the long term. That's because the capital value of bonds, for example, does nothing to maintain buying power (unless one considers relatively new inflation-linked bonds). There is no concept of *real* return—investment return in excess of inflation.

Because the definition of income has such a great impact on investment policies, the definition of income must be revised before we can consider investment policy.

Fortunately, a concept has been developed, and is being used more and more widely, that does a pretty good job of meeting both of the above criteria. It is known as the *Total Return Approach.*

The Total Return, Imputed Income Approach

The Total Return Approach begins with the concept that we should recognize as income only that amount that might, long-term, be considered *real* income—income in excess of inflation. So the first question is: How much *real* return can we realistically aspire to earn on our endowment fund over the long term?

That depends on how we invest the endowment fund. It's obvious, then, that the way to maximize the endowment's real return over the long-term is to maximize its *total return*—the sum of accounting income plus capital gains, both realized *and unrealized*. We go right back to Chapters 3 and 4, "Investment Objectives" and "Asset Allocation," as they are the starting point.

Let's say we decide on an asset mix of 80% common stocks, 20% fixed income, or 75/25, and after consulting historical returns of those asset classes, we conclude that we can prudently predict a *real* return over the long-term of 5% per year. That says we can recognize 5% of market value as "Imputed Income" each year.

But with this asset allocation the market value will fluctuate widely from year to year, and if Imputed Income equals 5% of that fluctuating value, then the fluctuation in annual income may be greater than our sponsor can live with. Therefore, let's define Imputed Income as 5% of a *moving average* of market values. We have found that a sound definition of Imputed Income is: *The average market value of the endowment fund over the last five year ends (adjusted for new contributions and adjusted for withdrawals in excess of Imputed Income, if any).*

Advantages of this approach include:

- The sponsor gains a fairly predictable level of annual income, not subject to large percentage changes from year to year.
- The sponsor learns early in the year the amount of income it will withdraw from the endowment fund. This is a big help in budgeting.
- Investment policy cannot be manipulated. The only way our sponsor can increase Imputed Income is by investing more successfully—by achieving a higher rate of *total return*, long term.

What is the downside of the Total Return Approach? The concept is long-term oriented. There may be intervals when the fund's principal declines for several years in a row. There is no way to avoid this possibility, as all markets are volatile. The same risk exists under traditional approaches to endowment and foundation investing. But markets, over a great many years, have eventually bounced back each time. As they do, the fund, under the Total Return Approach, regains the buying power that it lost—provided the rate of Imputed Return was established responsibly in the first place.

Appendix A (page 291) illustrates how such an Imputed Income method would have worked in the 1970s, when real investment returns were negative. Clearly, there was pain. Imputed Income dropped by almost 13% from 1973 to 1979 but never by as much as 5% in any one year. Then by 1982 Imputed Income was again above its prior high-water mark of 1973—although not in real terms.

Appendix B describes the functioning of the Imputed Income method. Once the amount of Imputed Income for the current year is determined, the sponsor has the flexibility to decide *when* during the year it will withdraw the money. Almost always, a withdrawal necessitates a sale of stocks or bonds (or mutual funds), as cash should not generally be allowed to accumulate. Dividends and interest should normally be reinvested promptly.

Warning: After a long interval—like the 20 years ended 1998, when investment returns far exceeded a 5% real return assumption, which forms the philosophical basis of our Imputed Income formula—members of the fund sponsor may agitate to raise the Imputed Income percentage (such as to 5½% or even 6%). That is the time to re-visit Appendix A relative to the 1970s, modify it by the increased Imputed Income percentage, and see how happy the fund sponsor's members are with the result. Not very happy, I suspect.

It is easy to forget that an investment period like the 1970s *can occur,* and the higher the market goes, the higher the probability that it will occur. My advice, therefore is: *Don't touch that dial!* If we have established our Imputed Income formula soundly in the first place, let's not tinker with it.

"Owners" of the Endowment Fund

We speak of a sponsor's endowment fund as if that sponsor is the sole owner. That's true in one sense, but it's a little more complicated than that. There are two basic kinds of money in the endowment fund.

Donor Designated and Board Designated Endowment

One is Donor Designated endowment, money that was designated by the contributor for the purpose of endowment. This is the only true endowment. To keep faith with its contributors, and the law, the sponsor should withdraw no more than annual income; the sponsor may not withdraw principal. Under most endowment statutes, Imputed Income meets this requirement of not withdrawing more than annual income, provided the definition of Imputed Income has been rationally defined. In fact, I would contend that the Imputed Income approach meets the intent of endowment statutes far better than the traditional definition of interest and dividends, and so on.

The other basic kind of money in the endowment fund is Board Designated money. This is money the sponsor's board of directors chose to treat as endowment. It is not legally endowment, and future boards may at any time withdraw the entire principal if they so choose, as one board cannot bind a future board in this regard. But the sponsor has every reason to treat Board Designated endowment as true endowment, investing it with a long-term approach in the hope and assumption that future boards will treat it similarly.

Why would a sponsor's board choose to designate contributions as endowment?

- Many sponsors encourage its supporters to include the sponsor in their wills. Bequests are a wonderful support for any sponsor. But bequests come in a lumpy fashion—a whole lot one year, very little the next, with no way of predicting the pattern. Few bequests are specifically designated by the donor for endowment. But bequests should generally not be put into the operating budget, as they can't be budgeted for. Hence many sponsors have a standing board resolution that *all* bequests should automatically go into endowment.

- Sponsors receive other unexpected gifts during the year, such as gifts in memory of a supporter who has just died. These also are best shunted directly to endowment.
- If the sponsor is fortunate to end a year with a budget surplus, one of the things the sponsor might consider doing with the surplus is directing it to endowment, where it can benefit the sponsor for years to come rather than artificially easing the sponsor's operating budget for just the coming year.

Use-Restricted Endowment

Many donors restrict their contributions to particular uses that are important to them. For example, a sponsor might receive two large contributions—one simply restricted to Program X, and the other designated for endowment *and also* restricted to Program X.

The sponsor would now have four endowment fund "owners":

1. Donor Designated, Restricted to Program X (the donor designated the gift to endowment and restricted it to Program X).
2. Donor Designated, Unrestricted (the donor designated the gift to endowment but didn't restrict its use to any particular program).
3. Board Designated, Restricted to Program X (the donor restricted the gift to Program X but the Board, not the donor, designated it to endowment).
4. Board Designated, Unrestricted (the donor didn't restrict the gift to any program, and the Board, not the donor, designated it to endowment).

A large sponsor, such as a university, could conceivably have dozens of restricted endowments, some of them Donor Designated, and some Board Designated. *It is necessary that each of these endowments be accounted for separately,* so the income from each can be used for its particular purpose.

If we have a dozen such endowments, we can invest each separately, receiving from our custodian a separate statement on each. Or we can do things a simpler way, a way that both saves cost and leads to better investment returns: we can co-invest all such endowments as a single endowment fund.

But then how do we keep each endowment separate? Through unit accounting, just like a mutual fund. That means we must *unitize* our endowment fund, starting with an arbitrary unit value, such as $10, and changing that unit value based on the total return earned by our investments each quarter.

If we start our endowment fund with two owners—Donor Designated Unrestricted (DDU) endowment of $30,000 and Board Designated Unrestricted (BDU) endowment of $70,000—we would start with 10,000 units, each valued arbitrarily at $10.0000 (($30,000 + $70,000)/10,000 = $10).

During the first quarter, let's say our fund has a total return of 3.628%. Its unit value would rise to $10.3628 (1.03628 × $10.0000). And at the end of that quarter let's say someone contributes $50,000 and designates it for endowment and restricts it to Program X (DDX). Our endowment would now have three "owners"—DDU with 3,000 units, BDU with 7,000 units, and now DDX with 4,824.95 units ($50,000/$10.3628).

Appendix C provides an example of unit accounting and a procedure a sponsor can use to maintain that unit accounting.

Investing Endowment Funds

Some of the most advanced institutional investors are the largest endowment funds—such as those of Harvard, Yale, Duke, and Stanford. They understand diversification, have large well-paid staffs, and are on the leading edge of institutional investing.

Few endowment funds are as well endowed. How should an endowment fund go about investing when it has only $50 million, or perhaps only $50,000?

Such endowment funds also should invest under the same principles outlined in Chapters 3 and 4 on Investment Objectives and Asset Allocation. This has not been the typical approach, however, that most such endowment funds have used.

All too often, members of the board or staff of the fund sponsor know a local banker they trust and hire the bank's trust department to manage the endowment fund. The banker is usually highly trustworthy, indeed, but the approach is often submarginal—for two reasons:

1. Few bank trust departments have the expertise to invest with real global diversification, and
2. While the staff members of bank trust departments work diligently at their jobs, they are rarely world class investors, for a very simple reason. Hardly any bank trust departments can afford the kind of compensation that will attract, or keep, the world's best.

Alternatively, many endowment funds place their money with a local investment management firm that has a strong reputation in the community. But the same questions should be raised: Does the firm have global expertise, and if so, is it really world class in all areas? Few if any firms meet that criterion, anywhere.

Well, how can a small endowment fund access world-class managers? True, they can't be quite as sophisticated in their approach as large funds, but they can gain most of the benefits of diversification—thanks to mutual funds.

Among the thousands of mutual funds, there are world class funds in every category of marketable securities. Even an endowment fund as small as $50,000 can diversify among 5 to 10 highly diverse mutual funds.

But which ones? Certainly, there are many mutual funds we wouldn't want to touch. How can we know which are the world's best?

Role of the Mutual Fund Consultant

Few endowment funds have the expertise on their boards or staff to know which mutual funds are among the best in the world. They must therefore hire an outside consultant who understands the benefits of diversification and who specializes in finding the best mutual funds in each asset class.

Such a consultant could be one's local bank, but few banks have developed expertise in mutual funds. Banks would rather guide us into investment programs managed by their own trust departments.

Many brokers and insurance company representatives offer mutual fund expertise. But can we expect totally unbiased advice from them when they are motivated to gravitate to the range of mutual funds that compensate them? Many such consultants are paid through front-loaded mutual funds—those that charge an extra 3% to 8% "load" (read *selling commission*)—or those that charge an *annual* 0.25% through a 12(b)(1) deduction from assets (read *another form of selling commission*)—or those that charge a back load when we sell the mutual fund, even after we have held that fund for a year or two.

I suggest a criterion for the hiring of a consultant should be that *the consultant's only source of compensation be the fees that he charges to his clients.* The consultant should then have no biases. His direct fees will be higher, of course. But we will know fully what he is costing us because none of his compensation will be coming through the back door.

Such a consultant will typically steer us toward no-load mutual funds that do not charge 12(b)(1) fees. Many world class mutual funds fit this category. On occasion, the consultant might steer us toward a load fund or one with 12(b)(1) fees. If so, his only motivation should be that he believes future returns of that mutual fund, *net of all fees,* will still be the best in its particular asset class.

The consultant should also be able to provide quarterly reports on the performance of our fund, including the endowment fund's composite benchmark and comparisons with each individual mutual fund's respective benchmark.

It is easier to draw up the criteria for such a consultant than to suggest how to find and hire one. Our selection should be based on the consultant's track record with other institutional funds and the predictive value we feel we can attribute to that track record when we evaluate all the subjective factors—including breadth of diversification in his approach, and continuity of staff.

So much is published about mutual funds today in sources like *Morningstar* that we might try to select our mutual funds ourselves. Today, such an approach is more viable than ever, but I still would not advise it. A consultant should know a lot more about mutual funds than just what is published, and much of his value added is his subjective assessment of the predictive value of a mutual fund's track record.

Exclusive use of mutual funds would entail a marked change in policy for many endowment funds that are either explicitly or implicitly wedded to the use of local investment management. There is no reason to discriminate against a local investment manager, but what should lead us to think that one or more of our local investment managers is among the best in the world? Our choice of investment management should be blind to where a manager's head office may be located. That blindness in itself is a key advantage of the exclusive use of mutual funds.

One role for our local bank may be that of custodian—the entity that holds the assets, executes all purchases and sales, keeps all cash invested automatically, and sends us periodic asset and transaction statements. The reporting systems of many local trust companies are oriented more toward taxable than tax-free investors, however, and their fees may be higher than the value of their services.

It is certainly possible for the fund sponsor to do its own custody of mutual funds and execute the necessary transactions. These functions, however, are an added responsibility for staff members who may not have much competence in this particular area, and staff turnover could lead to another source of problems.

Social Investing

A number of fund sponsors—churches and others—overlay their endowment fund investment objectives with a set of social goals that constrain them from investing in the stocks and bonds of certain kinds of companies.

This was most prevalent in the 1980s, when many funds avoided securities of companies that did business in South Africa. Other fund sponsors are sensitive to companies that do business in one or more other categories, such as cigarettes, alcoholic beverages, munitions, chemical fertilizers, and so on. Other funds consciously allocate a small part of their endowment funds to minority-owned enterprises or other companies they view as performing a particular social good.

Overlaying our investment policies with social objectives is one way to "put our money where our mouth is," and as such, is perfectly appropriate—provided the majority of constituents of that fund sponsor agree with the social objectives and with the cost in lower investment returns. Social investing probably does more to enable investing institutions to be consistent in their principles, and probably less from a practical standpoint to effect change.

But how can an organization gain the consensus of its constituency as to what industries to avoid? Tobacco companies might be easy. And maybe munitions . . . but should we even avoid companies for whom munitions is only 1% of their business? How about industries that pollute the environment? Which industries are they? Where should we draw the line?

The Cost in Investment Returns

If a fund sponsor is to take a social investing approach, everyone involved must be realistic about the fact that exercising social investing is likely to be costly, for the following reasons:

1. Competent investing is difficult enough. Avoiding any set of companies adds to complexity and reduces the investment manager's range of opportunities.
2. The best investment managers are competitive people and are driven to achieve the best they can. They tend to avoid clients who want them to observe any particular constraints.
3. Very few mutual funds observe social investing constraints and become eligible for consideration. Those few mutual funds that do social investing have—over the long term—achieved performance that is much closer to the bottom of the pack than the top. Moreover, one must consider whether the social objectives of any "social investment" mutual fund are the same as the social objectives of the fund sponsor.
4. Without the use of multiple mutual funds it is difficult for an investor to achieve the wide diversification I believe institutional investors should strive for.
5. Social investing has an unintended byproduct: Most large companies are so diversified that social-investing limitations eliminate many of them from consideration. Our remaining universe therefore is more heavily weighted toward small stocks, companies we know less about.

   Social investing might also limit us to investments in U.S. companies, because we may be too unfamiliar with specific foreign companies to know whether or not they meet our social investing criteria.
6. Members of the fund sponsor must expend a lot of effort to maintain a complete, accurate, and timely list of companies to avoid. Members must be willing to devote the time.

In short, it is unrealistic to expect as good long-term total investment return from a socially invested investment fund as from one that has no such constraints.

Whether or not an endowment fund pursues social investing, I still recommend the endowment fund to use the Imputed Income method for recognizing income. But whereas for endowment funds with unconstrained investments I have suggested an Imputed Income formula of 5%,[1] I would

---

[1] Of the average market value of the endowment fund over the past five years.

recommend no more than 4%, perhaps less, for an endowment fund limited by social investing.

The fund sponsor's board should recognize this reduced investment expectation and buy into it explicitly by lowering the Imputed Income formula. And I believe the board has a moral obligation to inform the fund sponsor's constituents and make sure they agree.

If everyone agrees, then of course the board should go ahead with its plans for social investing.

Proxy Voting

Some fund sponsors try to pursue their social objectives through proxy voting. They have at times introduced and supported motions on a company's proxy to effect some social or environmental change.

I believe such efforts have done more to sensitize companies to the issues than to effect change *directly*—and that has probably been the realistic expectation by the fund sponsors.

The investment downside of this approach is that we can only vote a company's proxy if we are direct owners of its stock, and that constrains us from using mutual funds, which are such a convenient and effective means of gaining strong investment management and broad diversification.

In Short

Endowments should set their investment policies solely in an effort to earn the highest expected total return within an acceptable level of risk, and without extraneous considerations about income recognition. Endowments free themselves to do this if they adopt the Total Return Approach. Under this approach they no longer recognize traditional accounting income, such as interest and dividends, as the annual income they can spend. Instead, they recognize Imputed Income—a set percentage of the endowment's average market value.

Appendix A

Pro Forma Results of the Imputed Income Method

To see how a 5% Imputed Income Method would have worked over a 15-year interval that included the disastrous 1970s, assume:

(a) On December 31, 1968, our endowment fund received a contribution of $1,000,000.

(b) There were no further contributions or withdrawals other than Imputed Income.

(c) Investments were rebalanced to a market value ratio of 80% stocks and 20% long-term bonds at the end of each year, and net investment performance exactly matched that of the S&P 500 and the Lehman Corporate Bond Index.

Results would have been as follows: ($000s)

	Income Withdrawn during Year (a)	As % of Prior Year-End Market Value (b)	Investment Return On			Year-End Market Value (f)	Market Value for Computing Imputed Income (g)
			Stocks (c)	Bonds (d)	Total (e)		
1964						$ 800	
1965						850	
1966						900	
1967						950	
1968						1,000	$ 900
1969	$45.00	4.50%	−8.5%	−8.1%	−8.4%	873	915
1970	45.73	5.24	4.0	18.4	6.9	885	922
1971	46.08	5.20	14.3	11.0	13.6	957	933
1972	46.65	4.87	18.9	7.3	16.6	1,065	956
1973	47.80	4.49	−14.8	1.1	−11.6	896	935
1974	46.77	5.22	−26.5	−3.0	−21.8	659	893
1975	44.63	6.77	37.3	14.6	32.8	823	880
1976	44.01	5.35	23.6	18.6	22.6	960	881
1977	44.04	4.59	−7.4	1.7	−5.6	864	841
1978	42.03	4.87	6.5	−0.1	5.2	866	835
1979	41.73	4.82	18.5	−4.2	14.0	942	891
1980	44.55	4.73	32.5	−2.6	25.5	1,132	953
1981	47.63	4.21	−4.9	3.0	−3.3	1,047	970
1982	48.50	4.63	21.4	39.3	25.0	1,254	1,048
1983	52.40	4.18	22.5	9.3	19.9	1,446	1,164
1984	58.20	4.03					
15-year annual return			7.6%	6.5%	7.6%		

Col. a = 5% × prior Col. g
Col. b = Col. a / prior Col. f
Col. e = .8 × Col. c + .2 × Col. d
Col. f = Prior Col. f × (Col. e × (prior Col. f − Col. a / 2)) − Col. a (assuming imputed income is withdrawn at midyear, on average). Exception is 1964–1967 when Col. f = 1968 contribution less 5%/yr.
Col. g = Average of latest five values in Col. f

Appendix B

The Total Return or Imputed Income Method

1. For any fiscal year, Imputed Income equal to 5% of the Base Market Value of the Endowment Fund shall be withdrawn and realized as income for that year.

2. The Base Market Value shall be the average market value of the Endowment Fund on December 31 of the last five calendar years. The market value at prior year-ends, however, shall be increased for contributions (or decreased for withdrawals, if any, other than withdrawals of Imputed Income) made subsequent to those years according to the following procedure: A contribution (or withdrawal) shall be valued at 95% for the year-end prior to the contribution (or withdrawal); 90% for the second prior year-end; 85% for the third prior year-end; and 80% for the fourth prior year-end.

3. The timing of withdrawals of Imputed Income during each fiscal year shall be at the discretion of the Finance Committee. At the time an Imputed Income withdrawal is to be made, the Finance Committee shall decide from which investment account (or accounts) the withdrawal shall be made. If such investment account does not hold enough cash to meet the withdrawal, the manager of that account shall sell assets sufficient to meet the withdrawal.

4. Withdrawals of Imputed Income shall be allocated to the various owners' accounts of the endowment fund[2] on the basis of the relative market values of those owners' accounts as of the latest year-end.

Following is a sample Imputed Income worksheet.

---

[2] Such as Donor Designated, Restricted to Program X, or Board Designated, Unrestricted.

Sample Imputed Income Worksheet

Date	Entry	Market Value	Contributions	Adjusted Year-End Market Values											5-Yr. Total	Income
				12/31/00	12/31/01	12/31/02	12/31/03	12/31/04	12/31/05	12/31/06	12/31/07	12/31/08	12/31/09	12/31/10		
12/31/99	MV	0		0												
Year '00	C		100,000	80,000	85,000	90,000	95,000	100,000							450,000	4,500
12/31/00	MV	100,000		80,000												
Year '01	C		56,500		45,200	48,025	50,850	53,675								
12/31/01	MV	165,816			130,200	138,025	145,850	153,675	165,816						733,566	7,336
Year '02	C		550,000			440,000	467,500	495,000	522,500							
12/31/02	MV	800,000				578,025	613,350	648,675	688,316	800,000					3,328,366	33,284
Year '03	C		300,000				240,000	255,000	270,000	285,000						
12/31/03	MV	1,210,000					853,350	903,675	958,316	1,085,000	1,210,000				5,010,341	50,103
Year '04	C		8,000					6,400	6,800	7,200	7,600					
12/31/04	MV	1,210,000						910,075	965,116	1,092,200	1,217,600	1,210,000			5,394,991	53,950
Year '05	C		12,000						9,600	10,200	10,800	11,400				
12/31/05	MV	1,390,000							974,716	1,102,400	1,228,400	1,221,400	1,390,000		5,916,916	59,169
Year '06	C		75,000							60,000	63,750	67,500	71,250			
12/31/06	MV	1,580,000								1,162,400	1,292,150	1,288,900	1,461,250	1,580,000	6,784,700	67,847

C = Net Contributions
MV = Market Value

Last column = % of 5-Yr. Total, times 5%

Appendix C

Unit Accounting

Unit accounting is conceptually simple for a mutual fund that is priced every day. A valid new unit value (share value) is calculated daily by dividing the fund's total market value by the number of units prior to any contributions or withdrawals that day. Money then goes into or out of the fund on the basis of that new unit value; the owner is credited with a number of units equal to his contribution (or withdrawal) divided by that day's unit value.

Endowment funds are not priced every day. At most, they are priced once a month. If (a) the fund is priced as of the end of every month, and if (b) contributions and withdrawals are permitted only at the end of a month, then unit value is similarly simple. There is always a valid unit value to determine the number of units attributable to a contribution or withdrawal made at the end of that month.

Many endowment funds are priced only quarterly, whereas contributions and withdrawals occur at any time during the quarter. Calculating unit values here is a problem. One must assume that the internal rate of investment return for that quarter, whatever it may be, occurred in essentially a straight-line manner from the beginning to the end of the quarter.

A sample worksheet of a hypothetical endowment fund that has two Donor Designated owners and two Board Designated owners follows. Let's review some of the entries.

The fund was begun on 12/31/00 with a $30,000 Donor Designated contribution and a $70,000 Board Designated contribution, both unrestricted as to use. We arbitrarily establish a unit value of $10.0000 to start off with. Hence we credit the two "owners" with 3,000 and 7,000 units, respectively.

In the quarter ended 3/31/01, there were no contributions or withdrawals until a contribution of $50,000, designated by the Donor to Endowment and restricted to Program X, was made on the last day of the quarter. In this case, the unit value is easy to calculate:

We divide the fund's 3/31 market value just prior to the contribution ($103,628) by the total units, which remained unchanged during the quarter at 10,000.00—for a unit value of $10.3628:

$$\$103,628/10,000.00 = \$10.3628$$

Sample Unit Record Worksheet

Date	Type of Entry	Unit Value	Donor Designated Endowment				Board Designated Endowment				Total Endowment Fund		
			Unrestricted		Program X		Unrestricted		Program X				
			Units	MV $	Units	MV $	Units	MV $	Units	MV $	Units	MV $	
12/31/00	C	$10.0000	3,000.00 30.0%	$30,000			7,000.00 70.0%	$70,000			10,000.00 100%	$100,000	
3/31/01	C	10.3628			4,824.95	$+50,000					4,824.95	+50,000	Wagner bequest
3/31/01	V	10.3628	3,000.00	31,088	4,824.95	50,000	7,000.00	72,540			14,824.95	153,628	
5/28/01	C	10.0690							496.57	$+5,000	496.57	+5,000	Conrad bequest
6/30/01	V	9.9092	3,000.00	29,728	4,824.95	47,811	7,000.00	69,364	496.57	4,921	15,321.52	151,824	
7/10/01	W	10.0049	−134.93	−1,350			−314.85	−3,150			−449.78	−4,500	Imputed income
9/30/01	V	10.8653	2,865.07	31,130	4,824.95	52,425	6,685.15	72,636	496.57	5,395	14,871.74	161,586	
10/21/01	C	10.9067					91.69	+1,000			91.69	+1,000	Davis memorials
12/12/01	C	11.0099					45.42	+500			45.42	+500	Wyatt memorials
12/31/01	V	11.0479	2,865.07 19.1%	31,653	4,824.95 32.1%	53,305	6,822.26 45.5%	75,372	496.57 3.3%	5,486	15,008.85 100%	165,816	
3/31/02	V	11.9750	2,865.07	34,309	4,824.95	57,779	6,822.26	81,697	496.57	5,946	15,008.85	179,731	
4/17/02	C	12.0247					124.74	1,500			124.74	+1,500	Merwin bequest
6/20/02	W	12.1921	−114.91	−1,401	−193.16	−2,355	−273.78	−3,338	−19.85	−242	−601.70	−7,336	Imputed income
6/30/02	V	12.2301	2,750.16	33,635	4,631.79	56,648	6,673.22	81,614	476.72	5,830	14,531.89	177,727	

C = Contribution
W = Withdrawal
V = Valuation

Because of the $50,000 contribution, we credit Donor Designated Program X with 4,824.95 units ($50,000/$10.3628 unit value).

In the quarter ending 6/30/01, there was only one cash flow—a contribution of $5,000 for Program X was made mid-quarter, on 5/28, and designated by the Board to Endowment. We calculate the number of units and the unit value as of 5/28 as follows:

1. The internal rate of return for the quarter[3] is –4.377%, based on the starting and ending market values for the quarter and the 5/28 contribution of $5,000.
2. The 6/30 unit value is $9.9092 (the 3/31 unit value of $10.3628 times one plus the quarter's rate of return (1 – 4.377%):

$$\$10.3628 \times .95623 = \$9.9092$$

3. We divide the 6/30 market value of $151,824 by the unit value of $9.9092 to determine the total number of units outstanding as of 6/30—a total of 15,321.52.

$$\$151,824/\$9,9092 = 15,321.52 \text{ units}$$

4. The number of units attributable to the $5,000 contribution on 5/28 must be 496.57—the difference between the 15,321.52 units outstanding on 6/30 and the 14,824.95 units outstanding on 3/31.

$$15,321.52 - 14,824.95 = 496.57$$

Board Designated endowment now has 3,496.57 units (3,000 + 496.57).

5. The 5/28 unit value is $10.0690 (the $5,000 contribution divided by the 496.57 units).

$$\$5,000/496.57 = \$10.0690$$

In the quarter ending 9/30/01, a withdrawal of $4,500 for Imputed Income was made on 7/10. The number of units and unit value relating to this withdrawal—since it was the only cash flow in the quarter—are calculated by the same methodology used in the prior quarter (we calculate the internal rate of return for the quarter to be 9.6486%, then follow steps 2 through 5 above). Then we allocate the $4,500 of Imputed Income on the basis of percentage ownership at the prior year-end—30% to Donor Designated Unrestricted and 70% to Board Designated Unrestricted.

In the last quarter of the year, there were two mid-quarter contributions—$1,000 on 10/21 and $500 on 12/12—both unrestricted as to use and

---

See page 25 for an example of how this is calculated.

designated by the Board to Endowment. Here the math gets a little more complicated:

1. The internal rate of return for the quarter is calculated as 1.6806%, based on the starting and ending market values for the quarter, the 10/21 contribution of $1,000, and the 12/12 contribution of $500.
2. The 12/31 unit value is $11.0479: We multiply the 9/30 unit value of $10.8653 by one plus the rate of return for the quarter $(1 + 1.6806\%)$, or:

$$\$10.8653 \times 1.016806 = \$11.0479$$

3. We divide the 12/31 market value of $165,816 by the unit value of $11.0479 to determine the total number of units outstanding—a total of 15,008.85 units.

$$\$165,816/\$11.0479 = 15,008.85$$

4. We estimate the unit value as of 10/21, the date of the first contribution, by multiplying the 9/30 unit value of $10.8653 times one plus the quarter's internal rate of return $(1 + 1.6806\%)$ raised to a power equal to (a) the number of days after the end of the last quarter, divided by (b) the total number of days in the quarter:

$$\$10.8653 \times (1.016806)^{21/92} = 10.9067 \text{ estimated unit value}$$

5. We estimate the unit value as of the 12/12 date of the next contribution the same way:

$$\$10.8653 \times (1.016806)^{73/92} = 11.0099 \text{ estimated unit value}$$

6. The number of units attributable to each contribution is calculated as follows:

$$\$1,000/10.9067 \text{ estimated unit value} = 91.69 \text{ units}$$

$$\$500/11.0099 \text{ estimated unit value} = 45.41 \text{ units}$$

7. The sum of these units, added to the number of units outstanding as of 9/30, must equal the number of units outstanding as of 12/31.

The above procedure should get us very close, but sometimes there is a small margin of error in the total number of units, as in this case:

14,871.74 (units outstanding as of 9/30) + 91.69 + 45.41 = 15,008.84 units or .01 unit too few.

The closest rounding in this case is to increase the units for the 12/12 contribution by .01 to 45.42 units. We can now calculate unit values for the two contribution dates by dividing each contribution by the number of units credited for it.

Chapter 18

Aphorisms

I *could* have titled this chapter "Miscellaneous Thoughts." But "Aphorisms" sounds more elegant.

It is actually a collection of various ideas that don't seem to fit elsewhere in the book or which I feel are worth expressing another way, despite the risk of redundancy.

Investing under Uncertainty

"The future is totally unpredictable," writes William Sherden.[1] "The only certainty is that we are destined to live in an unpredictable world filled with endless uncertainty." Sherden supports these statements by demonstrating the futility throughout history to the present day of efforts to forecast economic or political events, financial markets, scientific or technological advances, sociological trends, or even the weather (beyond the next two days).

I quote Sherden because his book meshes with my own observations and beliefs. I think it has profound implications for investing, and it serves as an introduction to a number of my aphorisms.

Playing the Odds

There is no sure thing in investments—only probabilities. Sounds like gambling, doesn't it? I draw a clear distinction.

---

[1] William A. Sherden, *The Fortune Sellers,* John Wiley & Sons, Inc., 1998.

Gambling is where the odds of winning are 50:50 or less. I don't understand the attraction of horse racing or casinos. The more we play the higher our long-term probability of losing.

Investing is where (1) the odds are in our favor *and* (2) we have a long enough time horizon to take full advantage of those odds. Many financial investments have a wind behind their back (interest, dividends, growth) that favor the odds of winning in an *absolute* sense—that is, of earning some positive return over time. But, net of fees, the odds do not favor our winning in a *relative* sense. Relative to investing in an index fund, blindly picking active managers is pure gambling.

It is said that an investor who, on a relative basis, wins two-thirds or three-quarters of the time is a spectacular winner. Three implications: (1) No matter how diligent we are, we will—by our own definition—lose on a significant portion of our investments, and we must be psychologically prepared for that. (2) We must be financially capable of sustaining such losses. And (3) if indeed we can win materially more than half the time, diversification and a long time horizon increase substantially the odds that we will end up in the winning column.

A key qualification for professionals in this field is a keen understanding of the laws of probability, both an intuitive and technical understanding, and a discipline to be guided by those laws.

What We Don't Know

Relative to investing, let's figure out what we don't know, then be sure *not* to base our investment decisions on what we don't know.

As a simplistic example, we don't know whether the stock market is more likely to go up or down tomorrow, so the success of our investments shouldn't depend on it. We do know there's a strong probability that the stock market will be higher 10 years from now than it is today. This begins to be something on which we can base investment strategy.

Notice, everything is probabilities. No sure things.

Reversion to the Mean

When we look at enough rates of return, our eyes begin to glaze over, and the Random Walk hypothesis seems more and more valid. Yet there is a strong force that I believe casts its net over the Random Walk and eventually reins it in—and that is Reversion to the Mean. That doesn't say that a poor manager will revert to being average, or vice versa. But it does mean the laws of economics are alive and well.

If domestic stocks outpace foreign stocks long enough (or vice versa), then the relative P/Es, currency values, and other fundamental influences will become so disparate that the advantage will ultimately shift to foreign stocks. Domestic stocks will become so expensive and foreign stocks so cheap relative to one another that investors will begin bidding up the price of foreign stocks relative to domestic stocks, and foreign stocks will begin to outperform.

If the interest-rate spread between FNMA mortgages and Treasury bonds becomes too wide, then investors will buy more mortgages and fewer Treasury bonds, leading to lower interest rates on mortgages relative to Treasury bonds, and the interest-rate spread will trend back into a more normal range.

Reversion to the Mean is a powerful force and should give us considerable pause as we project historical rates of return into the future.

Keys on the Piano

All things being equal, a manager with more keys on his piano should, over the long-term, outperform a manager with fewer keys, and with more consistency. Assuming the manager is equally competent to play all keys, that means he should have more opportunities to find undervalued assets. Also, the increased diversification made possible by the greater number of keys should result in the greater consistency of performance. But finding a manager that is equally competent to play all keys—that's a challenge.

Murphy's Law and Discontinuities

How many times has an investment manager shown us his eminently impressive performance based on a well-articulated investment strategy? As we analyze the strategy, we can see it is founded on certain fundamental assumptions about how particular statistics in the investment world relate to one another. And indeed, the relationships have worked that way during the years he has achieved such impressive performance.

But what if we run into a discontinuity? How nimble will the manager be in adapting to the change in the investment world?

That's a difficult but important thing to evaluate, as Murphy does indeed continue his perambulations.

The Dreaded Disease of Myopia

The signal-to-noise ratio of the investment business is abysmally low, that is, the fluctuation of the markets is so great that it is very hard to distinguish skill from luck. Well-chosen benchmarks can screen out much noise but they can't come close to eliminating it. The best means to screen out market noise is time, even though statisticians tell us that often a much longer interval is needed to develop a meaningful T-statistic than that to which we may be able to ascribe much predictive value.

The moral of the story is, let's avoid the dreaded disease of myopia. Let's not waste time getting exercised over daily or weekly performance. Investment committees might do well to ignore quarterly performance reports and should take great care in forming judgments based on 1-year results or even performance for intervals of 3 years and longer.

A key difference between investing and rolling the dice is time. Investing for a pension fund or endowment fund requires a long-term focus—preferably 10 to 20 years. That's a hard lesson—especially since it transcends most people's career horizons—but it's perhaps the most important lesson newcomers to the investment business must learn.

A Game of Inches

Once we adopt the concept of a widely diversified asset allocation—which has the most impact—the game of continuous improvement is one of inches.[2] But those inches add up.

A simple example is securities lending. If we have a great program, the probable increment it will add to our annual aggregate performance is only perhaps one or two basis points. But an incremental .01% in annual performance with little risk may be a great cost/benefit ratio when

---

[2] A term I first heard used by John Casey about 1980.

we consider the modest effort needed to set up and maintain a securities lending program.

Another example: Assume Account H holds 3% of our assets. We find a manager who we believe can deliver 2%/year more than the manager of Account H. Is it worth making a change to improve our aggregate bottom line by only 6 basis points per year (.03 × .02)? We should do it.

A further example: We find a great arbitrage manager who we believe should be able, conservatively, to churn out net returns of 12%/year with modest volatility and essentially no correlation with our other assets. These ideal characteristics are found rarely. The manager, however, can accept only 0.5% of our assets. If we really believe the manager can deliver these results, let's bring him on board.

Why fight so hard for a few basis points? They add up. If we can succeed in increasing our aggregate return by 50 basis points per year, that may raise us a full quartile in our 10-year comparison with our peers and add an extra $8 to $12 million over that interval for every $100 million we started with.

I Was Wrong

The investment business is certainly one of the most humbling. The scorecard is so clear that every investment manager has no choice with some of his portfolio selections but to say "I was wrong." The same is true of the plan sponsor relative to his choice of investment managers.

I'm talking here, however, of something more—about the *investment principles* we have come to follow, and the analysis we have done on any one investment opportunity. The name of the investment game is not to prove *I* was right, but to find out *what* is right. That can be very elusive and requires an academic mind set. This is not an excuse to be wishy-washy. But it's a call to be continuously open to the possibility of maybe, just maybe, *I might be wrong*.

The Open Mind

A corollary is one of the most important, and more difficult, traits for us to cultivate—an open mind. Each of us knows only a small percentage of what we might usefully know. We must strive constantly to know more and to test our convictions. We can do this only with an open mind.

I don't mean we should be like a leaf blowing in the wind. We must have convictions and act on those convictions. But we should always be open to the possibility that our convictions are not as well founded as we would have liked to think. We can test them by seeking people who take a different point of view, trying to understand the logic underlying that point of view, and seeing how our convictions stand up in light of that line of reasoning.

On Taking Advice

Whenever each of us is considering a material action or recommendation, or preparing a presentation, we receive lots of advice—from superiors, peers, and subordinates. And if we don't receive lots of advice, we should. We may have a great idea, but unless we know how it will play on others and what suggestions they might make, we are missing valuable input. From interested parties, we should *ask* for that input.

There's a catch, however. If we ask a person for his comments and suggestions, we can't ignore his input. If we're not willing to act on his input, we shouldn't ask in the first place.

How do we deal with comments and suggestions on our great idea? Our responses to advice come in several varieties:

1. To some ideas we immediately react: "Why didn't I think of that?" We adopt those ideas quickly.
2. Some comments send us back to the drawing board, because they identify a hole in our great idea. We must be quick to recognize such situations and be ready to deal with them on the basis of our intellect, not our pride.
3. Some comments show that the reader didn't understand what we said. Our reaction here must not be, "How could the stupid jerk fail to understand plain English?" We should recognize, "Someone missed the point here, so someone else is likely to miss it also. I'd better explain my idea in a different way."
4. Alternative suggested wording may strike us, frankly, as not any better than our own gems. In all honesty, however, might not the suggested wording be *just as good*? If so, let's *use* it. Why? By using

other people's ideas, we encourage them to suggest more, and we want that. Also, if we freely use other people's ideas and wording, they will be more likely to ask for and use our suggestions when the positions are reversed.

5. A suggestion does not seem appropriate. We must be sufficiently clear in our own thinking to agree to disagree in such situations. But we must articulate our reasons to the person who made the suggestion so he at least knows we appreciated his idea and didn't simply ignore it. Occasionally, through discussion, we find something related was bothering the person that we *should* pay attention to.

At the start we talked about advice from superiors, peers, and subordinates. Should we treat advice from all three the same? When the advice is from a superior, we may not be as free to avoid adopting it—although we should have the courage to defend our soundly thought-out convictions. But with that caveat, I think we should treat all advice the same— *on its merits.*

Ah, you say, all this takes time. True! But it can be time well invested.

Thinking Outside the Box

In creativity discussions, there is a familiar kind of exercise: Starting at Point A, how can we draw the following figure without (1) lifting our pencil off the page, (2) drawing more than eight straight lines, or (3) repeating any line segment?

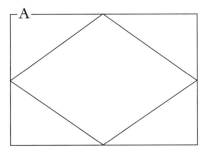

The answer is, we can't do it *unless* we go outside the box:

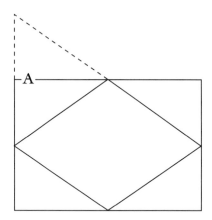

Most investing is generally done within certain parameters that we might consider the box—such as a certain universe of securities, for example. Some of the best investors have been successful because they "cheated"—they went outside the box. They went abroad when the box consisted only of U.S. stocks, or they sold some securities short when the box consisted only of long positions.

We all live in boxes, most of which we may not even be aware of. If we go outside those boxes, we do so at our peril, because others may laugh at us. But *provided* we have done our homework well, going outside the box is how we can raise our performance to a new level.

Opportunists

I admire opportunists and would aspire to be one myself. No, I don't mean opportunists who take advantage of other people. I mean those who recognize opportunities when they arise and are flexible and fast-reacting enough to take advantage of them.

It is highly desirable to establish a target allocation and to discipline ourselves to stick with it. But when a good opportunity arises—a valid opportunity, not a fancy—we should not confuse discipline with rigidity.

For example, we decide to target X% of our portfolio to real estate investments. We have reached our X% when suddenly we find a rare real estate opportunity with exceptional risk/return parameters. Should we mindlessly pass it up, or should we consider borrowing briefly from next year's allocation and give ourselves a *temporary* overweight in real estate?

Conversely, let's hold our fire until we find great opportunities. Let's say we target Y% of our portfolio to timberland, and the only timberland fund available has only mediocre risk/return prospects. Let's not "fill the squares" by taking the first thing that comes along. I'm an anti-square filler. Let's wait for great opportunities, or until we can recognize what those great opportunities are.

A word about opportunists. They are not persons waiting for a great idea to suddenly descend upon them. They are hard workers, constantly beating the bushes, enlarging their network of friends with whom they trade ideas, ever probing. That's where opportunities come from.

Leverage

Leverage is a highly charged word.[3] It conjures up the specter of speculation and wild risk-taking. And well it should—in some cases. But leverage is a very important term, one in which we should grow past the stage of an emotional reaction and into the stage of intellectual analysis.

If we are leveraging the S&P 500, which—let's say—has a standard deviation of 15% per year, is that speculative? If we leverage it two or three times, to a standard deviation of 30% or 45%, that would probably be considered speculative. But if we leverage it only 5%, to a standard deviation of 15.75 ($1.05 \times 15\%$), should we consider that speculative?

Let's say we have a fixed income account invested in T-bills overlaid by interest rate futures—and instead of buying a U.S. Treasury future with a 5-year duration and an underlying value equal to the value of our T-bills, we buy *five times* as many of those futures, with an underlying value equal to *five times* the value of our T-bills. Is that leverage? Relative to a traditional bond account, it surely is! But what if our account is benchmarked against 25-year Treasury zero-coupon bonds? We could buy Treasury zeros, of course, without leverage. The volatility of our "leveraged" futures would not be materially greater than a portfolio of Treasury zeros, as their equivalent duration would be no greater. But the futures would be less costly and

---

[3] Leveraged means paying for an investment partly with borrowed money, either *actually* borrowed, or *implicitly* borrowed, as for example, buying futures or options that have more underlying value than our net assets.

more liquid than the actual zeros. Now I ask again, is that leverage? Or might that just be a smarter way to do it?

Now let's say we want to arbitrage Interest Rate A against Interest Rate B (we buy one and short the other, depending on whether we think the spread between the two interest rates is too wide or too narrow). And let's say the spread between the two interest rates varies between 1% and 3%. While we are very good at making money on this arbitrage, we can make or lose only a little money when we are right or wrong, so our annual expected return is only 1.5%/year. Although the annual standard deviation of our returns may be only 1%, who would want to invest with an annual expected return of only 1.5%/year?

But what if we leveraged—10 times! That sounds wild, doesn't it? Ah, but it may not be. Let's say we can leverage in such a way that our expected return is 15%/year ($10 \times 1.5\%$, an attractive return) and our expected annual standard deviation is 10% ($10 \times 1\%$). Provided our expectations are realistic and that we can control downside risks of the leveraging mechanism, that is hardly a speculative investment!

The word *leverage* cries out for analysis and respect, not necessarily fear. And by the way, we should also check out the risk of UBIT. For tax-free money, leverage often, but not always, incurs UBIT.

Question the Numbers

Numbers . . . numbers . . . numbers! Investing is filled with numbers. Most of them are noise. Yet in the end we must rely on *some* numbers. Gleaning the message from the noise is a constant challenge. The kinds of questions we should ask about every number are:

- Is it accurate?
- How was it put together? Is that clearly defined? Do we understand the black box that spewed it forth? What does it *really* represent?
- Are the numbers consistent with other numbers we're aware of? If not, why not?
- Are there special circumstances we should keep in mind as we look at these numbers?
- Even if the numbers are accurate, are they the *right* numbers to look at? (We all are aware of how people can lie with statistics.)

- Ultimately, so what? The only thing we can do anything about is the future. What *predictive value* can we ascribe to these numbers?

A valuable habit when looking at numbers is to ask ourself "Is that reasonable?" This is especially true if we have calculated the numbers ourselves! The reasonableness test also applies to computer output, including programs like efficient frontiers, thanks to garbage in/garbage out, or the possibility that erroneous algebra may have been programmed.

We look at so many numbers, hence so many chances to go wrong; yet we rely on those numbers, and their accuracy is critical. Fortunately, most errors are of a size that we can catch them with our reasonableness test. For example, if a manager has earned 10%/year for three years, then 8% in the fourth, yet his 4-year return is 11% (higher than his 3-year number), something inside us should cry, "Tilt!" The more-than/less-than test is one of the easiest.

A side benefit: by habitually applying the test, we tend to understand the numbers better. And we gain an occasional insight when a strange answer turns out to be right.

Close Enough Is Good Enough— And Sometimes Better

Investments necessarily require us to deal with an immense quantity of figures. How accurate do they have to be? That all depends. There are certain times (as when calculating the daily multiplier in a Guaranteed Interest Contract) when we should go out 15 decimal places. And there are other times when it's close enough if we round to the nearest $100 million or even the nearest $ billion (as in discussing the market capitalization of a stock, for example).

The point is, if we understand *why* we are doing something, there is no point in our refining our analysis to any greater detail than might in the end impact our *so what?* Close enough is good enough—provided it *is* good enough, and not just a rationale for cutting corners.

And whenever we are presenting charts to committees or even our fellow staff members, we should be careful to round to the highest number commensurate with what we are trying to show. Extra decimals only add complexity and get in the way of quick understanding.

Why?

One thing I consider critical with everyone we work with, is that they understand *why*. This applies to our committee, all levels of our staff, our trustee/custodians (who should be considered an extension of our staff), and our investment managers.

It is not enough to understand what and how. Without understanding why, a person will sooner or later be doing something useless and not realize it. If he is doing calculations, he will not recognize when something is awry and he is coming up with garbage. He certainly won't be in a position to contribute constructive ideas.

If a committee member doesn't understand why, he is likely subsequently to make the wrong judgment as to whether a result is within the range of what should be expected or outside the bounds of what should be tolerated.

Whether a person is staff or a committee member, he should not simply accept our word. He should press us for why until he gets an answer he understands and makes sense to him.

Persons pressing us for why are not a nuisance—they are doing us a favor. They help us understand where the other person is and how well we have communicated. They help us articulate a rationale we may not have articulated very well before. In so doing, they often help us understand our own rationale better. And sometimes, we find we can't articulate our rationale very well—we find our argument doesn't hold up, after all, and it's time to head back to the drawing board.

So What?

In managing a pension or endowment portfolio, there are a million interesting ways we can spend our time. But time is a precious resource. We have only a limited number of hours each year. How should we allocate those hours? We need a criterion for the allocation of our time, and I suggest that a great criterion is, "So what?"

Unless we manage money in-house, there are only a few actions we can take. We can hire a manager, fire a manager, put more money with a manager, take some away, or change the guidelines for a given account. That's all.

How does every task we do contribute to our competency in making any of these five decisions? For example, we can spend an hour a day reading the

Wall Street Journal. That's interesting and it's relevant, but what does an hour a day spent that way do for us relative to the above five decisions? We can obtain hundreds of analyses of the performance and portfolio composition of each of our managers. Some of these are critically important in assessing our managers. But each possible analysis needs to be evaluated by "So what?" Yes, it's interesting. But does it contribute materially to any of the above five decisions? How much to the bottom line is added by the preparation of monthly or extensive quarterly reports to one's committee?

Applying the criterion of "So what?" has been a big help to me in staying focused.

Impatience

If we have thought through an opportunity thoroughly and concluded it is worth doing, let's get on with it as quickly as we can do it right. During the interval we delay, we may save ourselves a loss or may miss a gain, but on average—over time—we will miss during that delay part of the long-term incremental rate of return we anticipated. The magnitude of this average opportunity cost is probably well worth the extra effort required to get on with the show.

In the real world such impatience often conflicts with the schedule of committee meetings and the drudge of legal documentation, so we must learn to conform our level of impatience to the practicalities of life. But we should never lose our underlying impatience to get on with our opportunity as quickly as circumstances permit.

A corollary of impatience is, *"Do it now!"* If something special is worth doing for business (or pleasure), let's make time to do it now. Why?

- Getting things done well before deadline often gives us time to mull it over and improve it.
- Getting it off our plate lets us focus on other things. (Other special things are likely to come up as our deadline approaches, and we'll be able to do them too.)
- We'll sleep better without things hanging over us.

Trust

We must work only with people—staff persons, investment managers, trustee/custodians, and consultants—in whom we have complete trust. We may have the best auditors in the world, but if anyone on the team is smart enough, he can figure out a way to slip his nimble fingers into our deep pockets. Everyone on our team must have a high sense of ethics, a passion for his fiduciary responsibilities, and a dedication to the truth. We find this out through our due diligence and our own continuing sensitivities.

There are, fortunately, a remarkable number of people in the investment world who meet these criteria. And once we have added someone to our team, and established a reliable information system, we must be willing to let go. We must be willing to trust.

We are not the experts on everything. We must recognize that others are more expert in certain areas than we. When they suggest better ways to do things, we should always press for *why* and make sure they are defining *good* the same as we, but we should trust them.

When we hire a manager, what is the point of listing a litany of constraints on what he may or may not do? Right off, that means we don't trust him, and it only constrains his creativity and reduces his potential for long-term return for us. We should agree on a benchmark but let his investments stray from that benchmark if he so chooses. We need to stay informed, of course, but we should trust the manager to stray outside his benchmark only when he feels he has the competence to do so and when he is convinced the results will be beneficial.

There's a corollary to this: We ourselves must *earn* the trust of everyone we work with—committee members, fellow staffers, and our managers and service providers. We must at all times be totally candid, *with ourselves* as well as with others, in small things as in large, and avoid any perception that we are ever being cute or hiding anything. This means proactively anticipating the concerns of others and responding to them before they have actually expressed them, and then responding forthrightly and promptly to the concerns they do express.

Without trust—*earned* trust—all the way around, the system can't work.

Aphorisms of Others

Many investors have come up with better aphorisms than I, and I would like to share a few of those from several of the better thinkers in the investment field.

Joe Grills

Joe is a retired chief investment officer of IBM's pension investments and one who has contributed broadly to the field of institutional investing. Among his aphorisms that appeal to me are:

- While our fund will have losses, the goal is to avoid large losses that impact the fund materially. Ways to avoid large losses include (a) diversification, (b) cut and run before the hole gets too deep, and (c) don't throw good money after bad to fix a hopeless investment.
- Remember that the best quality assets go down with the market.
- Being prematurely right can be as bad as being wrong.
- How much time we commit to a project should be commensurate with the amount of the investment. It is easy to spend a lot of time on small investments that have a small impact on the bottom line while the big stuff goes unattended.
- Don't belabor decisions.
- If you can't explain an investment to your wife, secretary, or girl-friend, don't invest in it.
- Networking with the peers we respect can add great value to the day-to-day management of our fund. Also, periodically attending purely educational conferences with first-rate investment professionals can help us to broaden our perspective.
- Don't get too comfortable with existing sources of information.

Roy Neuberger

I first met Roy in 1979. The business day at Neuberger Berman had not begun yet, and Roy was the only one in the Neuberger war room. Roy was approaching age 76 at the time. Roy soon began managing a large equity portfolio for us and did a fabulous job of it until he decided to retire as he turned 85. At this writing, at age 96, Roy is at the Neuberger offices every day managing money, and he still considers himself a *student* of the market.

Roy didn't manage our account because he needed the money—far from it. He managed it because he liked playing the game, and most of all, he liked winning. That's my view of the ideal motivation for an investment manager!

Among many things, Roy taught me never to judge a person on the basis of his age. Roy has come closer than anyone I know to discovering the proverbial fountain of youth.

On my first visit to Neuberger, I was given a little booklet about Roy's sayings, some of which go like this:

- Stay in love with a security until the security gets overvalued, then let somebody else fall in love. (I think this is a metamorphosis of a version Roy once told me: "It's all right to fall in love with a woman, but never fall in love with a stock.")
- The essence of taking losses, which is ultimately a question of character, is to acknowledge when one is wrong.
- It is imperative that you be willing to change your thoughts to meet new conditions.
- Personally, I like to be contrary. When things look awful, I become optimistic.
- Sometimes after a price decline, some companies need to be rediscovered.
- Mr. Bernard Baruch was an advocate of buying a bit too soon and selling a bit too soon. His fame has endured.
- To walk at least one hour a day is a good way to improve your investing ideas.

Peter Lynch

I was fortunate enough to meet Peter Lynch in his Fidelity office in 1981, when he was reeling off performance that beat the S&P 500 by 15 percentage points per year, and to have him manage money for us until his retirement in 1990.

I remember sitting with Peter and asking him, in awe, how he managed to do it. Among other things, one of Peter's keys to success was extremely hard work. There was no simple formula to Peter's approach. The story may be apocryphal, but it seems that Fidelity once dumped a huge stack of Peter's asset and transaction statements at Harvard in hopes that the scholars there could uncover Peter's strategies that could be replicated—entirely without success.

Back to my conversations with Peter, his one comment that really stuck with me was, "I will listen to anything. When brokers come up with crazy ideas that they feel are so far out no one will listen to them, they call me first, because they know I will listen to them. I may not invest in them, but I will always listen. Some of those ideas are great money makers."

That's an aphorism worth emulating.

John Templeton

Sir John is another person who taught me to be no judge of age. He was over 70 when he and his associates began managing money for us in 1984. John is certainly one of the great investors of the twentieth century, yet his foremost goal in life has been to promote advances in the field of religion, as illustrated by his founding and nurturing the annual Templeton Progress in Religion Prize.

John's writings are full of valuable aphorisms—as applicable for everyday living as for investing. Among them are "helping yourself by helping others . . . putting first things first . . . finding the positive in every negative . . . making time your servant . . . giving the extra ounce . . . and winning through humility."

A key example Sir John set in the field of investments was his *willingness to stand alone* and *to think outside the box*. In 1972 when the U.S. stock market went off the deep end, John was entirely out of the U.S. market. And where was he invested? Some 50% in Japan! Japan was an emerging market at that time, before the term "emerging markets" had been coined. Then in the early 1980s, after the Japanese market had spiraled up and everyone seemed to be getting into the Japanese market, John pulled out and stayed out. Prices were getting too rich. And for the next half dozen years he looked foolish, as Japanese stock prices continued to go sky high. Of course, we all know how that story ended in the 1990s.

Jeremy Grantham

Jeremy is one of the more articulate thinkers in the investment business. British by birth, Jeremy was a founder of Grantham, Mayo and Van Otterloo in Boston during the 1970s—a firm that has had great success, because it has achieved great success for its clients. No one can outdo Jeremy when it comes to aphorisms:

- Equity investors over-pay for *comfort* (stability, information, size, consensus).

- Equity investors over-pay for *excitement* and *sex appeal* (growth, profitability, management skills, technological change, and most of all, acceleration in these).
- Everything concerning markets and economies *regresses* from extremes toward normal, *faster than people think.*
- Real risk is not measured by beta, which is compromised by overlapping with other characteristics. Real risk is a mix of career risk to the investor and fundamental risk (of bankruptcy) to the company.
- Ninety percent of what passes for brilliance or incompetence in investing is the ebb and flow of investment style. And never underestimate the importance of luck. This leads many plan sponsors to pick the wrong managers.
- Transaction costs are certain, but anticipated outperformance is problematical.
- There is no size effect, or P/E effect, or stock vs. bond effect, only a *Cheap* effect.
- The stock market fluctuates far more than would be suggested by its future stream of earnings and dividends.
- Size of assets under management is the ultimate barrier to successful investing.
- Foreign markets are less efficient than the U.S. market, but the process of investing is much more expensive.
- Never underestimate the effectiveness of idiot savants vs. conventionally bright people.

In Short

If I were asked to summarize briefly what differentiates my philosophy of pension investments from that of many of my peers, I would say:

- Diversify as widely as possible among asset classes with high expected returns, reducing our aggregate volatility to the extent feasible through this diversification rather than through low-volatility, low-expected-return assets.
- In each of these asset classes, seek continuously the best investment managers in the world that we can access, and don't get hung up on benchmark risk.
- Don't get distracted by "conventional investment wisdom" in whatever country we happen to be located.

Index